You are — to my life — Always treat the voice of your deepest self — With love always, Mom

Drinking

of the

Holy Grail

Iana Lahi

Thank you Shanna for helping to make this book a reality. It wouldn't have happened without you — Iana

Koboca Publishing

Library of Congress Catalog Number: 2006935079

ISBN-13: 978-0-9744997-1-0
ISBN-10: 0-9744997-1-4

Drinking of the Holy Grail

First Edition

10 9 8 7 6 5 4 3 2 1

Published by
Koboca Publishing
Tampa, FL

Printed in the United States

Cover Design: Bo Savino
Editors: Robert Yehling & Sharina Lahi

To contact Koboca Publishing:
E-Mail: Info@KobocaPublishing.com
URL Address: www.KobocaPublishing.com

Table of Contents

Side Bars

Acknowledgements

Drinking of the Holy Grail is a gift from the Masters of Light. Their presence in my life fills me with gratitude and deep joy. I feel blessed and eternally thankful to have their direct teachings guide my work and life. My heart is filled with thankfulness to Robert Yehling, who helped birth this book into reality with his masterful book development and editing skills. I thank my daughter, Sharina Lahi, for her superb and inexorable attention to detail as the book's copy editor. With deep thanks I acknowledge Clara Lasagni Morgan, Carla Roberts, Ginette Fertel, Jennifer Milligan and Marika DuRietz for their friendship, wisdom and unconditional love. I wish to thank my mother, Marion, for believing in me and growing with me. A special thank you to all of my clients and students I have worked with over the years who have touched my heart and helped me expand into greater love, and to my daughter Satia for the truth she carries.

Dedicated to future generations who know in their hearts it is time to discontinue living in separation. To all those who have lived before me, courageously drinking of the Holy Grail, and to all souls who long to taste and know its nectar.

Forward

There is something special that happens when snow blankets the earth. Besides the body stilling itself into the silence of the earth and hearing the occasional cocooned sounds of nature amplified, on this crisp winter morning the song of a red cardinal drew my attention deeper into my body and aligned me with the earth's song. The crackling fire in the hearth warmed the room as silent anticipation grew within my heart and within the hearts of the circle of men with me this morning. Twelve years ago, the invitation to experience union with the divine had been given to all of these men.

I had worked individually with all of the men present for differing reasons. The one thing they all held in common this morning was the open space of love in their hearts. Many thoughts had poured through my mind and heart the previous evening and earlier that morning while picturing this meeting. How could I honor the light of truth and heartfelt feelings in each of these men? How is it possible that a circle of men have asked me, a woman, to guide their group?

There have been three moments in my life when I could not get the words welling up from my heart and soul out of my mouth. One was this moment, the second was while I was reading a prayer at my father's gravesite on the morning of the mounting of his gravestone, and thirdly, during a sacred ceremony that I had created on my birthday to heal the wounds of my heart from past lifetimes and my lover called me to wish me a happy birthday.

As I opened the circle and welcomed these pure hearts to this precious time together, I began to cry. I felt so honored that they would ask me to guide their process this day; I could not even begin to describe my feelings. Their warmth and acceptance flowing out of their eyes flooded me with love.

This gathering had evolved not only from working with these men individually, but also from working with their partners and with many other women in circle. Over the years, I realized the profound affect women could have on men if they cleared the energies in their physical body and the emotional, causal and spiritual patterns created over eons of time. A woman's ability to hold space for a man and offer him the light and wisdom inherently present in her holy chalice assists a man in transforming his heart, mind and entire life. Women, I came to understand, need to learn how to communicate their intentions, feelings and desires while still honoring a man's cellular and emotional make-up. A woman can rediscover how to restore her own spiritual power through love and self-responsibility; from these realizations, she opens to the God-given natural gifts inherent within to become a transformer for integrated consciousness, divine sexual union and conscious relationship.

It took a very short time for this group of men to engage with the circle and express their most personal and profound truths. As they began to speak, I knew all I needed to do was just be there with each of them fully and completely as they shared sacred focus. They spoke about how they felt during lovemaking—their fears, apprehensions, dreams and realizations. They talked about how they could feel whether a woman held a lot of anger. If a woman was centered in joy and love, they realized, their desire to surrender and merge heightened. Entering a woman felt like moving into a dark void both frightening and inviting, depending upon whether the woman was one with her power or split off from it. They were all aware of being with women who held their pain, hurt and anger in their wombs and sexual organs. These men all wanted to open their hearts and feel emotionally safe with their partners, but were unable to when they had to interact with their partners' disowned emotions. They spoke about moving into the dark and feeling safe or unsafe. They all yearned for joyous expression and unconditional love and acceptance. They wanted to integrate their divine masculine and feminine energies within themselves and with their partners.

Over these past many years, I have assisted men and women to clear and heal their karmic, ancestral, sexual and life force energies that have been waiting to be illuminated and rewoven in their hearts, bellies, genitals and souls. My driving intention has been to facilitate the integration of their spiritual and physical energies and to rediscover the initiations of the body, heart and soul that men and women need in order to experience union with the divine, individually and together.

As I explored these ancient truths within my self, I began to remember who I have been over the past millenniums and about my own life 2,000 years ago during the time of Christ. The ways and practices of divine feminine and masculine union began to speak a language of its own, filled with energetic, emotional, spiritual and etheric knowledge. I realized that it is my basic nature to understand and interpret this language for others.

The Holy Grail Journey is a roadmap for those seeking to awaken, heal, align and creatively unite all of the subtle energy bodies and their physical and spiritual energies into the heart center; this is where God power lives, waiting to empower our souls. As these spiritual connections were revealed to me while working with my clients and students, I began to understand how to live in the meeting point where spirit meets the body. Over the course of years, I searched through historical records to realize that much of what I have grown to understand regarding the soul's healing journey can be dated back to the days before and during Christ and his teachings. After his death, and with the passing of Mother Mary and Mary Magdalene, these teachings were obscured due to intentional misinterpretation, and then destroyed to prevent their oral and written transmissions. These teachings and initiations of light and soul are presented in this book, making possible the *Drinking of the Holy Grail.*

I am honored to share these divine secrets with you, and present to you the time-honored teachings of the Holy Grail.

May they bring to your life abundant joy and love.

~ Iana Lahi

Authors Note:

Throughout *Drinking of the Holy Grail* I use the words "self" and "source" in ways that may be different than their usual application. The self dwells within Source and is an expression of its light and power.

The self that I am referring to throughout this book is an integrated state of soul, spirit and body. Beyond the personality and identity, the self is the union of pure consciousness and heart. The self lives in the balance point of the mind, body and spirit, experiencing life from a state of love as the receiver and giver of life itself.

When we think about the word "source," we naturally think about a source of electricity, the source of ideas being inspiration, the source of a spring, etc. As you read *Drinking of the Holy Grail*, think about living in the generator or source of all divine energy. Here, Source refers to God energy and the flow and momentum of all life meeting in every cell of your body. Instead of viewing Source as something outside of self, we have the opportunity to live in the center of Source. By shifting our perspective, we can be in the center of life instead of looking at it from the outside in.

The illustrations that depict the Holy Grail Energy Elixirs can be accessed at www.spiritgateways.com. And will provide guidance for the exercises found in *Drinking of the Holy Grail.* Follow the energetic connections in the exercises and make use of the illustrations as a visual guide to the heightened feelings that are possible by receiving your own imagery through the combination of word and picture. Allow the words in each exercise to seep into your understanding, so that it is your higher self that truly guides you through each exercise. At times, the exercises are intentionally left open-ended so that the exercises can become, through your own inner knowingness and repetition of the exercises, perfectly harmonized to your spiritual rekindling. Ponder the pictures, enjoy their beauty, but avoid becoming attached to how each exercise should turn out. Let each exercise instead become a gateway into your own self.

~ *Iana Lahi*

Drinking of the Holy Grail

Jana Lahi

Prologue

Jan's bright pink boots matched the reddish glow in her cheeks as she walked through the door of my Manhattan office on a cold winter day. Her long, windblown wavy brown hair seemed to mimic her swift body and arm movements as she took off her coat. Her gigantic smile and elf-like laughter caught me by surprise. Who was healing whom here? As I placed a cup of hot tea in her hands, she practically pranced over to the sacred healing corner of my office. As she sat Indian-style directly across from me, we looked at each other with wonder.

Both of us began to laugh and giggle. Then her demeanor became a little more serious. "I really don't know what I'm doing with my life. I seem to have it figured it out one moment, and then the next moment I am lost." Tears streamed out of her eyes. Her honest, straightforward flow of expression opened my heart further. As I gave her a tissue, she continued, "Everyone thinks I know who I am. I sure know how to look good to everyone around me, but I don't have a clue. Things just don't seem to be getting any better, even though I think they will everyday."

"What do you want to be doing?" I asked her.

"I thought I was doing it, but it just doesn't feel right. I want it to, but it doesn't."

Jan explained that her time dancing and acting on Broadway and her love for singing wasn't working for her anymore, but she didn't know who "her" was. When she was on stage, she could live through her particular character. Off-stage, however, she had no one to live through except men. They always seemed to be eccentric artists who needed heroin to help them connect to the astral planes of creativity; furthermore, they lived in these other worlds rather than maintaining a strong, stable connection to the physical plane. At least, she said, they were willing to try to find out what was beyond the physical constrictions of everyday life.

"I saw their pain and loved them in their pain. Their pain made them alive to me," she explained. "People with no pain, or out of touch with their pain, just pretended with life. Their creative drive was a desire so strong that I wanted to become a part of their world. They touched into raw creative energy and even though they did it though heroin, they went there. The source of their music, their art was through that drug, but wherever they went to, they sought that passion. Their world was rock 'n roll, where you go beyond the lyrics and through the darkness of the music to find insatiable creative power."

Jan let a deep breath out. "Rock 'n roll is not afraid of extremes or intense creative energy. It became a container for my creative journey. I became the icon, a guru, feeling how free you can be. I was not afraid of my creative power and in that atmosphere, the energy is just *held.* The unknown worlds, dark or light, were the places I danced into. They embraced me and sometimes I couldn't come out from where I was."

Jan began crying again. When she entered those altered spaces, her boundaries would collapse and leave her with no conception of personal reality. Jan's drug background was less checkered than most performers: She'd never tried heroin, used cocaine a few times, smoked pot occasionally, took psilocybin five times, and did not drink. When she danced, she would fall in love with the feeling of love—the rushing power of euphoria that filled her entire being with joy. She never wanted to emerge from that cocoon. Her nights were long and hard-driving, and several clubs and groups in New York City "anointed" her as their goddess of passion. Eventually, they drained the life energy out of her.

Time and again, Jan felt she found love, the real thing. Invariably, the latest boyfriend, after loving her free spirit, would crash up against the inner mirror she provided whether he wanted to or not. She herself did not understand why these men would run away from the passion, flames and power of the love that moved through her body. Jan shared her creative power with anyone who wanted to live through her love; however, she was unraveling with no place to go and no one to hold onto. As her illusions crumbled, so did her faith in her self.

Too afraid to live through herself, and fearful of what she would find, Jan helped those around her face each day. Some died; others lived.

Finally, Jan decided to find her true self.

Four years passed. Looking back at this time, Jan said, "I loved where I was. I was in a space of complete freedom—a beautiful place where the world was a playground. I was bouncing around from experience to experience, thinking that I found the one, although it wasn't happening. I had thought it was true love. I was in artist mode, wandering and experiencing—going with the flow, with whatever came and letting myself go with it. It wasn't a responsible time. I identified myself as the 'light,' the one that could take people away from their drugs. My best friend, Marcy, was using heroin and died; my boyfriend, Adam, was a recovering addict. Another friend, Roger, made a full recovery after heroin through meditation; he turned his energy around. I was an enabler for them. I gave them the space of an enlightened mind as a place to be—an anchor point. I knew what they were looking for through heroin. I could understand. They were looking for that connection with God, that bliss, that true connection to Source. They wanted freedom from suffering and away from everything negative. Their lives became drama even though they were trying to get away from the *drama*. They all had a lot of pain and suffering and could not connect to being here in the world. They were not accidental addicts; it was a conscious choice to stay in that plane. My friends did not lie, cheat or steal. They would go through withdrawal, but then go back on the drug.

"Men can handle and get off of heroin easier. Women can't or have a harder time getting off heroin. All of the women I knew on heroin died. Before Marcy died, she described her body as being unable to battle against her hormonal cycles and menstrual flow. The cycle itself brought her into states she could not deal with and the drug on top of that made it a losing battle. The pain level is different in the female body."

Before Jan found her own wellspring— the Holy Grail cup within her self—she listened and moved through the feelings and experiences of others, as well as her own experiences. "I provided a safe place to cry and release deep feelings. My friends—musicians, writers, dreamers—all seemed okay around me. They were able to let go of feeling like a horrible person for getting into what they were doing. I connected to their soul. I did not see their personalities."

By the time Jan and I began working together, she had cut herself off from heavy drug users. She was ready for a new opening in her life. Jan's vitality and love for life flowed through her every action. "I was playing on a cloud—complete Bodhisattva awareness—without a path.

I had an enlightened mind without a path. Everything wasn't real, the emotions were there, but I didn't know what to do with them. I had awakened to light, but it was separate from myself, and I did not have any spiritual discipline and was not connected to my body."

In our work together, Jan became aware of feeling numb in her body, though her heart center was very engaged. This split between heart and body often created many tears that alternately healed and expressed her sadness. She wanted to know and feel the full connection of soul and spirit—in her body. She didn't know how to do this. Even years as a professional dancer and actor could not help her access and integrate her spirit, soul, body and emotions.

Like most of us, she would experience these four integral parts of her being as compartments and at different times, in various ways. "In the dance clubs in Manhattan, I was trying to find freedom from the confines of society," she said. "I was breaking out of a tight sexual morality and puritanical Christian upbringing that no longer fit me. It was a place where I could release power, frustration and anger. I felt really empowered when I was dancing. Otherwise I was very quiet and shy. There I could completely express my soul."

Through our work of reconnecting her body and soul, Jan dove into her self—the first step of connecting with the Holy Grail—and discovered why she needed to travel into the dark. "I went into the dark, and what I perceived as light was not light. The world that I thought was light was not light, and was destructive. When I went into the dark, people could see my light and I could see myself as well. I had to go into the dark, so my dark could work its way out. I had to blast through the dark to find myself. My biggest fear was my sexual energy; I was connecting my sexuality with what was dark around me, but my sexuality was not dark. Drama became the expression of my dark. I enjoyed it while I was there. It became the door to my full expression, until I couldn't go any further with it. I knew the point when it could or would destroy me."

Most people play with their dark energies everyday without knowing it. Our society, customs, media messages and religious oppression make it very easy to manipulate, control and misuse sexual energies and personal power. Most of us stay with the same repetitive patterns until we want to venture beyond how we hurt others or ourselves.

"My relationships have been so extreme. All I have wanted is for my partner to come out with who they are, and not hide behind the relationship," Jan explained. "I was looking and still am for people who are willing to be real. Everyone is afraid, but we do not have to allow our fear to stop us. I kept getting hurt, in reality hurting myself, because I kept engaging with partners who weren't willing to confront themselves. I am a mirror to lovers, to their beauty and to their crap."

Jan realized she allowed her boyfriends to break her down, instead of persuading them to take responsibility for their own issues. Rather than cracking the mirror of self-delusions within their own psyches, they would crack her mirror. Her brilliant soul was too big of a reflection for those who didn't want to look into the mirror. In time, Jan learned how to keep her own mirror clear and to not give away her power so that someone else could profess love to her and then gradually destroy her reflection. She had no idea how clear her mirror could get and how powerful her presence could be.

Down the road in our work together, Jan shared, "A man can put in some dents, but can no longer crack me. The only thing that hurts me now is that I *feel* his struggle. I care and I have empathy, but I am inside my own self now and cannot be pulled out. I know his struggle: I remember that feeling."

As Jan began to remain connected to her deepest self through her body, chakras, higher self and spirit, she accessed the size of her universal connection. In the past, she wanted to be a part of everything—experiencing every moment of life to its max—and was willing to lose her self to feel connected to others. Her daily focus became the dilemma of whether or not to leave her self—a normal choice in our culture—or to move through the fear surrounding her *true self*. She learned to accept and love who she is, how to heal the separations in her soul, and how to integrate the spiritual energies in her body, heart and soul.

Then a day of reckoning came, the day we all reach when we work to know our true selves and venture through the dark to get there. She reached a point of no return. "In the movie *The Matrix*, Kevin Anderson takes the colored pill and he can't go back—I remember my first experience feeling that and wanting to fit in, but not being able to go back, and not being able to be a part of everything," she said. "All addicts love drama. I was the Tragic Beauty. Like Marilyn Monroe, everyone loves me, but no one loves ME. They all want me, until they find out who *I* am. *I* was projecting who they wanted back to them, but not letting anyone ever see me!"

As a performer and unfolding spiritual goddess, Jan's greatest fear of being seen for her most authentic self became the wall of separation between herself and life.

She decided to move in with her boyfriend, her martial arts teacher. I didn't hear from her for a few months. One day, I got a phone call from her, and we caught up. Her voice was quieter and less enthusiastic than usual, and dullness was present in her energy. I knew I was walking on delicate turf because her decision to move in with Carl was her own decision, one that she had never discussed with anyone. I chose to stay silent and listen. It was not until two phone calls later that I asked her why she had shut down to herself. It took her a while to figure it out. Jan chose to be in the relationship for a year. During that time she wrote a screenplay, closed her heart, stopped speaking her truth and gained thirty pounds. Carl wanted to give her what she wanted, but his spiritual path was a mystery to her. He worked with the deceased on the other side, and helped those souls on this plane who were possessed by demons. She felt uncomfortable in her own skin around him, yet they had great sex.

I asked her if she wanted to do some work in person. At our appointment, Jan experienced the power of the light within as we brought her soul and higher self together. After being shut down, the contrast between dark and light were very obvious to her. She wanted freedom more than anything, but did not believe that anyone could love the magnitude of her soul. She could live through Carl's connection to spirit after turning off the valve to her own source. We began taking the steps to creating a haven of safety, light and protection for her divine feminine self. Through energy and spiritual meditation practices that we practiced together, she opened to the light within herself. Stunned by the intensity of the connection, she grounded herself through the Buddhist deity Tara. Upon realizing her true feminine-masculine self was a powerful combination of love and beauty, she began listening to herself like never before.

Jan came to my first Movement Healers Training in Manhattan. We had an amazing group that has since stayed together as friends and colleagues. As Jan began to dance and move, fully integrated and supported by the energy connections aligning the spiritual forces in her body—the foundation of the training—she began to find the healer within. For years she had been losing herself while taking care of the deepest emotional and spiritual needs of others, all at the expense of herself. Now she opened to a power that lived within her, waiting to be found.

For the first time, Jan felt she could embrace the gigantic energy presence and power that defines her. She could express, contain and manifest this presence just by reconnecting the energies in her subtle bodies. Jan felt tapped into a source of creative and spiritual power that sustained her. By reintegrating parts of her soul that previously had been separate from her consciousness, she could embody currents of energy that brought clarity and profound joy. When her third eye opened in our second training, she immediately moved into the movement exercises and sequences, and resurrected her divine feminine and masculine selves until they united.

Eventually, Jan and Carl parted, though they remained friends. She made the decision to never again submit her feminine self to anyone. No matter how hard she tried, she could never get through his warrior exterior. When they made love, she realized she was the hummingbird and he was a grizzly bear. It just couldn't work. He never cried until she left.

She had a huge breakthrough during another of our trainings. While we were doing a meditation exercise that began by connecting the currents between the sacrum, skull and third-eye, she met her inner spiritual teacher, Babaji. His energy (with which I, too, am deeply connected) entered the studio space. He initiated her, similar to what I experienced in his presence; her face glowed with joy and light. Sitting there feeling this interchange was and always is beyond words for me. Jan had cleared her emotional, causal and etheric bodies to the point where she could draw to herself what she needed to fully succeed on her spiritual path.

Jan decided to leave Manhattan, move west and start a new life. Her goal: to create theater pieces originating from her whole self. So far, she is living her dream.

When she acts, sings or dances now, she doesn't "perform." Rather, she steps into union with herself and the forces of spirit she chooses to summon. She has integrated the necessary parts of herself that were in the dark. Jan now understands that the unmanifested dark is the divine creative force and that the void and raw creative power comprise two different zones. She has accepted the responsibility of creating and living from this union of power and love. No longer does she have to live in the fear of getting "caught in the dark." It was my great joy to help her journey through the tunnel into the light.

Later, while discussing how she could practice protecting her powerful, deep feminine essence, she realized how vulnerable she felt when immersed in this power. She wanted to remain the free, fun-loving goddess—her "fairy-goddess self" as she called it—filled with desires that were different now than in her past, but still very much alive with fantasy and openly shared love. I talked with her about creating 10 hoops that would be her spirit protection. These 10 hoops were energetic shields of self-respect and protection designed to protect her heart, body and soul. For instance, when a man entered the space of her home—her goddess temple—she was compelled to pay attention to how he honored both his presence and her space. She had recently opened to a man and slept with him, hoping to build for herself a caring and loving relationship. Instead, he ran from their exchange, choosing to escape out the nearest door. The next time she shared herself with this man, after creating the 10 hoops, he chose to begin healing and integrating his soul and spiritual bodies.

Realizing that she was ready now to be accepted and received, she began thinking about the 10 hoops she could create next time she was with a man, so she could *feel* and *know* if a man was ready to receive and reciprocate the energies of the love she desired to give. Jan had begun to love herself and treasure the gifts of her spirit, heart and soul. She could tap her inner power and channel the energies in her Holy Grail, but she didn't know how to protect and contain these energies without someone grabbing them and attempting to degrade her for holding such power. She practiced living in the center of her Holy Grail and receiving and giving from this place of grounding. By knowing where her spiritual center was, she could focus and begin to build the next level of her temple—her divine physical form. Here, her artist and goddess self could merge and build an inner fortress of love and creativity.

The soul's power and the heart's passion can open and transform our lives. When Jan first practiced an exercise to realign her heart center, she felt a deep longing and didn't know what it was. She had reached the point of feeling the Holy Grail, but did not know how to live within it. She felt she could sob for hours. We did a movement exercise to further open her body temple. As she circulated her life force energy through a circuitry of spiritual portals in her body, she entered into a high meditative state. We began to integrate her ancient feminine soul parts into her body through this energy until these aspects of light and dark were brought into full union. Her body was tingling and flowing with life energy and joy. A deeper realization filled her consciousness that became fused in her body; the awakened Holy Grail currents had a temple in which to reside.

Jan's next steps were to become the voice of her power so that others could *see* her. She had begun dropping the weight that she had put on over the last few years to protect herself and keep herself hidden, so that performing a one-woman theater piece could become attainable. "In this lifetime I am fighting to not remain silent," she said. "I am so afraid of being tortured and killed again for speaking my truth and living in spiritual power. Up until now, even when sharing a poem in a poetry reading is like putting myself up in front of people holding bows and arrows. In past centuries, if you had this kind of message, you were killed. Questions move through me all the time such as: Can I really have a positive effect on the world? Do I really know what I am talking about? Is the perception of who I am real?"

Jan's voice resonated with truth. I told her that I felt her voice would give strength to the world. Her past gave her the experience of feeling unsure about whether she could make a difference or not in anyone's life. But, when Jan did inner work to reach her spiritual center, she always knew that what she was experiencing was real. When she felt one in herself, she knew her perceptions and feelings about herself and others were genuine. She could witness herself leaving the spiritual-physical connection in her body, and choose to not go into her head, but return to the center. Her center of power was new to her, and magnified her inner confidence about moving into the world in a new way.

Jan did not miss sitting around and having a cigarette or a few drinks. However, she did miss socializing with peers and being viewed as the "way-out artist girl." "I could talk about spirituality and they would listen. They would hear from the place of: 'yeah, she is so open and free,'" Jan explained. "Now, I am a spiritually-free artist, one that most people do not know how to relate to. I just haven't found anything to replace being accepted and seen. I miss having a bridge to the world. I just haven't found a new bridge."

When Jan began teaching movement classes and helping others find their soul and spiritual connections in their body, she found her bridge to the world. Now, a choreographer, teacher and performer of theater, healing and movement stories, she has found her place by living in her Holy Grail.

Once we experience the doorways into the mystery of life within us, we each have a karmic (rising above past actions) and dharmic (true path) mission that is appropriate for our life and unites our personal and spiritual journeys. Our inner spiritual essence and our inherent God-given qualities form the outer commitment, providing follow-through for a chosen expression. Living in the Holy Grail becomes our life path.

For Jan, that path combines acting, teaching and writing. She realized she was ready to create another new bridge. She remembered a piece she had written a few years ago that was sitting in a file cabinet. It was time to rewrite and perform it. She asked me to help her fine-tune the work. I was delighted.

Her piece concerned a girl who refused to listen to the spirit guides who had accompanied her for eons. After she entered into a deep state of meditation, her past spiritual teachers assisted her in discovering why and how she progressed and often fell during her journey. To a soundtrack of Tibetan chanting, movement and rock music, a girl dressed in white sits in a jewel-lotus meditation position and confronts herself through conversations with her "gurus"—embracing her light and dark sides. Heretofore separated from the light, her dark feminine side faces her fears and breakthroughs, then light and dark unite. The feminine warrioress grows to understand and accept living inside her sphere of power and love. The inner and outer Jan join as one, finding true liberation on and off the stage.

When Jan first came to meet with me, her connection into spirit had already been evolving for eons. Her universal essence embraced the lineage of the Holy Grail without her conscious knowledge. Becoming aware of her spiritual roots helped her to accept her uniqueness and to focus upon her natural truths. They led her into direct connection with her source within, empowering her to embrace her masculine and feminine God traits.

Finding the light within our dark or hidden parts and integrating the two is the journey that returns us to the Holy Grail. The task of facing life's daily challenges can be all consuming and can deprive us both of our spiritual energy and our soul's greater purpose, until we surrender to accepting the perfection of our lessons. From there, we can shift how we engage our divine energies and relearn how to recreate our lives to benefit and serve our higher desires.

Jan flowered as the parts of her self that were sleeping in her spiritual past blossomed. Through the Holy Grail lineage of touching into her divine self, she could integrate the sweetness and power of who she is. Along her unfolding path, she remembered her divine nature through shamanic Tibetan Buddhism, the Goddess, her Druid connection, Shivaism, Kriya, Kabbalah, Taoism and early Christianity. These aspects of herself were in place and needed to be cleared and opened. Her inner teachers were waiting to return so they could help her fulfill the inner promise to herself—to again drink of the Holy Grail.

There are many ways to be gifted by the blessings of Spirit. We all have hidden talents and "spiritual gifts" that we have worked hard to attain, or have been given by the universe to further the enlightenment of this planet and ourselves. The codes of awareness of how to open to these gifts live in our bodies. They have been kept secret from us for over two thousand years, because if we had access to them, we would have access to the Holy Grail.

Light heals diseases and issues of the soul and spirit. We gain admittance to the codes of light within our bodies by integrating our soul, body and spirit. Leonardo DaVinci knew many of the secrets of the Holy Grail, including those of the codes of light. His drawing of the male universal figure with arms extended horizontally is the map to the light within.

For two millennia, the secrets have been hidden behind great violence, such as the Crusades and numerous bloodbaths. Now they can be once again revealed.

The ancient cup of knowledge has returned. Fill your cup with this divine, transformative nectar, savor it and practice its guidance in your life.

Part I

Legacy of the Holy Grail: Resurrecting the Truth

Chapter 1

What is the Holy Grail?

"The Self which shines as Sun within the Heart
Is real and all-pervading.
Twill reveal Itself as soon as false thought is destroyed
And not one speck remains."
~ Ramana Maharshi

Within the cells of our body lives a calling, the memory of a blissful, pain-free state of consciousness. It is sweeter and more lasting than the joy that hums in our bodies in the best of times. Some of us have felt it while sitting in a rowboat fishing, walking through the woods on the perfect day, gazing out to the ocean, swimming, meditating, making love, baking a pie, or holding a loved one. Feeling the divine presence within ourselves intoxicates us and makes us feel complete. Some of us would call it union with the divine and others would say nothing in their life could be better. How do we find the link creating union rather than separation? If, in these joyful states, we are so close to attaining the ultimate state of divine joy, and living in the fullest vitality of our cells, how do we take that elusive final step?

Throughout many past eons of our existence as spiritual human beings, we have tasted divine union—the merger of heart, soul and spirit. It is a sanctuary of bliss in the heart where there is no time but the eternal present. Everything is right here, right now. It stirs a desire to love so deeply that we embrace our own life spirit and walk through the doorways to eternal love.

However, we've forgotten this simple, ineffable truth about ourselves. We turn to Buddha, Allah, Christ, Mary and/or God to relieve our discomforts. We go through our day trying to comfort ourselves, engorging on whatever temporarily creates that comfort. "I will drink from the cup of life," we proclaim. But the cup is often empty. Thus, we conclude there is no way to fill it except to shop, eat, take on someone else's problems, workout, seek sexual pleasure, or indulge in our myriad quick-fix habits.

For the vast majority of us, the portal to this cup of eternal life closed a long time ago. When you track the roots of South American, African, Asian and Egyptian cultures, you will find ceremonies, dating back to the most ancient times, that keep the portals into the source of life open. Unlike those cultures, we dropped the veil to the source of true power, love, and creativity. We followed instead our mind's desires to control the forces of creation, rather than to co-create with them.

When we let go of the desire to control, we will find the portal into our inner Holy Land. Here, the proverbial milk and honey flow from the cup of eternal life, for we're drinking from the divine land of the eternal feminine that is our birthright.

The battles we presently experience between our mind and heart, spirit and soul, and body and soul create the pain and suffering that we consider normal. Unfortunately, it has been that way for a long time. Two thousand years ago we were at a crossroads between living in truth or in lies. The battle to keep the Holy Grail alive began; it is the same battle we are fighting today. For the last millennium, we have been counseled and warned that practicing direct connection with God was a sin, even though the master teacher-founders of the world's two largest religious movements, Jesus and Mohammed, *specifically advocated* direct communion. Some who defied this edict chose to hide; others were killed. Small sects openly practiced direct communion with God. How could such simple, direct devotion become the greatest sin on earth? In the midst of this organized sacrilege, how was the Holy Grail preserved? Some used their power to hold onto outer riches, land and position. Others composed music, wrote or sculpted. Many sustained spiritual practices in a secretive manner, thus becoming the miscreants, threats and "dangerous" renegades of their respective societies. These individuals could only live within the truth of their souls.

They would not permit anyone to shut their souls down. They were driven by a passion and often did not know what directed them.

We still see this in population groups today. The major difference between those brave souls of the past two millennia and us is that we have become numb to the repression and silencing of our spirit. On a daily basis, we're bombarded by mass advertising, political scandals, financial pressures, aimless wars and messages that promote dependency on prescription drugs, fast foods or other social narcoses. All are numbing to the soul. We have lost the knowledge of how to use the awesome power of the divine feminine, the Holy Grail. Ready examples of this in our entertainment-based culture include rock stars and movie icons, many of whom are caught in the dark side of their own prodigious creative flow. When I went back and listened to the lyrics of a few progressive rock groups of the 1970's, some 25 or 30 years after I'd first heard them, I was deeply moved by the level of spirit and wisdom in those words. What happened? How was it that these sensitive, attuned, creative giants could so readily engage in the flow of the universe—then turn away from that flow? Many artists, writers, healers and visionaries awaken to the Holy Grail moving through them; more accurately, they retain what they intrinsically know as children. They utilize it in their craft, but are unable to live fully from that divine center.

Unfortunately, we were not taught in school how to appropriately use the power of this God force. Instead we were instructed and directed to use our mind to feed, clothe, and build a capitalistic, industrialized and technology-driven society, rather than develop the powers of the soul. We were trained to be cogs in the machine, factory workers building the engine of an empire that casts its long shadow over the entire world—including our souls, bodies and hearts. In fact, the United States' first public schools were created in the late 19th century specifically to train children to become productive Industrial Age workers! Our intuitive faculties, those innate abilities to know, see, feel and tap the forces of life, are the tools that sustain, create and build our lives and cultures.

As long as we keep the soul, body and heart in separate compartments, we are sleeping in spirit. Once those walls between the compartments are down, the Holy Grail pours through to be received. This requires courage. Among those who have carried the power and magnitude of the Holy Grail in their lives and works are Johann Wolfgang Goethe, Richard Wagner, Ludwig von Beethoven, Claude Debussy, Frederic Chopin, Wolfgang Amadeus Mozart, Vaslav Nijinsky, Anna Pavlova, Joan of Arc, Michelangelo, Babaji, Mother Mary, Mary Magdalene, Sarah Brightman, Plato, David Bowie, Tori Amos, Justin Hayward and Mike Pinder of the Moody Blues, Ravi

Shankar, Anoushka, Sai Baba, John Lennon, George Harrison, Neil Young, Jon Anderson of the rock group Yes, Krishnamurti, Cat Stevens, Clara Schumann, Vincent Van Gogh, Leonardo Da Vinci, Monet, Chief Seattle, King Ludwig II of Bavaria, Abraham Lincoln, Martin Luther King, St. Francis, Nikola Tesla, Rudolf Steiner, Steven Spielberg, George Lucas, Rimsky-Korsakov, Jai Uttal, Bill Douglas, Tchaikovsky, Enya, Catherine of Siena, Ruth St. Denis, Martha Graham, Celine Dion, Barbara Streisand, Rumi, Shamiz Tabriz, Lalla, Sanai, William Blake, Ramana Maharshi, Lahiri Mahasaya, Gandhi, Milarepa, William the Conqueror, Swami Vivekananda and Paramhansa Yogananda. And who can forget the music that poured out of Julie Andrews and connected us with beauty and divinity in *Mary Poppins* and *The Sound of Music*?

These spiritual and creative giants are among many who have lived in co-creation with the One. They tapped into the Holy Grail, some in a single performance or magical composition, others over the course of their entire lives. They found it right where Christ admonished his followers to find the Kingdom of God—within themselves. All took the risk to live in it. Some battled with their forces of light and dark, and others ended the battle. The ones who concluded their battles did so by giving themselves over completely to their higher Self and living in love! They latched onto the supreme deity of creative and intoxicating light within.

Check this out for yourself. Listen to a piece of music by any of the musicians listed above, and see if it doesn't touch your deepest being.

These souls focused upon the courage and power of their will and explored the relationship of dark and light. Some fell into their own unresolved matters of sexuality, power, denial, and fear and created "dramas" to distract their lives, while others knew why they were here and found a way to manage without creating personal distractions. Among those who have since died, most experienced divine completeness in their lives.

The forces of light and darkness pull us into arrogance, pride, greed, ego, vanity, humility, selflessness, beauty, tenderness, truth, deceit, transcendence and radiance. Eventually, we reach an exalted place where we bring all of these states together to create oneness. Each emotion and thought is connected to currents of spiritual energy that flow into the physical body and create wholeness or separation. The nucleus of a cell can either be split or joined. Our minds and emotions have the power to split or unify God power. When a creative being, politician, world leader, spiritual aspirant or everyday Joe follows a current but never chooses to align the rest of himself to it, then chaos, split intentions, failure and loss rule. One way to interpret the present presidential administration in the United States is to see it as our collective shadow side brought to bear, because it outlasted our collective spirit side in the polls. When a shadow prevails, chaos, disorder and suffering manifest along the entire reach of that shadow.

Take the time to find your highest spiritual current and enter it fully! Instead of following the rules, beliefs and dogma of a particular religion or order, discover for yourself what Christ, Krishna, Buddha and the other great masters knew: All religions flow from the same wellspring of truth. Find the contradictions within yourself: They will exist between your body and sexuality, power and disempowerment, losing and "owning" yourself, direct or indirect connection to Source, fearing the dark and the light. Honor the fear but connect it to the truth that lives in the union of your heart and belly. Connect it to your light.

All of us descend from a religious and/or cultural lineage that was originally rooted in the harmony of spirit and Source. The ancient cultures of the Essenes, Greeks, Hopi, Lakota, Gnostics, Shivaites, Sufis, Tibetans, Hawaiians, Polynesians and oldest Egyptians and societies found in Africa, Australia, India, the Middle East and the lost continents of Atlantis and Lemuria all lived in union before eating the apple of materialism, worldliness and sensuality, losing their connection. Their lives were once filled with practices of purification, devotion and wisdom. They honored God within and listened to that voice, instead of their minds. They knew when they were attuned to their divine source—and when they were not.

The power of God can be heard in the heart. To keep the channel open, the ancients fed and nourished their bodies with loving attention as temples of the divine. They used water, fresh herbs and fruits and vegetables to cleanse and heal their bodies. They prepared for and practiced sex as a sacred ritual of God attunement rather than to seek immediate pleasure or to temporarily quench deep inner pain. Women operated as vehicles of light and carried the mysteries of creation. They knew how to move the vital currents of their bodies with the forces of the universe and nature. Their spiritual practices maintained their connection to the source of light, enabling them to heal, give birth, attune to the planets and stars to prophesize, strengthen their men through sex and maintain harmony among their peoples.

While the men presided over the gathering of goods, building structures and transporting tribes from place to place, women ruled the inner roost, from the inside of the dwelling to the inside of the heart. It was a perfect balance, and both man and woman fully honored each other's power.

Then something happened. It began (and continues) with the way women were treated. Through the course of time, women were degraded and killed to diminish and eliminate their powers. Turning against their own souls, women forgot who they were. Their own pain and hurt tore the threads of their remembrance. The knowledge of how to stay connected was erased from their memory.

When this occurred, the essence of the Holy Grail was lost to us.

Men began to seek the Grail in the form of a cup or a blood lineage back to Christ. This perspective spoke to the outer expression of male power, the outer warrior and leader: Maintaining control over one's body and soul through a straight line of rational logic and critical thinking was considered the norm. They sacrificed their inner kingdom, first for the sake of providing comfort, then for wealth, and finally to maintain social status and power. At that nadir, that lowest spiritual point, the hearts of men closed to the evolution of their souls. They fought to dissipate the precepts of love, union, creativity, higher service and expression. Greed and false power became the new God, and the cup of life became empty. The Catholic Church seized power by creating transubstantiation, a substitute for the Holy Grail in which cups were filled with wine on Sunday mornings and offered to parishioners as the Blood of Christ. Synagogues gave praise for life's abundance with a cup of wine, but lost the true meaning of drinking from the Holy Grail. The holy cup of wine became a symbol for sacrifice, loss and sorrow. The eternal union of Christ with Spirit became a story of suffering, unlike the kind of story involving inner redemption and resurrection we would expect from a self-realized man who taught the spiritually impoverished multitudes how to bypass external dogmas by finding God within themselves.

The bloodshed over who has the right to speak the word of God continued in the most personal ways—and still does today. Is not the current firefight in the Middle East being driven and defined by the hatred between fundamentalist Christians and radical Muslims (each of which claims to be the exclusive representative organization of God/Allah on earth) and their political and military representatives? We have lost touch with the ability to hear divine truth. It is an art form that needs to be rediscovered. Through religious corruption, both men and women have been uprooted from the inner connections that create the ability to feel and hear the deepest divine and universal truth.

Collectively, we were taught that our bodies were distractions to spiritual light and power. A woman's monthly menstrual flow came to be viewed as more of a dirty habit, if not a curse, than the celebration of her power that was respected as such by indigenous cultures from time immemorial…until the Church seized authority. Then, only the Son of God was honored in his bleeding. The rhythms of moving within and alongside Spirit perished. Only those who entered the rhythms through trance—mystics, some musicians, artists, some dancers, ministers, and new age adherents—felt safe enough to go with the flow. Yet could they do it by being fully in their bodies?

We breathe spirit every moment, whether we acknowledge it or not. However, naturally entering these rhythms without suspending the dense outer reality by smoking pot, having a drink, mentally obsessing or listening to hard rock has become a rarity. We use sports, creative obsession, alcohol, drugs, money, sex, dogma, power or junk food to numb the pain of separation; that keeps the walls up between the emotional, spiritual and physical worlds. Most of us cannot feel the currents of spirit moving our soul, body and vision without someone or something else doing it for us.

The flow of spirit in the body creates power. Spirit that moves in the body awakens the divine feminine. We move in and out of spirit. When the body and soul are energetically cleared and integrated, we experience God essence. When the mind serves soul realization, the ego's influence recedes like a shadow hit by the sun. Yet, simply opening to spirit and channeling it is not enough. Until we embody the consciousness of our whole self, we live in separation.

Chapter 2

Genesis of the Holy Grail

"Return to the center, where all life begins."
~ Iana Lahi

The Holy Grail Tradition, the lineage of the Awakened Spirit, began after the fall of Atlantis 12,000 years ago—an event metaphorically and literally captured in the Biblical story of the Great Flood.

The Grail's origins came from the civilization of Lemuria, also known as Mu. Leaving behind geologic remnants on the landmasses we now know as Hawaii, Fiji, Samoa, Micronesia, Melanesia, the Philippines, Easter Island and New Zealand, Lemuria was a civilization of balanced feminine and masculine souls. There were few splits in consciousness. Earth and human beings co-existed in harmony. Holy Grail Teachings evolving from Lemuria include healing with color, music, sacred geometry, herbology, light and sound, maintaining a clear physical and emotional body and heart center, balancing the systems of the body to the elements and constellations, universal love and unifying the physical and etheric bodies with the *tisra til* (third eye).

Ancient Tamil writings on palm tree bark still exist in the Vatican archives deep beneath Vatican City. They were pillaged from various cultures and transported to Rome by the orders of various popes. These writings describe a large landmass, Lemuria, that connected Australia and India before cataclysmically breaking up and sinking from a long series of earthquakes, volcanic eruptions, tsunamis and floods. Lemuria first came into existence 150,000 years ago and joined southern Asia, eastern Africa, the islands in the Pacific Ocean and the west coasts of North and South Americas. Approximately 100,000 years ago the land mass began to sink; within about 20,000 years, the land masses separated into islands of all sizes. They include the present-day Polynesian archipelago, Hawaiian Islands and Easter Island. Ancient Hawaiian legends tell of a "lost people" that followed a massive eruption of Kohala on the north end of the Big Island, some 60,000 years ago. This is consistent with the Lemurian breakup chronology. The Lemurians began to colonize these new land masses, and to head west to the Indian subcontinent and Australia, and east to the North American and South American coasts—planting ancestral seeds that became the advanced Incan and Pacific Northwest tribal cultures, as well as Australia's aborigines and India's ancient creators of yoga. All of these people carried considerable spiritual light and the keys to the inner divine kingdom; it was common knowledge in Lemuria.

The emergence of Atlantis brought further geological and cultural changes. When Atlantis rose from the sea, North and South American lakes, rivers, mountains and deep seas were formed from a previously swampy, marshland environment. During its first wave of cataclysmic events, Atlantis rose further, pushing seamounts above the surface in the Mediterranean Sea (now Greece and Cyprus), plus altering the elevation of the Alps and eastern North American mountains.

As Atlantis rose, Lemuria continued to sink. This geologic event contained a very powerful, consciousness- and soul-changing spiritual component that established a battlefield (depicted metaphorically in the *Bhagavad Gita* as the plains of Kurukshetra) on which our souls are still fighting today.

Atlantis and Lemuria manifested the two sides of God energies on the physical plane: power and love. Atlantis in its attempts to become the most powerful civilization eventually brought Lemuria down. The roots of the occult, astrology, magic and shamanism can be traced to Atlantis. Atlanteans directed powers that could resurrect, transform and shift energies through crystals. Their manifestation abilities, mathematical and scientific understanding of the functioning powers that sustained life were blended into their entire culture. Conversely, Lemurians used crystals to retain and hold high vibrations of love. They hid their historical lineage, knowledge, spiritual practices and order of universal peace within specially programmed crystals, as well as in secret scrolls and initiatory secrets.

These became the roots of the Holy Grail and later became the teachings of the Essenes.

By the end of the Lemurian civilization, the Atlanteans had learned to amplify and direct the powers of the third eye to control, destroy and magnify life force. The misuse of power had become so rampant that the life so beautifully woven with spirit by the Lemurians was destroyed. During this time, some Lemurian refugees merged into the Atlantean ways, but the Atlantean government forced Lemurian leaders to give up their own leadership order and follow a foreign spiritual protocol.

About 12,000 years ago, at the height of the Atlantean civilization—and dominion of the known world through seafaring means, not unlike the 18th and 19th century British Empire—an unexpected cataclysm caused the entire continent to sink. Only the highest eastern points remained above water; they became what is now the Azores, the Canary Islands, Gibraltar and the Madeira Islands.

The origins of Atlantis were kept alive by Atlantean and Lemurian refugees who lived and wandered in tribes, afraid to settle too long in one place lest it disappear as did their Motherland. These nomads spread to Asia, Europe, Central America, the Yucatan Peninsula and the Mediterranean; their descendants formed the Syrian, Babylonian, Chaldean and Egyptian peoples. Other groups formed the root ancestral tribe of the Cherokee nation in North America, and the ancient Druidic people that created Stonehenge in southern England.

The Fall

As I previously mentioned, the sinking of Atlantis and the Great Biblical Flood were one and the same. These events also coincided with Adam and Eve's fall from God's grace. The "fall from grace," as metaphorically described in the book of Genesis, occurred in the Garden of Eden. Located in the Tigris-Euphrates valley, this place was formerly known as Sumeria and Babylon. Once a verdant paradise, it is now the war-torn desert land of Iraq.

The fall happened as a consequence of man and woman losing sight of each other's powers. The masculine and feminine powers fell out of balance. They identified with their splits and differences rather than with their wholeness. Masculine and feminine parts of the self went into the abyss unnoticed and fell into darkness and separation. The power of God became identified as a force with which to control from, rather than as a source of co-creation. Leaving this inner "oneness" caused the beginning of world suffering as we know it. Rather than developing their spiritual power while linked into their feminine and masculine wholeness, the "Adams" and "Eves" split the circle. At this point Yoga was created in India to strengthen the connection between body and spirit and reunite masculine and feminine power into Source.

We have been trying to heal the split ever since.

Before the fall, ceremonies and rites of initiation filled and inspired every life. Chalices and stones were used in most mystery schools throughout the Mediterranean, Europe and Asia for initiatory purposes. Other items such as platters, bowls and spears were also ceremonial objects. The chalice held the herbal elixir drink of immortality, and the stone was held or placed on chakra centers to awaken the spine's strong alchemical force from tailbone (root chakra) to the top of the head (crown chakra). Initiations awakened spiritual forces within the aspirant.

Thus began the physical practice of the Holy Grail, the preparations, exercises and activations leading to full illumination and the usage of stones and chalices in ceremonies.

The original initiation stone was an iron-core meteorite that assisted in the spine's energetic activation. Initiatory stones in Crete, associated with Atlantean ruler (and Greek god) Zeus, were called "Thunderstones." Huge cone- and pyramid-shaped meteorites tied to Venus were used in Paphos, Cyprus and Heliopolis, Egypt. The "Stone of Heaven," found in the great Kaaba in Mecca and designed by Abraham (and later redesigned by Mohammed), was a meteorite believed to be from Venus and used to venerate the goddess' powers. The Chintamani Stone, known as "The Treasure of the World," now resides in the legendary Kashmiri kingdom of Shambhala. Within the Dome of the Rock in Jerusalem lies the *Even ha Shettiya*, "Stone of Foundation." King David purchased the rock for it to be the location for the Ark of the Covenant. His son, King Solomon, later used the rock as the foundation for his Temple, an alchemical cauldron for the divine masculine and feminine to coalesce into the presence of the *Yod He Vau He*—God.

Ancient Holy Grail chalices are found around the world. Two small cruets, or vials, owned by Nicodemus were placed in safekeeping in the head of a wooden crucifix before his death. They are known as the *Volto Santo*. "Oriental Cornerina," a red agate stone cup dating back to the time of Christ and known as Santo Caliz of Valencia, is in the possession of the Vatican. The Sumerian Grail was discovered in the "Oldest Sun Temple in Mesopotemia." The turquoise *Jami-Jamshid*, the Cup of Jamishad, was known to reveal the future and transform a human being into an immortal god. At least 20,000 years old, it was unearthed by Persian King Jamshid. The Chinese Golden Cauldron, a large golden pot, could manifest an ongoing immortality elixir to assist only emperors who governed their kingdoms in harmony with divine will.

One in Her Self

The Holy Grail's outer symbols of stone and chalice convey the inner message of the Awakened Spirit; the divine feminine, or Goddess, is the central point. Goddess religions and practices were very much the way of the ancient peoples who practiced the earliest ceremonies of the Holy Grail Teachings. The reason is profound: A woman advanced in her divine feminine powers could circulate life force power within herself and the universe simultaneously. The abilities to give life to others, transform the energies of death into life and return the soul to wholeness were everyday occurrences in ancient times. The divine feminine empowered a woman to become "one in her self." Her practice of circulating and regenerating the cosmic forces kept her whole and able to constantly conceive universal life force.

Mary, the mother of Jesus, was such a woman. She followed a millennia-long lineage of masters. In Sumeria, 3,000 years earlier, Inanna (also known as Nin-Khursag or Nintu) was known as "The Life Giver," "Mother of All," "Queen of the Gods." Her name also translates to read, "she who gives life to the dead." The serpents, with which she is often depicted, represent the divine sexual-spiritual forces and rebirth, the shedding of old skin and growth of new. By the time of the Eve mythology, the meaning of the serpent was already being contorted into an evil temptress. The Goddess, the feminine side of God, was about to be cast into myth as a lost rib, absent from her true source.

The Egyptian goddess Neith is said to have given birth to the Sun-God Ra by her own power. Both Egyptian goddesses Neith and Isis had the title "Queen of Heaven;" in central Asia Minor, Neith was Cybele, the Mighty Mother, ruler over wild nature. In the West, she was known as Artemis or Diana and honored as "Lady of the Moon." On the Greek mainland, she was the earth mother of all beings. Cybele, the mistress of the animals, was called such in Minoan Crete but was known as Aphrodite in Greece and Astarte by the Syrians. Goethe later lovingly termed her the *Ewig-Weibliche*, or Eternal Womanly. Her powers in ancient legends speak of her ability to consciously facilitate pregnancy by circulating her own inner male forces to the level of conceiving without having relations with a male partner—thus the fable of Mary being a virgin mother.

More myths shoot off from this crucial period. In one, a male aspect of the Goddess splits off and is turned into her own divine partner, her "god." A Greek myth portrays "earth" conceiving the Titans through intercourse with "heaven" or the "sky." In the beginning, as myths from other nations make clear, earth and heaven were not distinct. They were considered a single entity, the matrix of life, with the male-god arising from fission. With the Goddess' abilities to create and destroy life, a man honored her powers by moving through his own inner death and rebirth. He had to be willing to find his male power through the process of transformation through the feminine power. Only through his love and devotion to the Goddess could his emergence be whole. His awakening was a spiritual one, committed to building visions of abundance, civilizations, temples and industry, no matter how simple or complex.

The divine feminine, as practiced by Neith, Isis, Cybele, Astarte, Inanna, Mary and others, was responsible for allowing a man to grow, create and make decisions that reflected his soul truth. If a man did not receive of the feminine power, he prevented his male power from filling him, and he became an empty chalice, prompted to find satiation in non-sacred ways. A man's soul evolution required him to learn to drink from this Holy Grail and awaken his divine feminine-masculine forces.

A woman who misused her powers could drive a man down the road of emptiness, self-indulgence, relationship failure, loss or greed. A mother, lover or wife who tapped into her relationship in order for the male to fill her emotional and spiritual emptiness succeeded only in short-circuiting the man's creative, financial and spiritual life. Whenever a priestess misused her powers and withheld sacred connection, whether through ignorance or deceit, or a man destroyed others through his hunger for power for any reason, the divine sacrament of drinking from the Holy Grail ended.

The time of revering goddesses and gods in statue forms—practiced by the Babylonians, Sumerians, Egyptians and later Greeks and Romans—was the last period of honoring divine union. As men strove to destroy the powers of the feminine, women became victims of their tyranny and could no longer source the power of the Goddess to assist men in walking as gods. The memories were frozen, as it were, in stone and marble statues.

Moses, a.k.a. Pharoah Akhnetan

The second millennium B.C. brought in the institution of kingship—the third huge blow to the goddess religions and practice of the divine feminine. The greatest leader in this new, patriarchal way was Moses, who led the Hebrews from Egypt to the Promised Land in the Exodus. The Hebrews were descendants of the paganistic Patriarchs or '*ebrai* (Aramaic for "from the other side [of the Euphrates]"), who colonized the fertile valley between the Tigris and Euphrates in Mesopotamia. The *'ebrai* were the ancient ancestors of the twelve tribes who migrated with their pagan (literally "country person" or "of the country") heritage from Mesopotamia to Canaan around 2000 B.C.E. They were also the ancestors of Mary, Mother of Jesus. They revered fertility goddesses, were considered polytheistic, and ritualized sex to honor the Goddess. The *'ebrai* migrated into southwest Egypt where they dwelt until 1250 B.C.E., when Moses brought them to the Promised Land.

Moses' monotheistic thinking was difficult for the Hebrews to understand. However, his religious perspective was identical to the Egyptian Pharoah Akhenaten, who merged the Egyptian deities into one being named Aten.

Since Moses was adopted as a baby by a Pharoah, it made sense for him to embody the teachings given to those who sat on the throne. Still, Moses' true identity comes as quite a shock. Moses was, in actuality, Pharoah Akhenaten! Thus, the Jewish patriarch *was an Egyptian.* Akhenaten, also known as Amenhotep IV, ruled from 1367 to 1350 B.C., but was banished from Egypt when he was disposed for introducing the one-God concept to a people that had practiced polytheism for several millennia. He fled with his Hebrew servants, who looked towards him as the occupant of the throne from which he had been ousted—the *Mose, Meses* or *Mosis.* The deposed pharoah led the Hebrews and families of the Israelites out of Egypt. Specific similarities can be found between the *Egyptian Book of the Dead* (Spell 125) and the 10 Commandments. The Roman Catholic Douai Bible says the name "Moses" is Egyptian, signifying "heir" or "born of." It was often used with another name, such as Rameses (born of Ra) or Thothmoses (born of Thoth).

The name Moses does not appear in any Egyptian record, but the actions of Akhenaten do. It is well known that the Egyptian pharaoh not only constructed new temples to Aten, but also closed the doors to the many temples dedicated to the Egyptian gods and goddesses. Worship of Amun and the sun god Ra, both important deities of the people, was banned. Akhenaten imposed strict control over the devotional practices of the populace, and stubbornly enforced his patriarchal religion. The ways of the Goddess was suddenly and drastically obliterated from the lives of the Egyptian people.

Moses sought to eliminate all the old ways of worship. He blanched at the long-established teachings of transforming and integrating the inner desires of the lower self, which included: expansion of the inner eye (third eye) to see parts of self trapped in the dark terrain of the psyche; circulating spiritual currents through the lower chakras to purify, clear and integrate their powers; removing impure thought forms by re-establishing the energy of the soul's eternal grid; and clearing sexual energy through spiritual practices that aligned the base chakras with the heart and higher centers (third eye and crown). Instead, Moses introduced a strict code of abstinence outside of marital union, disregard for the physical body and its inner spiritual currents, and total adherence to a punitive, unapproachable male Yahweh from which few could grow. Women didn't belong to this equation except as submissive consorts to their men. Yahweh also issued Moses the Ten Commandments. The Essenes later incorporated the Ten Commandments of Moses and aligned them with the traditional devotional practices of the sacred feminine and masculine.

Upon arrival in the Promised Land, Moses and his followers encountered a more familiar practice to ancient cultures. The Canaanite god Baal, a fertility and agricultural deity along with his partner, the mother goddess Asherah, honored the creative, sexual and life-giving forces—the next evolutionary level of the Holy Grail. Moses and the people of the Exodus adopted the local Canaanite weather god, Yahweh, in a way that conflicted with and threatened the Canaanite way: they elevated the god's status to being the one-and-only God of the people. At first the populace did not find itself significantly moved by the change in devotion, since the people were able to continue to include the many gods and goddesses they had grown up with in their lives. When Israelite rabbis depicted Yahweh as the all-powerful God in Second Isaiah and in Exodus, however, the existence of all other gods was denied, and the people's lives were forever changed.

Moses' actions served as the decisive blow of the millennia-old psychic and physical battle between the patriarchy and matriarchy, at the expense of Baal and Asherah. The balance between the inner and the outer mirror of creation deteriorated as the inner feminine power was eliminated and the isolated workings of the patriarchy were externalized into outer dogma. As people moved further away from internal connection with spirit, the external laws of man became the greater force. The condemnation of the goddess-based religion created the devastating split between the Yahweh-Patriarchal religion and the Sacred Feminine way. Instead of celebrating and further developing feminine power in the temples, the practice was removed. Women were carefully and discreetly chosen for initiation and training in the temples of higher spiritual truths. Once, this had been as commonplace as young people becoming ministers today. They carried the responsibilities of a pure lineage where spirit and the body were seen as being holy. Too many sects had split off from the whole teachings of the Goddess. Power was being misused both on the Patriarchal and Priestess side.

Following Moses' passing, the Hebrews, along with other nomads, formed a tribal community. They briefly united as a kingdom under David (1010-970 B.C.E.), then split into two monarchies, Judah in the south and Israel in the north. The heavily edited and re-written New Testament erased the polytheistic, goddess-inspired teachings and practices of the "northern" race. The monotheistic Hebrews' disgust with the Canaanites' spiritual practices and customs, coupled with their desire to seize all spiritual power to control the masses, prompted total elimination of an ancient way. Jereboam of Ephraim, a ruling king of the north in 922 B.C.E., was an outspoken pagan who, in the first Book of Kings, "placed in Bethel the priests of the high places he had made." These "high places" were the goddess sanctuaries that the Bible consistently spoke about as the temples to be destroyed — sanctuaries dedicated to Baal. They were places of worship with the divine. During this time there was huge dissonance between the Israelites of Gilead and Shiloh. The Gilead Israelites followed Baal, and the Shiloh Israelites held the Gilead Isrealites at fault for destroying the sanctuaries.

Interestingly, the Holy Grail is first mentioned as a cauldron that resides in "high places" or *bamahs*. II Kings clearly states how the patriarchal leaders felt:

> "And the children of Israel did secretly those things that were not right against the Lord their God, and they built them high places in all their cities, from the tower of the watchmen to the fenced city. And they set them up images and groves in every high hill, and under every green tree." (II Kings 17:9)

Sexual Rites of Israelites Banned

The Moses-Yahweh religion banned the sexual rites of the Israelites. Before the time of Moses, tribes explored sexuality as an expression of worship, merging the boundaries of flesh and spirit. The gods and goddesses of the Canaanites, Assyrians, Babylonians, Hittites and Egyptians enjoyed full sexual partnership with their consorts. Yet Yahweh was regarded as a celibate, and the male scribes of the Old Testament were supporters of this ideology. The paid scribes of the Jerusalem Judahite royalty were not permitted to accurately describe the non-Yahweh based cultures, which later became known as cults. In 733 B.C.E., an ethnic cleansing exiled 13,000 people from the northern kingdom of Israel to Mesopotamia. Tribes from Babylonia mixed with the remaining Israelites to create future Galileans. Mary the Mother's parents, Anna and Joachin, descended from a Babylonian-Israelite union.

Meanwhile, the writings of the feminine from the "north land" were destroyed. The spiritual antecedents of the Holy Grail (and Mary the Mother), the combined Canaanite priestess traditions of Baal and his consort Asherah—the "outcasts" of Yahweh and followers of the Goddess sect—and the Essenes, who followed strict laws of sexuality and devotion to one God (as aspects of many gods to bring into oneself and worship), were seriously endangered. So was another Grail antecedent, paganism; by the time of Mary's birth, the split between the beliefs of the Moses-Patriarchial Hebrew lineage and the Canaanites' Priestess lineage had fomented to the verge of all-out attack on feminine power.

The fifty years before the birth of Christ looked like an end battle. The battlefield was Palestine and Syria, the home of Galilee, Judea and Nazarea, a land occupied by the Romans. Under the authority of Herod Antipas, who became known as Herod the Great, all civil rights ended. He set up his own council and withheld all political power from the Sanhedrin, the Jewish government. He created a powerful elite of Jewish and Greek families and ended the roles of kings and high priests. This resulted in an anarchic uprising among the people that challenged the Jewish community to either turn to the unseen God Yahweh, or to pray for protection to pagan masters.

During this time, the Psalms of Solomon were written to help establish guidelines for the sacred sexuality rites in shrines and sanctuaries. The Jerusalem Temple was home to ancient fertility rites. It housed the *asherah* — the altar to the fertility goddess and partner of the Canaanite fertility god Baal. The sexual ceremonies that took place there were the hub of religious life and were centered around devotion to Asherah. Because of this, it was around the time of Christ that Yahweh's divine feminine counterpart, Sophia—the Goddess—was rewritten back into the Gospels. The timing was ordained, since great women were about to work alongside Jesus and his dearest and closest disciples, the Apostles.

Chapter 3

The Carriers of the Flame

True power resides in the union of heart, body and soul while living in a state of divine remembrance with the One.
~ Iana Lahi

The faces of the Holy Grail are the same three people who personify the remarkable series of spiritually revolutionizing events that took place in the Holy Land two millennia ago—Jesus, Mary the Mother and Mary Magdalene. Each acted upon a soul mission to point the way into light. They were gatekeepers of the divine for the many who had lost the way.

The last thing Jesus wanted was to be viewed or remembered as the "savior." A true avatar, he had done his inner work—what the great yogis call *nirbikalpa samadhi yoga*—and walked on the earth for one purpose: to awaken redemption and the indwelling God within each soul that crossed his path. He did not live from his ego; material concerns, such as conquering others and acquiring wealth, were of no interest to him.

By the time Jesus returned to Israel to teach after a 20-year absence, the divine feminine power, once inherent in politics, spirituality, religion and culture, was virtually non-existent. Similar to our world situation today, those in control of the political (the Romans) and religious (Jewish Rabbis) processes did not want people to have individual practices in which they were able to consciously connect to the light. The reason? A soul filled with light from a direct connection to Source was an uncontrollable soul. The Jews and Romans battled for power over the people and their spiritual beliefs, an echo of which can be found in the way the Christian fundamentalists and extreme Muslim fundamentalists are waging war today.

Jesus the Christ, along with Mary and eventually Mary Magdalene, were trying to bring the divine feminine consciousness back into Judaism, Islam and Buddhism. Jesus' followers not only existed in the Middle East, but also throughout the Mediterranean crescent that stretched from ancient Rome to Greece, Macedonia, Thessalonica, Ephesus, Phoenicia (now Lebanon), and southeast to what is now India, Tibet and Nepal. Written accounts exist in India, Kashmir and Tibet of "Issa," the messenger from the West.

The later fabrication of Jesus' identity into the Son of God, instead of his true stature as a Christed One, changed history to fit a picture manufactured by a group of minds that desired to imprison people's souls in terror, fear and darkness. The difference between "Son of God" and "Christed One" is far more than a splitting of semantics. The Church uses "Son of God" to depict Jesus as the one and only person who deserved to be a child of God, labeling the rest of us as unworthy souls. In fact, in the Catholic communion ceremony, parishioners say before receiving the sacrament, "Lord, *I am not worthy to receive you*, but only say the word and I shall be healed." Conversely, Jesus' true stature as the Christed One meant that he achieved complete *divine* communion with God—and made it clear that we were all capable of working towards and receiving the same *inner* sacrament.

As a Christed One, Jesus showed his disciples how to see the light within and follow it into the kingdom of God. His brother, James, continued the techniques Jesus had taught the disciples through the Jerusalem Church, which James founded. The spiritual training both brothers had received from their elders and teachers continued their family's spiritual legacy, which was rooted directly from their mother's life experience and ancestry.

The life journey of Mary, the mother of Jesus, has become perhaps the most truncated and falsified story of the entire Galilean experience. Imagine shooting a four-hour movie, editing it down to ten minutes, then fictionalizing those ten minutes in a way that best appeases and controls the masses. The result: Mary's story as we hear it today.

The third participant in the innermost circle of Christ, Mary Magdalene, symbolizes how low humankind can stoop to destroy the reputation and life purpose of a person filled with the brightest spiritual light. How is it possible that the great lightbearer among Jesus' disciples—and the love of his life—was later described and regarded by others as a prostitute? Who *were* these others? They certainly weren't Jesus' disciples, who considered her a leader. Nor likely were they the Rabbis and Romans—there is no evidence of these groups having had interactions with Mary. In fact, these "others" never saw her alive. Nor did their children or great-grandchildren. The prostitute myth wasn't written into her story until several hundred years after her death.

The work of Jesus, Mother Mary and Mary Magdalene embodied spiritual states of consciousness on the physical plane—a matter of bringing christed light, sacred oneness and divine union into the human body. Jesus' performance of miracles was a natural act of manifesting the light of God. His practices of building light in the body constituted a science of opening, aligning and reconnecting the spiritual, etheric and physical currents. As Jesus exemplified and Mary Magdalene later carried forth, healing is a miracle that correctly uses the energies of God. As the spark of divine remembrance is awakened in the cells, the body opens to make room for this current. The chakras are ignited, transforming the karmic, mental and emotional mind. This activation brings to life what is dormant—as the pilgrims and multitudes of Nazareth and the Israeli desert experienced.

Mary the Mother: An Introduction

Why was Mary chosen by the Essenes to be the mother of Jesus? Why was Mary the one to plead to Pontius Pilate to spare her son's life? How is it possible that a spiritual giant was reduced to being recognized for having an "immaculate conception," an utter untruth invented by the Catholic Church? Mary the Mother birthed a son who entered this world with full consciousness. Mary was trained to competently bring higher consciousness into her body. This was her first mission as an initiate of the divine order. Why is this considered strange?

A sheep-farmer's daughter, Mary came from the rural surroundings of Galilee, a northern frontier province once a part of the northern kingdom of Israel. A descendant of the Israelites and Essenes and initiate of the Essene order (along with her future husband, Joseph), Mary was trained in the Essene School from the age of seven. She was expected to learn the ancient ways of union with the divine. These teachings included: ways to clear thoughts that cause harm to another or one's self; how to clear the emotional body of its angers, lusts and hurts, and of lingering internal wounds that create abusive behaviors to others; and the opening of the causal (memory) body that enabled people to remember who they were and the work they needed to complete within their lifetimes. Mary's training gave her the knowledge to build the spiritual body into a flame of light and provided her with access to the highest currents and states of consciousness. She was trained in the ways of healing, tantra (moving sacred currents of Spirit) and initiating others. She was able to educate her son, prepare him to train with the High Priests and Rabbis, and advise him to travel to India, Tibet and Kashmir to train with God-realized teachers and Avatars. Only after this training did he return to his homeland.

What about Mary's spiritual teachers, the Essenes? As the split of feminine-masculine power grew disastrously wide, there were tribes that worked to keep the oneness alive. The most significant, the Essenes, followed a way of life filled with disciplines to honor the God of creation. The Essences practiced and taught techniques to clear the physical and subtle bodies to maintain spiritual and physical health. They were adept at working with currents of energy that moved from the God Source to align the bodies—physical, mental, causal spiritual and emotional. These currents sustain life and create health, spiritual vision and purpose.

The Essenes understood that by clearing the bodies, the direct flow of Cosmic Consciousness could move through each of them. This healing tradition has existed in all civilizations in which the intention has been to live directly connected in God. They were not limited to a single religion, but studied them all in order to comprehend the great scientific principles. The Essenes considered each religion to be a different interpretation of a single revelation, a series of rays originating from the same light. They gave great significance to teachings of the ancient Chaldeans, Zoroaster, Hermes Trismegiste, the secret instructions of Akhenaten (Moses), founding Essene Masters who had transmitted techniques similar to those of Buddhism, and the keys of Kabbalah, the ancient revelations of the tree of life.

One of the Essenes' major preoccupations was to protect themselves from any contact with evil spirits, in order to preserve the purity of their souls. They knew their stay and influence on earth was to be short, and they did not want to prostitute their eternal souls. It was this attitude, strict discipline and absolute refusal to lie or compromise that made them objects of so much persecution through the ages.

The Essenes viewed their Brotherhood-Sisterhood as the teaching ground for the sons and daughters of God. The high priests worked to re-establish a code that integrated the feminine and masculine forces, through alignment in God. They personified the light shining in the dark, with the powers to transform darkness into light. When a candidate asked to be admitted to the Essene School, it was understood that a process of awakening the soul was set in motion within him or her. The student's soul was ready to ascend the stairs of the sacred temple of the divine. Only awakened souls could be considered for initiation into the mysteries of the Brotherhood-Sisterhood, thus beginning a path of evolution through the cycle of their incarnations.

The Essenes considered themselves the guardians of the Divine Teachings—later symbolized as the Holy Grail. They possessed numerous ancient manuscripts, some of which dated back several millennia to the dawn of written communication. A large portion of the Essene School members decoded and translated these manuscripts into several languages, reproducing them in order to perpetuate and preserve the advanced sacred knowledge. In 1947, these manuscripts were found at Qum'ran, an ancient Essene community near Jerusalem. They're popularly known as the Dead Sea Scrolls.

Long before the birth of the destined Anointed One, or Messiah, the Essene Rabbis knew of the coming event and prepared for it long in advance. The Messiah was a prophet, a guide for establishing peace amongst nations. He was to reawaken the forgotten precepts of living in the divine—the keys to the kingdom of heaven. The Essenes identified the appropriate mother to bring such a child into the world, a woman initiated in their ancient ways of connecting the human soul to God. An initiated mother was important, because when direct connection to the life-giving force of God is sought, initiations strengthen and magnify the soul's power. Once given these initiations, the well-disciplined, well-focused individual amplifies the bond between the inner powers of the soul and God force directly.

The chosen woman was a higher initiate, the teenaged Mary. She held the vision of the teachings. She was a bridge between the spiritual and physical worlds. Eventually, she spiritually ascended while in her body, during the lifetime of her son. She followed a more reclusive life as she transformed into higher states of consciousness. Her focus on sexuality was as an initiate who had entered higher states to experience the divine love that would enable her and her future husband to conceive and birth an extraordinary son.

Mary Magdalene: An Introduction

Mary Magdalene lived in the essence of the divine feminine. Her training with Jesus the Christ enabled her to attain the ability to channel life force energies for healing and manifesting. Through direct experience, she understood the intricacies of divine union. Her body was a temple where spirit and the flesh met in holy matrimony. Mary taught that the divine power of God emanated from the feminine side of creation, to be used with wisdom for the good of all. She recognized the shadow or dark side as the "forgotten one," or prodigal child; she always embraced it as the other half of a christed state.

As Jesus' most revered disciple and partner, Mary Magdalene carried forth the preparatory disciplines for receiving the Holy Grail and divine union. When Mary taught, it had become almost impossible for a woman to step forth as an anointed, christed teacher. This presents a striking similarity to our present culture, which takes a patriarchal approach to everything from religion to work ethic to ways of conduct. The feminine power was not respected and certainly not revered.

Still, she taught. The lost portion of her work first carried out with Jesus, involved entering the body of light by uniting the divine and human states. She taught that as currents of consciousness connect the mind, body and soul into the cosmic force, the divine soul energies of the masculine and feminine are ignited. These masculine-feminine powers meet in the body to create spiritual channels of sacred bliss, power and divine sweetness. This simultaneous union of God and body, *the sacred feminine*, opens the heart to take over the body and soul through the feminine container, the Holy Grail. It is within this sacred vessel that the currents of God flow and travel through the precipices, canyons, rivers and caves of our holy body temple, which becomes a chalice for creative power. The Holy Grail's nectar bursts from the opened heart and unites the emotional and physical body into a chalice of light. Its sweet wine anoints the heart—merging the spirit and body together. The body is seen as a temple of beauty and treated as a home in which a god or goddess may live.

When Mother Mary met Mary Magdalene by the well, they recognized one another as initiates of the Mystery Teachings—tools to directly access the power of God. They carried the active power of the Holy Grail and conveyed its divine essence to others.

The sacred mission of the two Marys was so crucial to the advancement of the sacred feminine Holy Grail Teachings for humankind that its essence is written into their names. The origin of "Mary" is just as spiritually significant and mysterious as the lineage and eventual teachings of both the Mother Mary and Mary Magdalene. It comes from *mara,* a common Hebrew root word. The Book of Proverbs describes *mara* as "bitter." The fate of the sacred prostitute could be "bitter as wormwood, sharp as a two-edged sword" (Proverbs 5:4). The Mesopotamia source of *mara* was the Akkadian verb *marau*, "to be bitter" — a state of bitterness caused from being rebellious.

The original name or designation that derived from *mara* was "Maryam." It was changed to "Miriam" in the Old Testament, then became anglicized as Mary. During the excavation of a third-century C.E. Jewish synagogue in Syria, a mural was found that depicted a woman rescuing the abandoned infant Moses from bulrushes alongside the Nile. She was Anahita, a fertility goddess who later became known in Greek mythology as Aphrodite. The priestess Anahita was also Maryam or Miriam.

Thus, the two Marys continued a spiritual lineage that included the adoptive mother of Moses, who was also imbued by the power and ways of the sacred feminine. Their lineage, and the spiritual significance of "Mary," was about to disappear from the face of the earth—but not from the hearts or hidden records of their safekeepers.

After the Crucifixion

After the crucifixion, the two Marys taught together and separately. Mother Mary taught quietly in communities, while Mary Magdalene taught throughout France and healed the sick, until she retired to a cave outside of Aix, Provence. Their work opened spiritual gateways to receive the Holy Grail within the bodies of aspirants. Many of their teachings focused on two particular bodies—the astral (emotional) and etheric (double). They taught that a clear emotional body looks like a sky filled with a million stars—and only then can the soul and physical realms be joined. The bridge between the spirit and physical realms, the astral body, is a connecting rod. Without a clear astral body, it is impossible to simultaneously live in the soul and the power of the third eye. The etheric body, or "double body," is the energetic component of the physical body. If it is closed, it creates illness, emotional imbalances and mental chatter, illusions and self-indulgence. When opened, it creates light, abundance, joy and love.

Mary the Mother and Mary Magdalene were also practiced higher-level initiates of divine or tantric sex, in its pure form a means to experience and worship God. However, the practice had become misunderstood and corrupted by societies, religious leaders, individuals and 1,000 years of suppressing the goddess religions. Its ultimate dissolution from the lives of all but the higher initiates came down to one thing: the tragic separation of God from sexuality. Sex without higher consciousness was inconceivable to women like the two Marys, divine initiators socially recognizable by the veils of adornment covering their heads.

They understood the role of *Qdesha,* holy women and once revered teachers who became high priestesses of the Sacred Marriage. Mary Magdalene was, in fact, a direct link in that lineage. *Qdesha* carried a distinguished position in the temples and carried on the fertility, birth and death rites of the human spirit. Those who did not misuse the power of their position maintained a life of discipline and service to the divine. They were as devout as present-day nuns, and undoubtedly the ancient inspiration for the Catholic sisterhood—though the latter's practices are much different. Their ceremonies, chants, dances and meditations served as holy, divine communions with God. The offering of the chalice of wine in Catholic communion ceremonies—described as the "blood of Christ" for the past 15 centuries—may have well been derived from the *Qdesha* offering of the *sacred womb, the original chalice, in communion with the One.* Their relationship to their bodies was the key to the universe. Through their connection to their power centers—their wombs, solar plexuses, hearts and souls—they developed spiritual powers. These feminine sexual-spiritual practices recognized that the male rebirths himself through the feminine power, internally and externally. The sacred priestess, *Qdesha,* was the awakener. She was the holder of the cup and taught disciples how to drink the nectar of God.

This cup was the Holy Grail—the womb of the Mother-Goddess.

Eventually, the *Qdesha* were called "sacred prostitutes." Thus began Mary Magdalene's ignominious descent into the underbelly of Church lore, and the submersion of the Holy Grail Teachings to protect the *Qdesha* from the fury of Church leaders hell-bent on their elimination and that of the women who carried the teachings in their hearts and souls.

Mary taught the discovery process of life. Like Mary the Mother, she was reduced to being a myth of shame—one that every woman must break through to find the truth. The Catholic Church took her viewpoint and turned it around to condemn anyone who sought the light within the dark, or the unknown of his or her own heart. She was perhaps the greatest saint that the Church refused to recognize; they vilified her and created the prostitution myth to tarnish her legacy.

Chapter 4

Destroying the Divine Feminine

"All that there is
Is worship—
To wash your feet
Like Magdalene
With my hair;
To make my heart's blood
Sweet ointment for your eyes,
To lie with You,
To lie alone,
To eat of the summer fruit
And remember the bitter hunger
When food fails us
In the winter storms."
~ Rumi

Before the conclusion of the 1st century A.D., an entirely different reality swept across the Holy Land. It minimized the contributions and influence of the two Marys and Judaism itself while simplifying and twisting Jesus' most sacred admonitions through councils, rewrites of gospels and destructions of other gospels. Eventually, his teachings were ground down to candy-coated half-truths fed to spiritually bereft masses.

In 90 A.D., rabbis revised the Hebrew canon, eliminating some sacred texts and adding others, thus creating 24 new books. This occurred principally because Christians were distorting the text of the Hebrew canon to suit their own views and enhance their religion. (Example: The Hebrew word *alma*, meaning "young woman," was translated to "virgin" in the book of Isaiah, implying Isaiah had prophesized Jesus' birth to a virgin.) The discovery of the Dead Sea Scrolls revealed another aspect of Judaic history: Like the early Christians, the Jews of Jesus' time utilized far more religious texts than the ones ultimately included in the Hebrew Bible, a text which was not "standardized" until the 2nd Century.

The disempowerment of women and non-Christians accelerated in the 2nd Century A.D. to levels beyond its already oppressive pre-Christ stage. The Christian followers of Peter and the converted Paul (formerly Saul of Tarsus) began to subjugate women and exclude them from all church services. Women serving as spiritual leaders were considered heretics—another convenient misuse of an old word. Heretic comes from the Greek *hairesis* and means choice. Meanwhile, all information about how the goddess practiced was being eliminated from the Christian Bible, a collection of writings and gospels that had only begun to be assembled.

In the year 220, Hippolytus, an early Church philosopher, declared Judaism heretical in his *Refutation of All Heresies*. There was more. After the Hebrew Bible was translated into Greek, and Christians had adopted the entire text, they added new passages and entire new books to the Septuagint. Then they accused the Hebrews of having *deleted* those newly added sections from the Bible, and used this as the basis for future acts of violence against Jews.

By the late 4th Century, the death penalty was creeping in as the ultimate punishment. Incomplete historical records show it was used only sporadically until the 11th Century, when it became standard treatment for "heretics." However, church suppression and persecution was widespread even before the introduction of the executioner as the "solution" for all heretics. Church leaders eventually began personally directing the persecution of the followers of competing religions.

Once Church leaders struck the fear of God into all men and women, they went to work to diminish the power of the uppermost teachings. A series of Church councils—Nicaea in 325 A.D., Constantinople in 381 A.D., Ephesus in 431 A.D., and Chalcedon in 451 A.D.—eradicated all records and teachings about Jesus being both human and divine, plus many ancient and mystery school teachings and nine sects of early Christianity. The Church did not honor Mary as the mother of Jesus until 400 years after his death, when the Council of Ephesus proclaimed her Mary, the Virgin Mother of God. This was hardly a thorough description of her enormous spiritual powers and abilities as a carrier of the Holy Grail.

Yet, the most egregious blasphemy was saved for Jesus' most powerful disciple, the one whom even the *Apostles* looked upon as the greatest among them—the love of his life, Mary Magdalene.

In the original *Questions of Mary,* quotations by Epiphanus elaborated upon the story of Mary being Jesus' closest confidante because she was his sexual and spiritual partner. Mary's true role to Jesus was gradually erased by the over-dominating rewrites of the Church.

It only grew worse. In 591 A.D., Pope Gregory I labeled Mary Magdalene a whore, officially sanctioning a characterization that remained official Church doctrine until 1969. To this day, this designation symbolizes and justifies the Church's suppression towards women in such deeply personal, vital areas as right-to-choose, birth control, priests marrying and women serving in the priesthood.

The desecration of Mary Magdalene's name and significance becomes more offensive when you consider the materials to which Pope Gregory had access when he stigmatized her. Mary Magdalene is the only woman besides Mary the Mother who is mentioned by name in all four central Gospels of the New Testament: Mark, Luke, John and Matthew. She is one of three people (John the Apostle and Mary the Mother were the others) recorded in John 19:25 as remaining with Jesus at the foot of the cross.

Furthermore, it is clearly stated in three Gospel sources (John 20:11-18, Mark 16:9, Matthew 28:9-10) that Mary Magdalene was the first to see Jesus resurrected after the crucifixion. Whether she saw Jesus first in his astral form (because he had passed from his body), or in his soul body (so he could comfort her while he reconnected, integrated and healed his soul and physical body) does not matter in this moment...Or does it? Is it that the occult evidence drove Pope Gregory I to depict Mary Magdalene as the whore of whores, the polar opposite of her true stature as a human embodiment of the feminine divine?

Once the sacred teachings of the feminine divine were banished, places of worship became the next series of targets. The Roman emperor Constantine, during the 4th century, ruled that temples should be destroyed and churches built in their places. In 601 A.D., Pope Gregory I urged Augustine of Hippo (later St. Augustine) to seek out "pagan" temples, destroy them and build churches on top of the sites.

The Loss of True Power

When the reign of co-creating with the Goddess ended in the first centuries after Christ's death, it ushered in a morose 1,000-year period, which history labeled the Dark or Middle Ages. Like so many conclusive chapters of a period of truth and power—the great rulers of Atlantis, the Greek dramatic masters, the Egyptian dynasties with their deep metaphysical underpinning—the light of Goddess teachings remained in our hearts only indirectly, through a fairy tale. Holy Grail legends spun from the womb of the buried feminine divine (see "Legends and Correlations" below). They are the stories of men trying to empty their own minds and bodies to find the spiritual passion that moved through them.

During the Middle Ages, the two greatest killers were the Black Plague and the Church. Any individual who carried the power of the Holy Grail was judged, exiled, or killed by the Church because he or she threatened the institution's position and hold on the masses. A perfect example is the courageous French teenager, Joan of Arc. The "evolution" of men during these control-hungry times produced those needing to retain physical and material power for themselves without developing the inner Holy Grail, the divine feminine half of their souls' blueprints. These men brought down civilizations by creating wars and religion to control the masses. Nothing exemplified that more than the Crusades.

The Church produced many leaders who, in the name of God, afflicted people most directly. Religious and political leaders split the autonomy of their people's power, stripping away their ability to access Spirit directly. By persecuting the use of feminine power, only false power could manifest. A religious middleman, the priest, was created by the Church to serve as a go-between for a person wishing to interact with God. Besides thoroughly diminishing a person's inherent spiritual power, this act was a blatant violation of Jesus' own words and admonitions inviting his followers to enjoy *direct access* with God— "The kingdom of heaven is within you" and "Where two or more are gathered, there will I be in the midst." Finally, the rise of the priest was the final death blow to any hope women had of remaining spiritually relevant.

Apparently, ecclesiastical edicts and Church-created practices weren't enough to wipe out the divine feminine. Church leaders went for the kill—literally. For many centuries after the deaths of Jesus and the two Marys, they slaughtered mystics, monks and female priestesses—a reign of tyranny that even crossed over to North America, in the infamous Salem Witch Trials of the late 17th century.

Ironically, only greater bloodshed could attempt to save what had been written out of history and destroyed by the Church. Battles were won and lost to defend the lineage of the Holy Grail. The Knights of Templar and the Royal Courts of England tried to preserve the way. From the mysterious Merlin, a master of light, to stories of the unicorn, the divine feminine went through various phases of being remembered and destroyed. The unicorn, once believed to exist on the astral plane, was woven into 13th century tapestries as a caged animal. This perpetual symbol for the christed divine feminine was depicted as no longer allowed to run free.

Legends and Correlations

The Holy Grail legends of King Arthur describe the final times of the divine feminine, when the magic of life, beauty and divine feminine power (personified by Guinevere) was the subject of battle. Holy Grail tales from the 13th century tell of the determination of Lancelot and other knights to meet their own soul struggles. This willingness to face the trials of the soul became known as the "Quest for the Holy Grail." The Knights Templars' pilgrimage for the way of truth and to preserve the dying mysteries of a past adorned with innocence and contemplation gave their lives purpose and clarity. This determined fight and agonizing loss for the divine feminine shattered the collective human heart for generations to come.

A new and darker type of fighting replaced this noble and divine pursuit. In the Crusades, warriors fought to strengthen and expand the injustice and lies perpetuated by the Church, rather than for the defense and preservation of true power. Humankind became filled with despair, longing, hatred and pain. Men began to betray and turn against anything holy; they became more and more emotionally blocked and armored. The search for the Holy Grail became the way to rediscover a hidden heart of gold that once upon a time, was melded into Spirit.

This search reached its ignominious low in the Americas in the early 16th century. While Spanish explorer Hernando de Soto canvassed the coast of what is now Florida for the elusive "Fountain of Youth," Spanish explorer Juan Pizarro plundered and destroyed the Incan culture in Peru while craving his personal "Holy Grail"—the Incans' plentiful treasures of gold. A thousand miles north, Pizarro's counterpart, Hernando Cortes, eliminated the Aztecs for the same reason. The Incans and Aztecs mined not only the precious metal, but also the inner gold of divine union—as indicated by their rituals and ceremonies honoring the sun. The Incan way was forever preserved in their word for God:

Apukontitiillateqsikayllawiraqochapachayachachiqrunakamaq.

It breaks down to a beautiful story of divine masculine-feminine balance: "*Apu*: the spiritual mountains. *Kon*: the cycle of water. *Titi*: spiritual energy. *Illa*: the complementary energy of life. *Teqsi*: the beginning cycle of all. *Kaylla*: the end cycle of all. *Wiraqocha*: foam is the water, the origin of life. *Pachayachachiq*: complete order of everything. *Runakamaq*: creator of human beings.

This is the power of the Holy Grail in living form—something the Spanish explorers, like the Church leaders on whose authority they operated, tried to destroy. While millions of women suffered and died horrible deaths, evolved spiritual sects like the Druids, Coptics and Essenes were vanquished and countless sacred records and writings were destroyed, the quests of those who sought to preserve the teachings of the two Marys, and the goddesses and priestesses who preceded them, were not in vain.

The Holy Grail lives again. It starts in the center of your chest.

Part II

Aligning with the Holy Grail: Integrating Light and Dark

Chapter 5

The Power of the Holy Grail

"Imagine you have transformed your entire
emotional body into Spirit Self.
Your Spirit Self would then imprint itself into your etheric body
like a seal into sealing wax, and give it form. In this way, your
etheric body is transformed into Life Spirit.
When this is done, the Life Spirit penetrates
the physical body and transforms it into the Spirit Human."
~ Rudolf Steiner

Only now can we see how two millennia of humankind's addiction to fear and confusion have led to tragic consequences for civilization as a whole. As both Marys would have said, unless the light shines forth from the self, hatred and pain will be the master. A cleansed and purified emotional body, connected to the heart center, creates clarity. It is *natural*, in our human-divine nature, to feel aligned to spirit and to think for our self. It is natural to feel good, to feel free, to feel attunement (at-one-ment) with our inner and outer worlds and the people in our lives. By returning to clarity, we're returning to our body temple's natural state.

In order to live fully aligned with our spiritual power, we must make a choice: Do we serve the light or the dark? One cannot serve two masters. Serving the dark maintains a state of denial in our emotional and memory bodies. We find reasons not to stretch our comfort zones. We align with soul patterns that repeat themselves over and over again in our every day lives, carving grooves like worn-out records in our psyches, rather than pulling out the roots and finding the source of joy and light. Serving the light furthers our sacred commitment to create projects and relationships that open portals of well-being and prosperity for others without sabotaging our divine nature.

If the differences between light and dark are so vast, why don't we just turn away from the darkness and stream to the light en masse? The answer pertains to the pain we've held within our emotional body over time—and the short-cuts we've often tried to take to numb ourselves. Drugs such as marijuana activate the emotional body and help the user travel into other realms. It is like jump-starting a dead car. The current from spirit has no way to move. It must first go through the emotional body to reach the physical body.

When congested and filled with the aberrations of pain and karmic wounding, the emotional body prevents spirit, the flow of God force, from fully moving into the soul and body. There is always a gap that seeks fulfillment through more substances, mind candy (TV, movies, entertainment, escapist magazines) or food. Access to the divine feminine has been cut off for so many soul lifetimes that our DNA has become cluttered with the genetic blueprint of prolonged suppression. A few of us have so strongly desired a full connection with spirit that we've been able to rise above it; we've found and tasted the Holy Grail. For the vast majority, however, it is only by having a drink, joint, other narcotizing prescription drug, junk food or sex with many partners that the emotional body can be fully activated and opened. Once opened, it is our responsibility to keep it that way.

Our bodies need to be re-trained to be able to feel life's rhythms and vibrations without the aid of drugs, sugar and alcohol. Our nervous systems need to be reconnected to receive the high voltage of the feminine power. Women who are addicted to high levels of sugar are unable to maintain the balance of their masculine-feminine energies. Let me give you an example. Several years ago, a successful and well-known West Coast yoga teacher came to one of my trainings. At the end of the first day, she vomited for three straight hours. A day later, her physical response was the same. She finally admitted to the group that she smoked marijuana "a lot" and couldn't get through a day without the common sidekicks of marijuana dependency, candy bars and cookies. Her body could not handle the vibrational increase from the meditations, teachings and movements. The anger stored in her feminine self was being unleashed, and she could no longer keep it down.

Unfortunately, her story is the story of most of us before and even during a spiritual awakening. Not all of it is our doing. Since the 12th century, Catholic and Protestant churches and powers have done everything possible to dilute, shut down, suppress, neglect and judge our spiritual-physical and emotional bodies. They have treated any manifestation of feminine power as evil (*Eve*-il), socially threatening, despicable and (you pick the negative description).

However, like feminine power itself, we cannot be placed in such a stifling box when our powers are alive and at our beckoning. When the feminine side is activated and co-creating with the masculine aspects of God, perfect union results. If we split them in half, then war, control issues, power struggles, poverty and hatred dominate. Nothing can offer a more graphic example than the decades-old struggle of women to enjoy equal rights with men, who presently control the global social and political agendas.

Men and women in our culture are not supposed to possess the powers of a Jesus or a Mary, even though *Jesus himself* admonished people to out-perform him when he said, "Greater works than these shall ye do." Once the soul journey of union begins, these powers naturally blossom like a dormant bulb exposed to a most brilliant sun. We must be willing to work through our own pain, not live through others, not have others live through us, and surrender to the greater feminine and masculine God power within ourselves. When we step into the divine feminine and reconnect ourselves into Source, the fire of our souls causes us to experience all that we are. That fire contains the holy mysteries of creation that no longer can remain hidden.

The Holy Grail is that feminine container of power and light, the lineage of spiritual truth passed down to those who can listen and receive from within their deepest selves. These Lost Teachings of the sacred feminine were once written down, but for all the reasons described above, were hidden and became dust in a box. This was the fate, as well, of the Nag Hammadi manuscripts (historical writings that date from pre-Crucifixion to four hundred years after). The Lost Teachings were hidden because they promoted awareness that the light of God existed within oneself—"The kingdom of heaven is within you," Jesus famously said—rather than in externally imposed beliefs. The Lost Teachings chronicle the holy connection between body, soul and spirit and how to maintain the consciousness of the awakened state. The teachings have traveled secret societies and circles since the time of Mary the Mother and Mary Magdalene.

Lost Mystics

The last teachers of the Holy Grail lived in the 13th century. These mystics were executed by the Church, suffering the same fate as tens of thousands before them. They held the rites of life, sacred prayers, dances, meditations and chants that helped them keep their containers open and pure. The women who carried the ray of the christed light were eliminated completely by the 15th century. By then, the teachings were only known through symbols and codes of light that bridge the spiritual currents of God with the physical body. These energy circuits created (and still create) a direct link-up with Universal Consciousness. They are the powers of the Holy Grail and can be experienced through dance energy movements and meditation practices.

Christianity and the Roman Catholic Church are not the only spiritual bodies to suppress the feminine-masculine balance and the sacred feminine power of the Holy Grail. Hinduism removed the understanding that the human body is the temple of the feminine, charged with deep feminine vibration, and cannot be transcended without first opening the powers of the inner feminine and merging them with the masculine powers. The 108 Hindu gods and goddesses were taught as existing outside the person, rather than as representing various expressions of feminine and masculine power. Sects such as the Shivaites knew the secrets of divine union and maintained their existence through discreet and hidden initiations. Buddhism removed the expressions of spiritual and sexual power off this plane and placed it into cosmic consciousness separate from the physical vehicle—*even though the Buddha himself understood and practiced divine union*. Buddhism that integrates body and soul carries some of the greatest power of any religion to restore the broken spirit. Its most enlightened adherents understand the battles of the psyche and mind, and know that to transform human consciousness, the ferocious spirit of the divine must be embodied.

Right Use of Power

As our global culture accelerates to higher and higher levels of technological breakthroughs, multi-national relationships and subsequent control by those holding the money, oil and military might, the exalted tradition of living from deep body and soul wisdom faces extinction. Unless we strike a balance within our culture, we face a repeat performance of destroying our civilization, much like Atlantis. The global warming crisis is an early warning sign, but the continued actions of political powers in the United States, Israel, Iran and China underscore the seriousness of this danger.

It is inevitable that the world culture will learn to drink from this cup again, but we may destroy most of civilization before that happens. We still have a collective choice, though time is running out. The severe imbalance of power governing the planet will have to be rebalanced. Until the feminine and masculine manifestations of God are no longer separated, there will be war, destruction, massive death, starvation, huge contrasts between rich and poor, and pain. The divine partnership of the feminine-masculine, when reunited within our spirit, will begin to turn around this era of hatred and bloodshed.

The Holy Grail is the missing half of the light needed to run nations, homes and communities in a harmonious, balanced, spiritually uplifting way. It was the "cup" from which Christ and the two Marys drank. Christ was condemned because the powers-that-be feared his might and influence to bring the cup directly to people's lips—in other words, they feared his ability to spiritually transform and empower an entire populace.

The Holy Grail's main secret is that it is a state of consciousness that gives direct connection to the source of life—which leads to a right use of power. *The ability to feel deeply within one's body is the most important quality a seeker of the Holy Grail can possess.* That which lives within the Grail can only be felt. When this communion with highest vibration and energy occurs, the divine feminine registers the heightened experience. As described in my forthcoming book, *Spirit Gateways*: *The Union of Love and Power,* the right use of power is something that is learned and practiced. Without this integrity, the power can be misused.

The journey back to Oneness—to God—has universal dramas. One of the most visible is how we use power. We can repress the power of others—and ourselves—or we can build spiritual power in every situation with the intention of creating, perpetuating and expanding life. During the average lifetime, every person experiences this test on several occasions. Power creates states of elation so consuming that it can seduce the mind into thinking it is the ultimate source. The great Indian yogi Paramahansa Yogananda, in his commentaries on the *Bhagavad Gita*, called this power "King Ego" and warned his readers never to ascend that throne.

The balance of power within our inner masculine-feminine energies nourishes the Holy Grail vessel. The quickest way to dissipate this power is to allow King Ego, the ego self—the part that defends and justifies how we survive, and freezes our beliefs and perceptions—to block the interchange of this divine power. When both feminine and masculine energies are in balance, there is a consistent interactive flow of life force and creativity, giving and receiving. The sense is one of expansion and joy. The Holy Grail went underground because the power it contained was unattainable unless the individual practiced the spiritual disciplines to carry and manage this great spiritual nectar. For thousands of years, women held this power in differing levels. In man's search to become sovereign and source his own spiritual power, he created inner walls. By cutting off his own feminine and becoming spiritually empty, he sought to conquer land—and woman herself. This ignited greed for possessing and owning what was not rightfully his. The land became a material replacement for the vast landscape of *spirit* that his soul so desperately sought. The split between male and female power became so extreme that the masses docilely began to accept whatever social system was created for them, rather than co-creating their own social systems in conjunction with a powerful mother-father role model leader. After collectively making this drastic choice, man forgot that divine power cannot be possessed. It's not ours; we don't own it. It is impossible to possess or exercise this type of power without creating an imbalance of existing spiritual forces.

As we learn to recognize the misuse of power, it becomes easier for us to recognize those in religious, political and social positions who identify themselves as master controllers. To change things politically and educationally, we need to harness our own balanced power. When religion is used to disempower the masses, it is easy to become prey to those who play Creator. Those wolves in sheep's clothing are everywhere we turn.

Becoming a Solution for Peace

How we utilize God power is our choice. Each person on this plane of consciousness is tried and tested as being either a co-creator with God power or a self-glorified magnet of duality by his or her own God self. The God Self has "parts." When they were free enough to manifest themselves, they lived as deities, gods and goddesses. These parts are aspects of our soul. We all have manifestations of these gods and goddesses within us.

When we open the gateways to inner vision, hear spirit whispers and soul calls and accept our purpose as it is revealed to us, our lives become solutions for peace. This is the true Christ Power. This is the promise of a life anchored in spirit. This is the power of the Holy Grail.

We are so accustomed to living in separation that we do not know what living in feminine and masculine integration is like. We charge into life (or avoid it) with our ego-centric minds holding the reins; this is a violation of spiritual law. Our minds were divinely intended to be servants of our hearts, rather than the consumptive power of our whole being. In order to re-create our future steps, we need to first recognize where we abandoned our souls, individually and collectively. We can continue to give away our spiritual and personal powers and define ourselves through belief systems that deny the knowledge of directly sourcing God power.

Or, we can end this two-millennia cycle of self-betrayal and rejection.

When we come into union with all of the parts of our self and cleanse, purify and rediscover their essence, we will be working through the feminine ray. Underneath our pain, hurt and anger, the divine feminine and her endless power is ready to be resurrected into life.

Only then will we hear her voice.

Chapter 6

Voice of the Divine Feminine

To dance again in the flower of union
God's essence dances in divine understanding
This way of grace imparts miracles
I know for I have drunk from the cup
Now as I offer its sweetness to you.
May you come to drink of the Holy Grail
As you prepare to receive the Grail
I offer my prayer.

You do not know me.

I live deep inside of you. You haven't known I am here except for the moments you have felt me in the trees, Earth and mountains. I do not want you to find me. You have done well to protect me and carry on with your busy life, making it safe for me to hide far, far away. Even when you consciously co-create with the rest of the parts of yourself, you have been afraid of me. I have made sure you are busy with worldly concerns. This way, I can live in my own world. I see how much you have united with your inner spiritual essence, your inner feminine and masculine, and have freed these powers within yourself. I watch you become heated or angry, because you feel so alone, unseen and unheard out there. Meanwhile, my divine trinity, the inner mother-father- child, is asking me to come out.

I have been hurt. Deeply hurt. Tales of my plight seldom come out in history—after all, it is history. I have been tortured, whipped, burned and beaten until only my shame of existence remains. I have been persecuted because I defy the mind. I live in a world where logic does not exist, but compassion and caring reign. I hide away so deeply that you may think I do not care about anyone. This is far from the truth, for my eyes see your pain and how it became so deeply imbedded in you in the first place. I see how you have run from your truth. I see how you have been trained to please everyone around you. The ancient fear of retribution for not pleasing a stern, fierce God is deeply engrained within you.

Many of you have been stabbed in the back and punished for not leading those who eventually found my dwelling place and attempted to destroy me. I know you have suffered through great confusion over whether to let me live in the deepest realms of your psyche or allow me to emerge. I know I have made it difficult for you, for I would not have come out even if you wanted me to.

At this time, I see that you are no longer able to live your lives fully without me. What has changed? Why has everything been going along so smoothly, and even at times incredibly intensely, as you seek to open deeper to your own core? I know you have spent years perfecting how you relate to others and the world, totally respecting the space I have needed.

After so many years of learning to listen, only now can you hear me. I want you to know that I respect and honor the devotion you have shown to your own personal transformation and growth. You have decided to become the authenticity that you seek. You're standing at the threshold of joy and love. I see you standing there, awkward and confused. You do not know what you have been waiting for. The reason you have felt as though you know nothing and yet can receive and appreciate your own hard-earned wisdom is understandable.

To find me, you had to unravel the tale of your life— the agreements you made at birth, during your youngest years and those made to me. You abandoned yourself to respond to how your elders needed you to be, and the expectations they put on your shoulders. You worked to make everyone else feel good at the expense of yourself. You left your own heart of joy and love to be responsible in the world. You chose to judge yourself when you were distant from me and felt fear. You rejected yourself when you were just trying to survive and fit into a pre-structured world of expectation. You learned well how to give of yourself even when it felt wrong, just to receive the love you wanted. You were willing to stay empty to keep another from leaving you, denying the power of your own existence. You worked to make everyone else's reality appear safe so your life was given meaning. You chose to be responsible for everyone's feelings so they would be appropriate and less invasive to you. You chose to act as if you knew what you were doing so you would not have to feel the pain of being seen as unworthy whenever you had the opportunity to receive. You chose to connect your energy to others so you were guaranteed to be loved back, even at the risk no real love was coming your way. You agreed to conditionally love yourself instead of unconditionally loving yourself; this kept you contracted in a box. You based your life upon self-lies, to avoid the fact you might actually be powerful.

You agreed to come for me when you were whole. When you were ready to feel complete. When only joy and love could remain. When the prospect of living your life fully from who you are was ready to burst through.

O, sacred one, you have given so much. You have stretched to feel another's pain and goodness. You have lain awake at night crying until tears of longing for oneness dampened your pillow. You have asked God to show the doorways into the kingdom of Itself, and be shown how to help others live in this union. Now, it is time once again for me to lead the way. I am keeper of the prayer, keeper of the dream, keeper of love.

Now that you are ready to open your heart, I offer my prayer.

May you recognize the purity in your heart.
May you honor the goodness in your heart.
May you exclaim in joy the power of your birth.
May you wander no more away from yourself.
May you ask for what you need without shame.
May you devote yourself to yourself without guilt.
May you cease blaming yourself for being imperfect.
May you see that you are a blazing fire of God.
May you see yourself in the dawn and sunset of each day.
May you seek God's creations in each moment.
May you embrace your fears instead of judging them.
May you understand the perfection of your being.
May you accept the wisdom of your duality.
May you unite in the love existing in the parts of your Self.
May you play in the rhythms of your heart.
May you accept the power in your heart.
May you know that I am you.
May you regain your trust in me.

May you enter home into yourself gracefully.
May you give thanks for the peace that already exists.
May you remember me in the wind.
May you remember me in the Earth.
May you find your heart in my heart within the Earth.
May you receive blessings from Earth and heaven each day.
May your purpose be united into fulfillment and fullness.
May you graciously receive the blessings of your ancestors.
May you receive the strengths of your past.
May you forgive your actions based upon needing love, giving love and creating love that took you away from yourself.
May you learn to surrender to your highest self with peace.
May you recognize the ferocity of Light that pours in your soul.
May your body and mind receive your soul and heart with thankfulness.
May the power of your light fill your world and others.
May you always remember that you are here to be YOU.
May you receive in every cell the beauty of the oneness of your Self.
May you create wondrous acts of expression from your union of Self.

I am the Creatrix,
The divine Feminine of Life.
I am the Soul known as Mary, Ishtar, Astarte, Aphrodite, Innana, Hecate, Demeter, Isis, Kali, White Buffalo Woman and Tara.
The all-embracing, I am.
I am the Light of the World.

Chapter 7

Preparing to Receive the Lost Teachings

"If you stop walking on eggshells and are honest about it—dominating another human being, needing to control another human being, even if it's in that person's best interest, treating someone like a possession, taking advantage of another human being because you can—all of this is... [the] misuse of power. Not all of us are willing to admit where we're misusing our power."
~ Tori Amos

The power of the light is ready to be ignited. The force of enlightenment, the force of love, and the precious momentum of illumination are dawning all around us. We blossom as we bring light to every aspect of our divine self, creating a diamond of resilient luminosity.

Some will get caught in the darkness of their own consciousness, while others will triumph and discover the portal beyond their illusions. It is only possible to get stuck in the dark when we hold onto what makes us feel secure. The dark is our own disowned power. If we avoid our own darkness and the games of how we delude ourselves, we battle with self, others and the world. The battle manifests through dueling with our own creative life-force: how we use our power, how we give it away or push it down, how we love one another and how we love self. We fight over whether or not to fit into containers that are outside of our selves. The more we fight, the easier it becomes to deny the pain of living in separation with our self and others. Bouncing around in the splits of the soul binds us to emotional pain. We get caught up in these thoughts rather than soul knowingness (*gnosis*) and empowerment.

However, this walk through the darkness to access the light constitutes a major gateway we must traverse on our road to liberation.

No longer can we continue to find completion from outside experiences and sources alone. The passion found within our physical, mental, emotional, spiritual and etheric bodies creates a doorway into the eternal. As we reconnect the energies that make up our hearts, souls and spirit, we discover oneness. The anxieties, angers and fears created by the splits of our soul and psyche are transmuted into usable, living energies.

Have you wondered how some people always seem centered and full of vitality, while others seem like they're always swimming upstream with teeth bared? Where do you stand, right now? Here's a quick way to check: Visualize a spinning atom of light. Perceive its nucleus, then its outer rings. If you are standing in the center of this spin, you are balanced. The yoga tradition has an axiom for this: "center everywhere, circumference nowhere."

This same interplay with balance happens with the energy circuits inside your body. If the currents are connected, you will enjoy a good energy day. No one will prevail upon you in a negative way, nor will you need to fight to get something your way. You will not eat for the wrong reason, nor argue with someone you love. A feeling or inspiration will hit you and you will trust it. Instead of reacting out of fear, rejection or judgment, you will stand strong within an inner peace. Creative ideas and solutions will pour into you at your beckoning, and while others around you are filled with anxiety and worry, you will follow your inner voice.

By owning and utilizing the powerful unity of our life force and sexuality, our soul and emotions, our body and heart, our lower and higher self, our inner masculine and feminine selves and our eternal self and mind, we fulfill our soul's original promise to live in union with the One. It is our birthright and our mission. The way in which we accomplish it will first change our inner world, then the phenomenal world around us.

The Lost Teachings interpret the consciousness of living in the center, living in light, the nectar of divine knowledge and sweetness. It can be very challenging to know what step to take next on your spiritual journey. We get pulled in so many directions, or we practice a style or form of meditation that provides us with only a limited amount of growth because we have practiced from our parts rather than our whole being. While these are all good steps, wouldn't it be wonderful to emerge from our necessary walk through the darkness with the pieces of our selves aligned with our light-filled center? When we are connected in this way, our soul accesses spirit with ease.

Once we understand how to transform our lower self into light by passing through its darkness, we will stand on solid spiritual ground like well-rooted oak trees.

When we overcome the gravity of duality, our souls lift into flight. Let's merge the two aspects of duality and live in its union by viewing the dark from light and drawing the two together. By doing so, we merge into who we really are, our soul's eternal blueprint, instead of playing aspects of our self against each other. Universal consciousness opens and the connecting nucleus of life energy becomes a magic carpet ride through the stream of creative cosmic consciousness. We no longer find the need to prove anything, get entangled in an issue or someone else's drama, be intimidated, complain or throw a tantrum.

Sometimes it's hard to release that which keeps us separated and distracted from what is really trying to happen. Will—the focused intention of soul—and heart—the portal into truth—fight one another until the will serves the heart's alignment in God. Our will unites with our belief system to integrate power and love. We take that one step beyond separation and enter the gateway to joy. We are grounded in happiness instead of careening through the emotional and spiritual upheaval of living in the parts. We become a source of power that rises from the seed of creation. We experience a power without pain and struggle.

Before our souls separated into pieces, we could feel the presence of God at all times. Before our minds knew separation from God, we lived in peace. Through ignorance and fear, many of us have closed the doors to the kingdom of heaven. That action has, through the ages, brought forth great masters who walked among us and mingled with us for one reason: to give us the keys to the kingdom. All of the sacred texts speak of this. Out of fear, we have closed so many doors that it is challenging to find the right key.

A New Planetary Blueprint

Right now, we are at the crossroads of living a new planetary blueprint—and our bodies feel it. We can reconnect the parts shrouded in darkness to those basking in the light. As we each come back into our wholeness or holiness, we can step into the new planetary blueprint. The spiritual hierarchy, the beings of light that serve the planet's upliftment, offer this roadmap. Consisting of archangels and ascended masters committed to the healing of this planet, they hold the gateways open to restore the physical life force energies with the creative forces of God. They serve humanity by guiding us beyond separation into oneness. When called upon, they respond. They are Archangels Michael, Gabriel, Rafael and Uriel; and Ascended Masters Kuthumi (St. Francis of Assisi, Pythagoras), Sant Kumara, St. Germain, Babaji (serving for more than 1,750 years from his Himalayan temple), Christ (known as Sananda on the inner planes, also lived as Adam, Enoch, Elijah and Joseph of Egypt), Paramhansa Yogananda, Ramana Maharshi, El Morya (once Abraham and King Arthur), Mother Mary (Isis) and Mary Magdalene.

Here is the blueprint they have given us:

- Reconnect all of the energies in the body, soul and psyche.
- Clear the ancestral, genetic and karmic energies.
- Align the matrix of our true self into the awakened design of universal power—God.

This new design takes us beyond dogma and fear. It works with the higher chakra centers and instigates the clearing and reconnection of all the chakras. This process brings about the healing of innumerable energetic and lifetime blockages, including those surrounding survival, emotion, life force and memory. The soul, too, is freed from that which restrains its magnificence, and everything that allows us to see our state of being as it is in the moment (our perception of truth itself) is brought to the fore. Forces awaken in us when we are tapped into the God essence, and as our energies are reconnected, we find ourselves gaining an intimate relationship with the powers of creation. It is only by aligning our cleared chakras into the ray of our highest consciousness and purifying the underlying energies that feed the emotional soul, however, that we are brought to the point of leaping into our core power and becoming illuminated in the awakened Christ Consciousness. This process is activated both by our desire and by our direct request.

These are the Lost Teachings, the Holy Grail Teachings. They're ready to be given once again.

Our culture has eliminated a great practice enjoyed by our distant ancestors. They sat by the fire and listened raptly as their elders, wise men and women, spiritual leaders and shamans passed information through oral storytelling of resonant truths that blended real-life experience with legends and myths of distant pasts. The Vedas, India's sacred song-scripture, is derived from more than 100,000 pieces of wisdom transmitted orally for several millennia until they were written down beginning about 5,000 years ago.

It is different today. Many false teachers and healers who have not fully completed the darkness-into-light spiritual journey for themselves bombard our airwaves, church pulpits and the self-help shelves of bookstores. Their works lack the purity of spirit and the clarity of spoken word—which, when practiced, connects the listener to the truth and wisdom of the teller's experiences and divine messages. This loss of direct transmission from the wise storyteller has made it difficult to connect where we are on our own path, and how to fully understand and grasp the true meaning of circumstances that appear in our lives. Instead, we have our "spiritual experiences" and then we have our lives.

Tools are needed to help us find the direct connection with our source and self. These tools include shifting focus, reconnecting, allowing and receiving. Cracking the shell of our energy bodies—and tapping our deepest divine stories—takes patience and love. With open-eyed wonder, we can touch grace. We can begin to learn about our self in a new way. It all starts by trusting your self and refraining from judgment in every possible way.

Listen to the messages within and distinguish whether they are emerging outside or inside your core power. When you think you have figured something out, put it aside and stay flexible, open and discriminating. First open to your self, then to others. If you block the voice of truth, you will function from separation. Learn to live in the unknown and embrace rather than reject what feels out of control. Try this simple step, taught in some yogic disciplines: Whenever you have a sudden revelation or come upon a solution, or, when someone makes a statement that upsets, offends or otherwise troubles you, stop, take ten deep breaths and ask, "What is trying to happen here?" By that tenth breath, you will likely have replaced the initial excited burst of anger or annoyance with a measure of perspective, which will then lead you forward with clear eyes, mind, heart and soul.

We feel a greater enlightenment by illuminating one part of our self at a time. We connect the dark to the light until our whole self is ignited. The Holy Grail guides one to attain enlightenment by uniting the soul and body. Joy takes the place of sorrow as we step beyond the grids of our mind and emotions and experience the opening of who we truly are, while bringing into our body the full configuration and highest frequency of light, the christed vibration. Our cells begin to vibrate clearly in union with our source. We become awakened and free.

Be clear how you work within this current and how you step from it when engaged in action. Your way may be to help others, forget others, forget yourself or dominate others. Be aware whether you hold onto your perspective or are able to drop it in the moment. Come closer to allowing those you know or encounter to be their most authentic selves, rather than exerting your influence upon them. Stay in the power of your current. Trust that you do not have to move into darkness to merge with another. By staying in union in your self, you magnetically begin to pull another out of his or her darkness. Become aware of how you keep yourself living in the dark.

Pay attention to how you repeat patterns. You become that which you connect to in your life force power. Be conscious of who and what you connect yourself with. Living in your power remains a roller coaster ride until you stop connecting to other's dramas, beliefs, sentimentality and pain.

The ways in which our parents dominated others and suppressed their own selves set the stage for what we have to transcend. Sometimes patterns of control extend several generations into our familial past. By releasing them out of our heart, DNA and energy fields, we can change our life. We are no longer drawn to others who live by draining the energy and spirit of those around them. Those who live off of others in this way do so after cementing themselves into a pattern of withholding their own light and unique gifts from the world.

How we confront our inner controller in relationship to our inner feminine and masculine will either freeze us on our path or melt us into God. We reach a comfort level and identify with who we are and what we have; we then choose to live in this well-controlled framework. Love your divine self in your body, and passionately connect to the life within you. The waves of the sea never stop. Neither do we. Becoming one with the current is the act of mastery that breaks us out of control. What we fear is obtaining and utilizing this gift itself, and the outer and inner changes it might elicit in our lives.

When the genetic and ancestral energies are cleared in the body, we become free to be our most authentic selves. Talk about incredible adventures! The patterns passed to us strengthen and weaken us, and are encoded in our bodies, but when neutralized, give our soul the command of its own blueprint. When we overcome the avoidance of our ancestral patterns of denial, fear and control, we emerge as carriers of new codes of light consciousness. No longer encumbered by the rules of false power, we can lift the lid on our creativity and sexuality.

When the gateways between the bodies are closed, it is impossible to access our unique spiritual design. Our devotional and loyal side might prevail so that we become carbon copies of another's spiritual teaching. Or, our curious and flighty self might take over so that we become spiritual window-shoppers who bounce from path to path without stopping long enough to plant a seed or grow roots. When our spiritual essence is unblocked, however, and allowed to live in all of our bodies, we carry the spark that is unique to ourselves. Then, we find the path that is unique to our selves.

Get Thy House in Order

The admonition is in all sacred texts: "Get thy house in order." We must honor the lost parts of our self, reclaiming them as messengers from God. We must remove blame and shame from our bellies and minds and learn to sit and feel in the temple of our body. We must view the darkness within from the highest light of our heart.

Each moment is an opportunity to choose love over fear, and honor the teaching power of that fear. The cup of the Holy Grail is the container we fill by being willing to sit with our pain and not project it outside ourselves. This is the way of becoming the jewel, the eternal diamond—a full-faceted spirit being. The driving mind is merged with the soft, compassionate heart, integrating empathy, action, death and rebirth. Our soul is the chalice of creation that feeds our hearts, body and the world. As we drink in the center of each atom of light, every thought becomes another entry point into the divine.

The Holy Grail teaches us to:

- Care for the body with food, herbs and beverages that feed the longevity of body and soul
- Open the life force currents in the body to connect earth (feminine) energies with heaven (masculine) energies.
- Hold a focused, single-pointed consciousness of the divine in the third eye, the *ajna chakra* or Kutastha Chaitanya (Christ Center).
- Take responsibility for the power of ignited divinity in your body.
- Love the body as a shrine of the Holy Masculine and Feminine God dwelling within.
- Awaken the sexual organs with devotional love and with the intention of moving God energy through the circuits of the body to maintain health and divine connection, both individually and as a couple.
- Release shame as an expression of the body and replace it with joyous expression, love of the body and loving God through the body.

The Perfect Grid

Imagine for a moment that the perfect grid of God consciousness exists in your body. It has been covered by layers of emotional, mental and etheric untruths, illusions, karmic and genetic codes that lay deep within your DNA. As you clear these false programs, and reconnect to your true self, you discover the gateways into all transcendent and God-empowered qualities of your self. These gateways of spirit are the initiations that heal body, mind and soul, allowing the experience of conscious atonement, or "at one-ment," with all life. They are the openings that awaken your life force power, the authentic connection into God power. They empower the design of God already living within you.

Like a figure-eight loop moving between the heart and belly, love and power co-exist together. When the gateways are opened, the emotional body heals. The emotional body is a less dense physical body and expresses the soul and spirit in divine union. The mental body seeks to understand how it is connected or separated; it heals when the emotional body and soul are reconnected. The physical body heals as the spiritual powers unite the soul. We achieve full remembrance of who we are. The gateways can now support the interchange of cosmic current, the divine universal intelligence. Healing the bodies and seeing through our spiritual center unites our wounded parts with the essence of our inner home—the Holy Grail.

Enlightenment is not something that happens to us. It is something that happens *within* us. It is the stark sensation of standing in a cave and suddenly seeing a large piece of gold glisten from the opposite wall. It shines brightly under the intensity of the flashlight beam that blazes forth from our higher self. It strikes something in our heart. We walk across the room and try to chisel the gold out of the wall. When it doesn't budge, we crumble the wall with dynamite. All that is left is the gold. We become rich.

An initiation gives us what is already ours. It connects us to the true reality within. You must know that everything exists within you, because when you directly experience the flames of God burning in your heart, or experience the joy of who you are for the first time in your life, you must trust it is not some mistake. *It is your birthright.*

We are in a peak moment of dark and light separation. The battle of dark and light is encoded in our body. Feminine expression is denied in 90% of the population. There is a powerful connection between hormonal imbalance in women and suppressing the enormous power in the vital organs. The increase in heart disease, diabetes, cancer of reproductive organs, breast cancer and arthritis are connected to denying the feminine force in the body. The expression of the feminine through sexuality is often the only way we can allow her presence.

The power of the feminine to heal, create, manifest and regenerate is beyond what we presently accept in our culture. The virgin-prostitute split (Mother Mary-Mary Magdalene) keeps the feminine disempowered. The raw assertive power of the feminine is considered the "whore," and the passive nurturing feminine is considered the "virgin." By bridging and balancing the virgin and the whore, we restore the divine feminine. A great deal of today's obesity issues with women occur because we shut down the energetic connection between our spiritual, physical and sexual power.

Women can take charge of their lives and own their authentic feminine power. The energetic matrix between the perineum and pubic bone and medulla oblongata, located at the base of the skull, is a figure-eight loop that can be reconnected. When that happens, hormonal balance is restored. Dizziness, depression, menstrual problems, low blood sugar and blood pressure recede or disappear entirely. The need to fill the emotional and sexual vacuum by eating ends, as does the tendency to soar too high or swoop too low in the storms of moodiness and mania.

To reconstruct and align our spiritual-physical matrix, we need to move inwardly and outwardly. Even the act of reaching stillness requires the ability to move inwardly. Spirit is moving consciousness that unites matter and mystery. Moving in spirit melts the blocks that cement our mind and cast our body into its concrete.

To move requires the ability to feel. Any situation that demands an unfeeling response from us is asking us to not be our most authentic, deeply feeling selves. Vitality—the full experience of being alive, is the result of energy in motion. E = motion is the interchange of energy between cells in the body and the universe. Living in the center point of our energy bodies activates life source, the raw creative power of dark and light in union. "Good" and "evil" exist only when light and dark are separate from another and are attached to the wounds of the emotional body.

Your Emotional Body, Your Chalice

The emotional body is a chalice within the body that holds the divine feminine. Higher consciousness is grounded into the body through this chalice. Mind, body and soul are integrated through the emotional body. Thus, the emotional body serves as a bridge. A blocked emotional body prevents the divine feminine from awakening and fulfilling our soul's mission. Political and religious leaders, spiritual teachers, gurus, healers and artists who have not created a chalice for their emotional and soul body to live within break agreements with themselves and others, and are pulled by financial, sexual and power offers.

The chalice resides in the deep belly within the pelvis. When connected into this wellspring the mind has a place to settle and nurture itself. The mind becomes a still lake, and life debris at the bottom of the lake is left there or cleared out. By clearing the waters we do not have to repeat the same patterns over and over again. When stones of life's circumstances are tossed into the lake, waves ripple to the shoreline, then dissipate. The lake returns to stillness.

There is no way to remove a pattern from the mind permanently until the waters of the emotional body are clear. Only then can the chalice be filled in an atmosphere of light and expansive presence. The door opens with grace, and we are never the same again. We are not sure how we got here. The stories in our bodies are worked out, and we are done playing in our lower creations, the dramas of self-rejection.

Physical Illusions

The physical plane's illusions are entry points into what is spiritually authentic. We have to pass through our illusions enough times to finally recognize that deeper reality exists beyond the weighing and balancing of duality. We first see the illusion, then choose to end the further perpetuation of it.

Some of the illusions created in our bodies include:

- Separation from God
- Creative, spiritual and sexual power exist separately
- Intuition is a sense separate from the rest of everyday reality
- Love is meant to fill momentary needs rather than build a whole person
- Sexual passion decreases in time when with the same person
- The notion that pain must be ignored
- Our power must be used to serve others
- Infinite consciousness is separate from how we must live in order to survive
- Separating the body, God and sexuality helps us to attain enlightenment
- Reality can only be seen with physical eyes
- Mind is overlord of the soul

Light of the Holy Grail

Light contains pure consciousness. As it travels into the physical realms, it moves through subtle and finer vibrations into the etheric. Our physical body fills with love and power as we open to these vibrations. Qualitative in nature, they are experienced purely through the primary elements. Spirit carries the interwoven, mutually supportive creative and regenerative powers of the elements: fire, water, air, earth and ether. Our bodies—spiritual, emotional, mental, etheric and physical—are made up of these elements. Fire predominates the spiritual body, water the emotional body, air the mental body, earth the physical body, and ether the etheric body. All the elements are in all of the bodies. Each aspect of our soul can also be experienced through an element. Wind (air) is the messenger of God. The waters of God cleanse and purify. The fires of God transmute and transform all energies. The earth of God is the container for power. The ethers are the interlocking web of life.

When the elements within us separate, or when we carry too much of one element at the expense of another, they divide the bodies and create imbalance. When we reconnect soul and body, and our elements are in balance, our hearts open—transforming mind and feeling so that we are able to soar with our higher self. This balancing of primary elements in the bodies constitutes the basis of Ayurveda's doshic system (vata-pitta-kapha), Chinese and Tibetan medicine and Shamanic medicine.

Surrendering to spirit permeates the body with divine truth and helps to facilitate the reconnection of our split parts. Surrender not to false emotions, concepts and dogma of the mind, but to relationship between spirit and your body. This awakened consciousness is the interaction of soul and spirit. The mind surrenders to the wisdom living in the temple of the body. The faculty of intuition no longer comes and goes. We start living multi-dimensionally, simultaneously interwoven like a shimmering tapestry touching the yarns of a universe comprised of poetically vibrant designs of music, color and shape. We become lighthouses. We live in union with many strands of consciousness, the DNA of the matrix of life. We are able to access information, know things and feel the truth of the big pictures of our lives. No longer fluctuating from a lack of wholeness, we are present in divine flow. We know the outcome of situations before they happen, whether a person will betray us, if a person will fulfill their soul calling, whether they will honor or dishonor their karmic challenges, etc.

The Holy Grail is a blessing and a gateway to the infinite love and power of the divine. It grants the opportunity to prepare for and receive its sweet wine. It is the body of the beloved; the heart of God in our bodies; the chalice of grace, beauty and wonder ready to be held and drunk in eternal oneness. It is the container created by the potter's wheel when our wet hands touch the clay of everlasting life, the union of the feminine and masculine within ourselves. Our boundless devotion serves as the firing kiln.

It is time to complete the quest of the Holy Grail to understand the mysteries of the divine feminine and masculine. We can shift the future of all societies on this planet by healing the splits between the masculine and feminine powers. It is time to share the mystery teachings and put an end to their long-enforced slumber.

Chapter 8

Understanding Sexuality and the Dark

Listen to the power within your sexuality, listen closely, feel your soul's desire to unite heaven and earth. Come to your fire and burn through the darkness surrounding your true light.
~ Iana Lahi

When the consciousness of the divine feminine is separate from spirit, it manifests as a dark, negative and controlling power. In such a state, the feminine power lacks movement and can be used destructively. It is captivating, building a connection to ego rather than to spirit consciousness. When caught in such spiritless darkness, there is no light at the end of the tunnel. The unawakened dark side of the feminine is revered in our culture. In contrast, the light-empowered woman in her full feminine power continues to be reviled, as she has been for centuries, because of her perceived threat to the cultural status quo. Yet the dark side of the feminine that exists in a man or a woman's soul yearns to connect to that which is presently unmanifested. This is the creative process!

Darkness is the home of unmanifested feminine energy. Many spiritual power seekers journey into the dark. Alcohol and drugs open doorways to the dark, but may also sometimes provide a glimpse into the light. There are energetic openings that once accessed link us directly with the spiritual void within the dark. Without knowledge of these energetic openings it is easy to become addicted to the false power we experience upon stumbling into this spiritual void. When this happens, we find ourselves withholding love and power, stealing the power of others and failing to fulfill our dreams and/or complete projects. Many of us will claim that our visions of power are God-inspired when, in fact, these "visions" are only applicable on a survival level; eventually they cause fear, mistrust and illness in other people or nations. The entire crusade-like energy behind the "war on terrorism," and how it has created a blanket of doom over millions of people in the Middle East—and killed countless innocent women, men and children—illustrates the effects of misdirected vision.

There is a difference between dark power that exists separately from the light and raw, creative feminine power found as the counterpart of the light. When the feminine power is awakened, integrated and initiated, individual empowerments, ideas and solutions are birthed. We create lives of beauty and happiness. Our lives become multidimensional expressions of feeling. When we look at the sky, our hearts inhale expansiveness. When we hug someone, our bodies and souls give and receive the hug. Our patterns of self-rejection and self-hatred no longer have room to exist. No longer do we fear who we are. We feel connected with the forces of life, giving us the real food we need to live deeply. When this power opens, it restructures our life. Our creative dreams and aspirations can become reality. We are in touch with a force so deep and powerful that our old mental and emotional habits must be reconfigured. Our hearts feel connected to the universe and to others, and our motivations become creative and life giving rather than self-serving. What we do with this power is the single most important action of every moment.

A lot of power exists in the dark, the wellspring of feminine power. Part of our self stays in the safety net of the dark for protection until we no longer feel afraid and can let go to the next level of unfolding. Opening to the light requires expansion, while the dark commands contraction. Both make us up. Dwelling in the feminine and absorbing its power expresses a level of mastery. The container of the divine feminine is a fueling vessel for our soul. Here ideas, healing energy and life force build momentum.

Living on this planet is an evolutionary experience of interacting with light and dark. If we know how to recognize and work with all of the qualities of our dark and light selves, we evolve with greater ease. We stop repeating the same mistakes and instead apply our experiences in the conscious exploration of God power. Instead of facing our power with fear, we will welcome it with joy and heightened anticipation.

We have the ability to transform dark into light. Innately, we know how to do it, but this is something we have forgotten. We have lost the knowledge of how to participate in the eternal dawn of creation—the point where light and dark interact. "Let there be light," God commanded the heavens, and so began creation. As creative power moves from the dark into light, idea becomes form. When uninitiated energies of nature infuse with light, life begins. Unifying the sun and moon within us awakens the eternal moment. Stillness and movement are united.

There are so many times when we do not know what is going on within us. We live in a dream that is created by being cut off from Source, and we mistrust our abilities to manifest our soul's purpose. Are our dreams of the dark or of the light? What about our conscious actions? Do we create situations that utilize our power to unite companies, countries, lovers, and families for our own unspoken needs—or to bring others closer to freedom and life abundance?

The soul journey of the Holy Grail forces us to face whether we elude or unite with who we are.

In each lifetime, we explore this relationship differently. All of us want to personalize God power. We want to think that *we* are the power. When our mind, body, masculine and feminine natures are separate, our mind will always think it is right. This distortion of God power insulates us from experiencing true perception. We are unable to feel and see at the same time that our feminine (body) and masculine (mind) are disconnected. We separate from our heart and the feminine power of God; we think the power we feel in the dark is everything. By illuminating the power in our darkness and reconnecting it into the light, we raise our vibration and become whole.

Fear of Leaving the Dark

Many of us are afraid to leave the dark. Its familiarity holds us tight. Leaving the comfort of darkness can feel like death because our souls often equate living in the light to past life memories of persecution and death. If this cellular memory of being out of control and at the mercy of others overcomes us, we become chained to the urge to dominate our reality. Our survival is determined by how we relate to the dark—yet the penalty of remaining in the dark is severe. The light of love is not allowed to live in its entirety and the feminine is confined. Sexuality and creativity remain separate.

The fine line between living in union with God and using the power of God to feel empowered creates mental separation. We are trained to identify with the illusions of power, and then we strive to become those illusions. Doesn't that seem a bit insane when you read it? Yet, this is the overriding extent of our relationship to 21st century society! We forget our relationship to creation and go back into separation. Then in the next lifetime, we feel ashamed, judgmental or religiously pious, and we try to hide from the world or we find we have difficulties making money. A cycle begins that feeds upon itself, keeping us in greater separation.

As our state of separation intensifies, our soul parts lose their sense of connection, and we settle further into the dark. The journey through the gateways of the Holy Grail Teachings begins when we call all soul parts back into our body. We have a responsibility to complete the configuration of our soul, body and spirit into light. We also have a responsibility to treat our experiences of betrayal, abandonment and rejection as true mentors of pain, denial and disempowerment that push us closer to our divine self.

Choosing to embrace and heal this split between light and dark takes courage of heart. The choice itself begets power, for healing occurs even as we choose to rescue and resurrect our own darkness into light.

Ignite Your Resurrection Process

This simple exercise heals the split between spirit and your body. Breathe into your solar plexus and visualize blue light, then gold light filling this space. Bring your consciousness into your solar plexus and sit in the light. Look up through the inside shaft of your body. Look for light pouring down in through the top of your head and experience it as a waterfall of color and brilliant light. Remain centered in your solar plexus and allow the light to pour into you.

From ten feet above your head, enter into pure white light. Shine this beam of light into an elevator shaft corridor within your body. Let this be a laser beam of love, and focus it into the corners and base of the elevator shaft corridor.

Now, look for a part of your self that is standing or sitting in the dark. Look to see him/her from the side of their head, see their hair, and as if behind a movie camera move until you see their face and—especially their eyes.

Send him/her a message that you are here and ask him/ her if they know who you are. If not, tell them and explain that you have come back for him/her. Ask what he/she has needed others to know about him/her. Listen and receive. Ask what he/she needs to you to know about him/her and tell him/her that you are here completely, right now.

When it feels right to you, ask him/her if he/she wants to come live with you. If the answer is "yes," invite them to come live in any part(s) of your body that they choose. If not, ask them what he/she needs from you to begin to feel safe and able to trust you. Let your heart beam your love to this part of your self. Feel this part of yourself bathing in light in both your second chakra (between your navel and pubic bone) and in your heart.

Maintain this focused connection several times a day for eight weeks.

Conscious Transformation

Conscious transformation, regeneration and alchemy are beyond the dogma of good and bad. Transforming darkness into light completes the circle of creation. Light and dark brought into union explodes a force of God so powerful it can heal anything—uniting the brain with unlimited intelligence, returning sexuality to its true purpose and awakening the powers of the soul. This innate power is light years beyond the culturally popular religious concept of a God who perpetuates lack, disempowerment and disease, yet is also the way spiritual practices on Earth took place for dozens of millennia before religion took over!

Learning to see and live clearly takes diligence, for the mind plays many tricks. For example, if you had a controlling father and you always yearned for a relationship with him, you may have internalized his presence in your body-psyche. Or you may have chosen to abandon your own power in one of your chakras to allow his needy power into you, as part of your agreement to accommodate him. In your healing process, you have to choose between keeping him alive energetically or choosing your own life. You may fall into the need to change others around you who deny the misuse of their own power, or you may project onto someone else that they are the cause for the pain you are feeling.

The key to handling this through the Holy Grail Teachings is to unite the darkness and light of this issue, to claim full ownership, and to dispense with the residual father energy that lies in all five bodies—spiritual, mental, physical, emotional and etheric. The Holy Grail Teachings supports living in the center of oneness. We are re-taught to reconnect the wiring of our God-realized self.

The marriage of your soul, body, heart and spirit is not a psychological concept. It is a natural feeling state, inspiring solutions that heal the world. Controlling the feminine has been the downfall of our planet's social system. We need to shift into acknowledging wholeness and union of the awakened feminine power as a cultural and personal norm. The feminine power of God interconnects all highways of creation within and without. It is a weaver, a uniter. It does not know how to serve lofty, split-off beliefs of the mind. The feminine power works in acceptance, surrender and interpretation of the One.

Oneness lives in the temple of the body. We go to our inner temple to clear, reconnect and align to our highest truth. The sacred marriage, or *hierosgamos*, of heart, body and spirit honors the power of the united feminine and masculine. Control does not exist when we live in the union of our feminine and masculine powers in union. Instead of controlling our feminine from the mind, we need to understand that to live in balance with God, we need to surrender our mind to the feminine force within our bodies. After all, we are uniting with Source—where the feminine naturally co-exists.

This is the first step to living in divine union.

Sexuality and Divine Union

The yearning for union in body, spirit and heart enlightens sexuality. Whether we are in relationship to another or to our self, when we connect and move core energy through our chakras and energy bodies, we heal.

The pure power of divine feminine and masculine coming together in the body constitutes the first orgasm. The feminine moves up from the earth in pure light and meets the light of the masculine energy. The two energies unite and travel through each chakra, continuing the subtle reunification of heaven and earth in the body. The Star of David (also known as the Shield of David) represents the union of the descendent and ascendant currents of God meeting in the body. The triangle base, with its point reaching up, is the feminine energy. The down-turned triangle point is the masculine energy. The central space in the Star of David is the heart. The symbol can be traced back through Hinduism, Buddhism, Judaism and Islam. In Hinduism the two locked triangles are called 'Hrim' and 'Om' and represent Shiva and Shakti. In south Indian Hindu temples, the Star of David is known as *satkona yantra* and represents *Nara-Narayana,* the divine state of perfection and union between woman/man and God. In the Buddhist *Tibetan Book of the Dead,* also known as the *Bardo Thodol*, the two overlapping triangles are known as the "origin of phenomenon" (*chos-kyi 'byung-gnas*). In Islam, the Star of David is called the *Najmat Dawuud.* The Mormons make use of the Shield of David in their architecture and represents the Tribes of Israel. The symbol of the Star of David can also be tracked to the Theosophical Society founded in 1875, the Freemasons and the Zion Christian Church in southern Africa.

The purpose of divine love is to meet God in the heart and initiate the power represented in this symbol.

Two currents of God move through every cell of life. Their polarity creates magnetic energy, the basis for vibrant mental and physical health and dynamic sex. The two currents divide into sub-currents, connecting levels of spirit and soul. They become strands of liquid light that flood the body in love. When they connect, like a plug into a socket, the sensations fill the temple of the heart with currents of love. This is an anointing—union in the divine. The light of God illuminates the body and soul to meet itself.

Sexuality is meant to be life giving and restorative. The sexual organs are the flames of God energy, and express power, love, surrender and devotion. If fear is absent from sex, opportunity exists to receive the pure power of the dark (feminine) and channel it into pure light (masculine), thus completing the circle of creation. So many people still equate the dark with primal negativity. However, this raw, pure power is really *creation* energy.

The Holy Grail shows us what to do with this power. First, we must feel, open and surrender to its existence in our hearts and souls. Instead of cutting off from the power and trying to love from a split circuit, we need to embrace and receive the power in the depth of our feminine, whether we are male or female. As women, it is our responsibility to be at one with the power that lives in our dark feminine and raise this power into light consciousness.

Most women are ignorant of their power. Most men fear this power, so they steal, dominate or use it—or worse, all of the above. They also seek out women in a primal, predatory manner who don't own their power. That is the deeper instinctual nature of the abusive male. Women look towards their sexual partner for their temporary "empowerment," rather than nurturing their own sexual power. Women use men to be empowered, and then wonder why they get burned. As a woman feels more at home in her flames of power, she can assist a man in finding his feminine side so that he can draw from his own feminine energy instead of hers. She anoints his chakras with her divine light after he expresses his desire to receive her. The currents of love are circulated and regenerated in her body, giving the man abundant life after the woman learns to do the same for herself. The act of receiving the currents and experiencing the magnitude of the feminine self releases the fear of both partners. Their love becomes a generator for life energy.

At first, the feminine feels bigger and more potent than we are accustomed to. Most women try to ignore the power currents of the earth that move up through our legs and ignite the fire in our vaginas.

Many women carry excess weight to smother the power. Others block or short-circuit the power, thus manifesting diseases such as cancer, arthritis and diabetes. When a woman has not done the work to clear anger from her second chakra—vagina, womb and belly—a man will sense her anger on some level. He will try to deny it, run, set up defenses or control. Women need to make it safe again for men to enter their temples, but they also need to be attuned to the energies and power that reside within them.

On the other side, men separate themselves from transmuting the power in their own dark side. They repress their own true power, then seek to control and deny the power of others. This separates men from their hearts and causes heart disease, strokes, drinking problems and obesity. Men innately know how to access the feminine power of creation. Whether they do it or not is a question whose collective modern-day answer presents itself in the hard-edged, bellicose state of the world. Each time a man bridges his creative soul with his deeply rooted knack for initiative, he heals the wound within his divine feminine.

To save our world culture, men and women must stop abusing the power of sex and return it to its sacred place. Contrary to the devastating teachings of Christianity, Islam and Judaism, which continue to strangle the power and sacredness of women to this day, the body must be honored as the holy temple Christ described to his followers two millennia ago. Honoring the body, soul and spirit is the true communion. Abstaining from sex because you abhor it or have experienced unfulfilling past sexual liaisons is not the answer. Having sex consciously is the answer. If the heart, body and soul are in union, sexual union becomes the act of the beloved, as I elaborate upon in great detail in Chapter 29. Devotion to the beloved becomes our spiritual and life practice.

Such a life practice makes living in the Holy Grail an interactive experience with pure vitality. We are able to express our impressions, weave images and feelings, become raw essence and light, and immerse in the ocean of life. Our minds, bodies and souls are united as the poet, painter, writer, dancer, healer, lover, seer and gatekeeper of our soul and planetary heart.

Part III

Mary the Mother: The Divine Essence of Love

Chapter 9

I Am Mary

My love embraces the world to remind you of who you are.
~ Mary

The blue waters part around our boat as we move through the currents on our way to southern Gaul. Summer casts its sweetness through the wide-open scents of seaweed, wild roses and rosehips. The warmth off the sparkling water reflects upon my face, melting the grief of my shattered dreams. Its cooling mist settles upon my woolen cape. I remove the hood and turn my face up to the sun as my cloak ripples in the wind against my cool skin.

A building anticipation to arrive rises within me. It is very sad to have left Jerusalem; I struggle to accept that I will probably never return there. As we near the port of Massilia (Marseilles), the sounds of docking ships, transporting cargo and voices commanding others to finish their chores fill my ears. I prepare to enter the bustle and activity.

My three devoted brothers of spirit escort me. John, the Beloved, will continue on with me and two will return to continue the work. I live in the oneness of my heart, unafraid but searching for my new life. We gather together drinking from our chalices. It is late, but the warmth of the fire blazes on. We see the times ahead, of madness, of destruction and we mourn life's losses. We drink from the cup, relishing in these sweet hours knowing we are here to hold a truth that will take over two millenniums to accept. We hope we are never lonely and can come together again some day to recite the longings of our hearts to a world that will be ready. We live in the flame and give our hearts to the way.

My son, Issa, is safe now. He has left for India and someday I will travel to where he is.

Since Joseph's passing five years ago, I no longer practice the duties of a householder. I miss our practices of devotion to one another. He always laid me down with the tender touch and glance of one who adores God and the Goddess within me. Through our mutual love, we could maintain our holy sacrament of living in the One. Little do people know the true meaning of the Star of David—once a symbol for holy heart union of the divine feminine and masculine. The true inspiration for my son's teachings has now become a sign of control and restraint.

My son was not a traitor to the Roman Empire, but a teacher to reunite man's heart to God and unite nation to nation. I'm not speaking of a God to die for, but a God to treasure life. Issa's life was an expression of living in the oneness of God; those living in separation were tormented and threatened by his absolute authority and power. Obsessed by separations in thought and body, they felt his waves of love entering their hearts, but had no container in which to hold them.

As a temple, container and chalice, the body holds the light for the Holy Grail. It is through our body that the light meets the dark and the remembrance of creation is ignited. It is here in the chalice, free of fear, the ray of our eternal self, that the soul of our unity has a place to dwell. This home can never be forgotten. For here resides the eternal chamber of light, the flame burning from spirit's song of life. It is through my daughter-in-law Mary's body that the way of the holy temple shall be taught. She carries this union in her radiant form and through her children and through her children's children.

My vision opens in the wind. I peer into the distance and know there will be bloodshed to determine who owns the holy temple. No one can own the temple of the soul. Many will believe that its light should be shut down and obliterated. They will try, but it will not happen. They will continue to silence the women who proclaim they are vessels for the Word. Then the Word itself will be cast into bronze, hardened by the powerlessness of man's misuse of will. They will fight for the wrong ideals.

As my travels take me through Nemausus (Nimes), we stay near the Rhone River before we begin our journey to the north. From the south of Lugdunum (Lyon), we travel first northwest, our destination

Caesaromagus Turonum (Tours), and then to Condate (Cherboug) where we will board the ship to take us north to Venta Belgarum (Southampton, England).

We are met by Ancient Ones of Light. These brothers and sisters are my family, the Essenes. We are to spend many months visiting and exploring this beautiful land,. People are more than kind as I lay my burden into the ocean at land's end.

Before spring comes in, I will leave, this time alone, to venture north through England, enroute to Scotland. It is here that I am drawn. I will head to northern Scotland and then travel the east coast of Scotland throughout the summer. Only when the winds of autumn begin will I pull myself away from the majesty. The kernels of my work will be laid in northern Scotland.

I see what I must do. I need to return to Glastonbury to the community, sending word to Martha to bring Mary my daughter-in-law, granddaughter Sarah and grandsons to Gaul. Hopefully, Mary of Salome, Mary of James, my sister, Maximin and Lazarus will be with them. They must leave discreetly and travel lightly to protect the children. Since the death of James, Jesus' beloved disciple, it has been too dangerous for them to stay. Then they must journey to England so the children can be cared for and begin their Essene training before Mary Magdalene receives her inner callings to begin her teachings in the world.

I have much to practice and teach. The breeze cleanses and sweeps away my grief. I am rocked gently in the embraces of the sea, waiting for time to pass, for day to move into the starlit night. I am living in the center of the sun and the moon.

Issa appeared one day in a vision and asked me to travel to the east, where I would find him and spend some months together before it would be time for me to leave this world. When I arrive at his sanctuary, there will be many coming in and out of his small hut. I have seen his face many times in my mind. To see it in the sunlight is more than I could ever imagine. We will spend many afternoons that grow into evenings discussing our lives and futures. He has come to realize that only a few have the craving in their hearts to seek the infinite. Most are content with their illnesses and lacks. He instructs only those whose hearts were purified. This way, the knowledge retains its essence and has the best chance to thrive. His sons have ventured to see him, and he has instructed them in the ways of the One. He has lived his life in union with the Father-Mother God and is content.

I see the course of my life: I will write for the next few years and in the last ten years bury my works. They will be buried in a box, along the hillside close to where Mary Magdalene, the children and I are to spend our summers in the mountains in France. Over time, I fear they will be destroyed. People will fight each other to the bloody death over these teachings, the purpose of my life and the foundation for my son's teachings and work.

I want to share them again. I have tried before. Hopefully, this time they will exist forever.

Chapter 10

Lost Teaching #1: Completing the Circle

"Today you will drink deeply from the fountain of my love. Tomorrow you will be the fountain. Tomorrow you will carry the gift you have been given into the world."
~ Paul Ferrini

We are here on earth at this time to complete a circle. Do you remember this as your agreement? We first came here to fulfill a dream. We dreamt this dream together. We want to experience all of God—shadow and light. We want to know the secrets of creation and become the creative flame of God power, our home, as our deepest inner voice beckons:

The only way I can return home is to bring you with me. I have walked over every bridge that I can create in these realms. I cannot walk any further without you. I ended up on the edge of the cliff once again and said, "Dearest God, I am here again. Please show me the way."

I prayed and opened and cried. I could not receive an answer. I began losing my faith. Maybe I was faltering. Maybe my inner sight was decreasing. God finally answered me as I sat in silence. "There is no bridge, because you are the bridge."

We stand at various levels of being birthed into divine light. Many are on the fence. Many are in the dark, filled with self-loathing, pain, anger and sickness. Many can feel the new frontiers of light but carry the energetic engrams, or designs of living from control and fear. Many are in complete denial of their designs of consciousness and claim to be spiritual aspirants.

To complete the circle together, we must come through the darkness within our own consciousness, access the center of light and implement its power correctly. This darkness is where the unknown lives. We were once courageous adventurers of the unknown. We came to this planet to create visions of beauty. When we separated from Source, we created a void. It is easy to get stuck in the vacuum-like darkness of the void.

So, rather than completing the circle of darkness into light, we split the two. The journey we all seek is to reconnect light and dark and live in the wholeness of creation. Whatever healing form you choose to utilize, travel all the way through yourself to see how you have been aligned to the powers of darkness—illusion, fear and doubt. Just let them go. Stop trying to figure it out.

We do not know what the feminine is. Many men want to touch and be touched by the Goddess, but are afraid of being consumed. They do not know what to trust. The true Goddess has lived outside of the body. Most women disembody their Goddess, making it impossible for a man to surrender to her power. The undercurrent of manipulation and control keeps him angling in the way of caution, rather than opening fully towards divine intimacy. This causes confusion and fear. When a man looks to the power of the feminine creator within himself, he learns to love. If the woman is asleep, he can only try to arouse her sleeping power. A man who denies his inner Goddess destroys all possibility of union with God. We are afraid of this power and of being stuck in God's birth canal.

The feminine creation demands a clear masculine energy to complete its circle. As a woman clears her own divine masculine she is able to support her feminine self. A clear man can support a woman's integration.

Being in the fire of God's light brings up every fear. Some might say darkness is what arises, but really, it is only the absence of light. When we rejoin the heart of the divine feminine with the power in the dark, we heal fear, pain, struggle and anger.

Today, everyone is being given the profound opportunity to complete his or her circle and to awaken the gateways of living multi-dimensionally. The "now" is not stationary. It moves and weaves though time and space, bridging what is present and yet to occur. The rippling current of light known as tantra ignites the spiritual essence of passion within. It will break you free of your controls. It is the life force meeting the divine. This divine fire is meant to consume and transform while you come to understand what mystical liberation is all about.

Completing the Circle: 10 Practical Steps

Step 1
Identify, write down, observe and then stop all the ways that you hurt yourself. Begin to substitute new actions and thoughts in place of those that bring you hurt.

Step 2
Listen to yourself. Pay attention to what your divine power is saying at every moment. Listen and respond.

Step 3
Stay with your authentic self. Do not leave yourself. Be the guardian of yourself. Refuse to abandon yourself any longer.

Step 4
Love your anger. Know that beneath your anger lies greater power. Make a pact to bring this power forward.

Step 5
Return to your sweetness. Feel the honey in your heart. Nurture a sweet smile, and glance with delight at the sky, birds and heart of the person sitting across from you.

Step 6
Ask your body to express itself to you through music. Listen to the melodies that are embodied within you, waiting to be heard. Each time you listen, plunge deeper into the vibration of the sound, until you can sense the *first note* of the melody, the origination point.

Step 7
Go back to a time in your life when you left the circular flow of freedom, expression and spontaneity. Re-choose your path from that moment.

Step 8

Forgive yourself for every time you left your circular flow of life's self-generating energies. Acknowledge how you forgot to give to your self. Forgiving means learning to give to one's self in the true unconditional spirit, while also detaching from the negative energy of not honoring yourself at a previous time.

Step 9

Refuse to live out or enact a spiritual value from your head. Always bring a realized truth into your body. See from your hips, heart, knees, belly, toes — all of your body. Refuse to live for one moment without your whole body and soul interacting.

Step 10

Every day, start from the beginning. Learn to be alive each day in the same new way that trees, birds and animals exhibit. Begin anew as many moments in a day as you can, as though each moment is the very dawn of creation. Start with one moment and work your way up to ten new moments each day by the time the sun goes down.

Chapter 11

Lost Teaching #2: Choosing the Path

"Before thou standest on the threshold of the Path; before thou crossest the foremost Gate, thou hast to merge the two into the One and sacrifice the personal to Self impersonal, and thus destroy the 'path' between the two."
~ Madame Blavatsky

A friend of mine gives people a concise answer when they ask him how he developed into a creative, free-spirited and deeply meditating yogi despite being the son of a military officer and a woman who, had she not married, would have become a nun. "He was discipline; she was devotion," he says. That certainly sums up a *bhakti* (devotional) yogi's path.

We are born onto the path of our families of origin. This path is filled with the perfect gifts and challenges needed to master our present lifetime. Much to our surprise, the path of family always takes us face to face with our fears, illusions and limitations. This is the legacy our birth family bequeaths us, besides (hopefully) the support and guidance needed to become an integrated person in one's community. Our families can show us the wholeness of love, or how love is denied and separated into parts.

The path of life takes many forms and incorporates many transitions. The more we separate through fear, the more difficult we make our life path. The underlying challenge at birth is to refrain from separating from our whole self. We have the cellular pattern deeply engrained within us to move out of our self to find and be filled in love. The joyous child knows itself as the source of love, and the family of higher love mirrors this back to the child.

The choice of our true life path—what the Hindus and yogis call *dharma*—is the most important decision we can make in our lifetimes. It is not through living an outer path devoid of understanding our connections or relationships that takes us home, but instead the liberating of ourselves from limitations and the going beyond the boundaries of this path that brings us to the center of wholeness. At this point, our actions and responses to every day life become the practice of our path.

When you reach the state of not-knowing this is when you can finally grow. Many wise women and men have said, "The older I get, the less I seem to know." This realization of not-knowing ensures the soul's ability to receive. By living in the connection point where the spiritual and physical meet, the soul can enter a home of knowledge. This means you have gone beyond needing to control.

In our child-like world of innocence and wonder, we did not know the answer to who we are. We just *were*. And if we could not be our highest selves, we became someone that could convince everyone else that we were special or significant. From what place do you exist? Can you embrace the concept that knowing the origin of your existence creates your whole world?

Your choice can result in the re-creation of your life. You are not in existence because of anyone or because of any situation. Why remain in situations that give you a false sense of life, that keep you in a state of imbalance? You are doing so because you still fool yourself. You are still pretending. Instead, if you seek to love the sky or the earth more than your own existence, you will begin to live in authenticity, living in your soul's truth. Your existence only becomes liberated when you are aligned to your higher self, which is much bigger than your worldly images and attachments.

Each time you find yourself identifying with the substances of life that confine and define you, refuse to surrender your power to it. Why have you chosen to remain contained? To be free you must throw away your crutches, unhealthy foods, habits and choices and return to the sea and the sky within you. This is where you will find freedom.

Choosing your path is a feeling. Furthermore, the actions you take during your life will define the design of both the path and the walk. Choose the feeling with which you want your life to be filled, and gratefully open to the experiences that come your way. If you correlate feeling with action, you can make the shifts. Separating the two creates confusion. The energy and prior experience you infuse into your actions creates your degree of soul alignment. The energy becomes the true teacher; the person who might provide you with guiding or healing information is merely a human messenger of that energy. If we work to become one with everything in our life, we begin to feel what we want and what we do not want. Our choices become more clear and guided by our soul, which expresses our highest divine self, so that our choices always promote our spiritual growth and evolution.

Living in a state that leaves us drifting halfway between life paths never directs us to our true path. If we stay with our most challenging choices, we will avoid laziness, greed and unhealthiness. We will have the energy and determination to stride forth onto our path of paths.

The masculine patriarchy has preached a gospel of action without emotion and feeling. This is the prevalent energetic structure in which we live. This passionless state of mankind has become overwhelming. Part of the journey consists of being consumed by passion, which we confuse with lust. Many individuals convert their personality structures into their "religions," which they follow with the zealousness of an extremist. Over identification with their perception of reality, as well as their preoccupation with the objects and actions of lust, keeps them off their true path.

What is the path? It is a direct connection to the source of life. The path brings profound wisdom and a thinking-feeling structure that encompasses the whole instead of the separate personality structure. We find the path within ourselves when we choose to live each action with passion. Gone will be the days when each man or woman just thinks about his or herself.

The feeling nature of our body is the bridge to divine freedom. The embodiment of light opens us to a new patterning. The anchor to which we are connected in our bodies defines our experience on the spirit realms. Without the anchor, we preach words without living them and create physical circumstances that block entry into our true home.

Chapter 12

Lost Teaching #3: Finding Your Heart

"What a wonderful lotus it is,
that blooms at the heart of the spinning wheel of the universe!
Only a few pure souls know of its true delight."
~ Rabindranath Tagore

Men and Women of the Flame

The feminine essence of illumination peels away the layers of our hearts, much the same as ocean waves cleanse and renew the body. When allowed to enter the heart, this power of beauty and love magnifies its life force through expression. Freedom comes from expressing the feminine and masculine energies in union. This new era will teach us about the powers within our hearts and souls. We must put that information into action with the light of freedom.

The structures and systems of the world, along with the media, hypnotize us into the delusion that we must create more and more controls to protect us from the dangerous plots of others. This has never been more evident than the years since 9-11, when the U.S. and its allies have preached "security" while depriving citizens of more and more basic freedoms—right down to domestic spying. How do we stay free of the metastatic fear that is being created all around us? Will we be able to pull away from the reality being painted for us that separates the language of our soul with the angst surrounding survival? How can we tell our friends and family to stop deadening their bodies and minds and awaken from the deep sleep in which they are submerged? As each of us ignite the passion and fire of our soul, and illuminate the reason we are here, we will break the spell of living in separation from the One.

We are being drawn to a living presence that seeks to fill and reunite us with our divine birthright—God. Our hearts must be reunited with the purified power in our second chakras, lest we give our power away or seek to control others. We must set our hearts free from the controller within our minds, and live in the design of our authentic selves. This both requires and ensures that we will fight for our inner and outer freedom, while refusing to allow others to limit what we need to nourish and further expand our souls.

When we create freedom in our life, we are tapping the spiritualized power in our hearts and connecting its radiance to the rest of us. As we receive love with an empty mind and an integrated body and soul, we become the divine. The feminine-masculine union in God IS love. The illuminated feminine wants to love. It lives to unite. The masculine power must learn to surrender to the consciousness of love. The masculine cannot remain standing separate and alone from the flame of the feminine without causing great harm to self, others and society. Until we receive the feminine flame, we will push away the feminine expression. The masculine must learn to surrender and be devoured by the light of the flame. Whether male or female, our masculine side must learn to open, serve and grace the vision of our feminine nature.

Women and men of the flame refuse to create separation of the heart and soul in any way. Their minds do not ignore the intelligence created by the soul, spirit and heart in union. They acknowledge a difference between the fire of the ego and the fire of the divine. The ego fights for its own existence, while the divine fights for nothing. The divine co-exists with the forces of nature, God and spirit. The ego defends and removes itself from everything around it, then proclaims itself Master of the Universe.

Become aware of the social and political forces that attempt to create separation in our minds about others. Watch the forces in your life that create fear. Stop the urge to live through another, and thrive upon your own life energy. Walk into the spindrift where the surf meets the sand, and become the power within the dissolving wave. Walk on a mountain and become the force that transforms rock into soil.

Stop identifying your personality with your projections. Strip your self to nothing; lean upon your soul. Feel the raw space, the nothingness. Remember: You are the power that transmutes beauty into form, love into matter and nothingness into fire. Return creation into its form. You are the tantrika, master of heaven and earth. Know your heart—the connector between the masculine and feminine forces. Live within it. Apply this wisdom and light. Instead of living in confusion, stress and self-imposed hardships, center yourself in the power of oneness. Instead of living moment-to-moment in reaction to your separations and thus creating more pain, live in the center of love as the creatrix and creator.

Fill your mind and heart in light and hold it for as many hours as you can each day. As soon as you fall away from it, return to this light. Keep your attention deep within you, thinking of your self as a generator of light. Allow this light to create all that is needed for you in your world. Allow this light to extend in purity without harboring any agenda for those that you love.

To find your inner heart, you must lose your mind and prior conceptions of your self. Return to the universe all of the projections people have ever placed on you. Focus on the flower in your heart. Keep it active and alive. Watch how it wants to close, and constantly choose to keep it open. Master your life.

The feminine power constantly attracts the fountain of life. We have a responsibility to merge into the waters of the feminine divine and learn to receive its graces. No matter what is blocked in your life, you will melt into divine bliss once you know that you are light.

The feminine power knows death as change and transformation. It lives in the rippling, soaring, engulfing waves of creation. Clear out all of the emotions in your belly, so you can enter pure power. Death is the shift from one state of consciousness to another; the final death is the shift of the physical body into spirit. Death of the identity of self prepares us for eternal life.

Allow the greater face of God to see you, then touch and embrace you. As a divine lover who holds the heart of creation, the spark within your heart is ignited. As soon as you separate from Source, your heart closes.

Your decision to become empowered by the light makes possible the ability to transform all that is in the dark into the light.

The Wound

Each person has a wound within his or her psychic body, created by separation from Source. We dance around our wounds and become attached to the mystical, devotional, creative, powerful or addicted lifestyle we live. Healing the wound sets us free to live. We wander from situation to situation trying to heal the wound. One segment of society says, "Ignore the wound by living your life." The other part of society says, "I have no wound."

However, you do.

The wound is the gateway to our soul's karmic completion. Facing the wound makes it possible to enjoy a complete, fulfilling relationship with a partner while flourishing in partnership with God. How we deal with our wound determines the level of emotional and soul freedom we realize in a particular lifetime.

Here are some examples of how the wound is created:

- A son is born and the father sees his son as an extension of himself.
- A son or daughter is born and the mother has little or no emotional support from her partner. She relies upon the innocent baby to fulfill her emotional needs.
- The mother has zero interest in her baby or in being a mother.
- The father is preoccupied with making a living.
- One or both parents silently grieve that they had to abandon their life dream to support a family.
- The mother has miscarried a few times, prompting her to regard the baby who survived as "too" special.
- We enter life carrying the burden of saving or rescuing others.
- We enter a new life after being killed for our beliefs or spiritual power.
- We enter life after abandoning our self and others in a previous life.
- We enter life without being recognized for our talents.
- Our parents never felt good enough in their lives, then drop that burden on us.
- Our parents see the light in us and expect us to carry their weight.
- We are perceived as a threat to our parents' or siblings' authority because we are more intelligent, sensitive or beautiful than they.
- We continue to manifest shame and self-blame from our past because we ran from love, controlled others, controlled when and how our heart center would be open, chose money over love, lost those we cared about and thought it was our fault.

- Our parents had boundary issues, and our energies were used for their life survival. Consequently, we learned to equate being used with surviving.
- A sibling died, and we were left to carry the pain.

We often create our present-day wounds while trying to heal wounds from previous incarnations. Often, our health conditions are manifestations of our deepest wound. We draw people to ourselves who will expose our deepest pains by how they treat us. Although often ignorant of their actions, they will interact with the dark energy of the wound rather than the wholeness.

The only way to stop creating more pain is to heal the wound. The wound is healed when our heart no longer carries the pain, grief, anger, resentment or fear. We find our deepest heart when we have accepted and healed our wounds. The person we were prior to the wound is restored. The wound created by interchange and loss of power with another is healed. We choose not to carry the denials, abuses or fears of others, and we reclaim our hearts.

Healing the Wound: Six Steps

1) Feel into your body and self and acknowledge the presence of the wound.
2) From your heart, ask what specific feeling is connected to the wound.
3) Allow images and sensations from all of the senses to "speak."
4) Receive what your body is transmitting and communicating.
5) Trust the message—no matter how traumatic it might be.
6) Give the wound over to your heart to be basked in light.

Chapter 13

Lost Teaching #4: Letting Go of Control

"Dive thou into the Ocean of sweetness: thus let all errors of life and of death flee away."
~ Kabir

The cells within our body resonate to both negative control and the divine light that prevails when control has been transcended. This struggle between the mind and body became the centuries-old battleground of the Holy Grail, for many an instrument for the balancing of the body and consciousness so that one could enter into the vibration of the highest ray of light. To enter into this spiritual place of power beyond control, we are guided step by step through how we love, think, eat and create. Take a quick moment to focus on your breath. As you breathe in, picture light moving through the pores of your skin and entering your body. Then exhale light, through the pores of your skin into the universe. See how liberating and strengthening that feels?

Imagine an entire lifetime built upon that feeling, a lifetime minus the tethers and gravity of control.

All of us have shadows, parts of our self that have been separated from the light for varying amounts of time. These parts seek to control our thoughts, deeds and relationships with others. By touching into the essence of our heart, we can face these controlling parts and make the momentary choice of embracing them. Only fear can create control or define a controlling environment. We fear not having enough money, comfort or possessions. We fear our gifts and our power. We fear that someone else will take away our power.

The Holy Grail teaches that when we connect into a consciousness of oneness over fear, we become divine co-creators. Every cell in this universe is connected: We are here to love and work together. Each of us is connected to the source of life. The knowingness that we are connected through the vibration of light, through the codes of light in our DNA, helps to move beyond the need to control. The power within Source can be used for good or evil. It is our responsibility to learn to recognize when it is being misused.

Our yearnings for comfort and nurturing keep us tied to what feels safe. Many of us have been willing to stay in uncomfortable work situations and relationships in exchange for the sense of belonging. This drives us so forcefully that we are willing to numb our bodies so that we feel secure. All of us have experienced this or are experiencing it; we define our lives through this "creature comfort." To remain in this state of comfort, however, we keep the divine separate from our physical lives. Unfortunately, when we identify with any thing other than our divine eternal self, we lose sight of our path. As soon as we suppress or close off the divine, we are in separation. We are tossed to sea by our own action. To be immersed in the warmth and joy of life's most nurturing energies, we need to redefine our comfort zone.

Effects of Separating Divine Masculine and Feminine

The moment that our mind began to separate the divine masculine and feminine aspects of our soul, the power generated by living in union began to weaken. In this separation within Source, the mind scrambled to find ways to survive while diluting its essential connection to divine masculine and feminine. One can compare this ego-driven panic to passengers on a ship who, shipwrecked and marooned on an island, desperately hunt down food, water, fire and ways to stay alive. The longer they remain marooned, the less their hopes for being rescued, and the more willing they are to make compromises of their lifestyles to survive.

During these trying times, the mind was able to expand into the unlimited reaches of the sky, but it was not able to travel as easily into the feminine divine. As the body became more and more denied, entry into the gateways of God— what Jesus called "the kingdom of heaven within you" (Luke 17:21)—became increasingly less accessible to the masses. Those who still carried this truth were forced underground, under threat of being killed. The feminine was labeled as "dark." Its power, either dark or light, was unattainable by those living in the mind, yet the mind became what Indian master Paramahansa Yogananda termed "King Ego," the ruler of a world completely broken off from the Holy Grail, from spirit.

Subsequently, the wars and battles created within the self and within political, educational, religious and scientific arenas executed the truth of spirit. Many souls became male and female warriors of the light. Their connection of oneness was so strong that they gave their lives for this truth. Today, many are fighting for truths that have materialized through their own separations. Instead of surrendering into God union, they're engaging in material, cultural, social and international battles and, by doing so, interfering with their souls' common divine path. Only by reconnecting the inner feminine and masculine energies into divine union can we rediscover the truth of our souls and know what to fight for.

We are all manifestations of the light of God. Each of us carries a flame that, when ignited, lights the way for the person beside us. As we stay open and aligned to the full spectrum of creation, we hold the gateway for the next person to join us in this sacred way. We also hold the responsibility to refuse to support another's darkness or misuse of power. When we assist others in recognizing their patterns of control, sexual indulgence, creative egotism and business superiority, we often find ourselves fearlessly standing on a cliff with other angels who dare to expose what is false. Learning to offer the truth without hurting or bashing another is an art form, and something we all must learn in order to stand unwaveringly next to precipices.

The darkness of false power and control will not win out on this planet as long as we are able to identify light and dark. As soon as we let go of our fear of survival, we are free to take our next spiritual step.

It is our deepest challenge to stay open when all we want to do is close down. If we close the gateway to God in our heart, we lose the opportunity to love, and we abandon our birthright to become a vehicle for our soul's highest expression.

A New Body Blueprint and a Planetary Alignment Beyond Control

We have a blueprint in our soul body that states the past and the future. This blueprint is perfectly aligned to spirit, and exists in the union of our higher and lower selves. It is "read" by opening and connecting the inner gateways in the body. In preparation for receiving this blueprint of spiritual discipline, we must practice mental focus, clarity in the heart and an alignment to God. The Holy Grail teaches the preparations, which I briefly mention here: The physical body must be cleansed so that the channel of spirit is open and pure and made strong so it can handle the power of spirit flowing through us. The emotional body must be elevated in vibration to reconnect the source of its pain into spirit, then taught how to transmute negativity into positive joy. The mental body must fill with light so it can perceive from compassion, patience and forgiveness.

The spiritual alignment entering the planet today corresponds with our soul body's blueprint; together, they constitute a new design that combines intellect, spiritually discriminating love, compassion, union of self and God power. This alignment has the power to alter the culture so that we can become a society of co-creators. We need to co-create with spirit to develop pathways of education, medicine and politics that build life force intelligence instead of destroying it. No matter how hard the negative forces try to keep people in fear and disempowerment, the evolutionary pull towards oneness will win out. It is important to make our spiritual practice one of living in the center, where all consciousness meets. When our focus merges into this center point, we can simultaneously think, feel and perceive in total consciousness. When connected into this seed of consciousness our natural spiritual gifts open. We can see the inner planes, and hear, feel and sense other planes of consciousness and levels of awareness. Quantum physics calls this center the nucleus of the cell. We merge with knowledge—*gnosis*—and experience the union of light with all of creation.

As soon as we contact the divine aspect of our self, we become more attuned to this body blueprint and planetary alignment. As students of our own divine nature, we need to hand over the reigns of control to this divine aspect. We need to ask our fear-based parts to surrender to the divine power that runs our consciousness. This level of courage opens our hearts.

One of the biggest and hardest areas of release concerns work—especially for men. When we let go of how we identify with our life work, we release the need to have an identity. It is important to let go of our identity because when we do not, we become sorely attached to it, often ramming into a wall composed of our own self-perception. This wall becomes stronger as we create beliefs about the level of significance and meaning we have to others and to our workplace. It is easiest to relinquish our identity by replacing our feelings of attachment with a new perspective of living from a place of honor and awe of our true spiritual nature. In doing so, we frame our existence not by who we are, but by what level we are one with the co-creative process. Such a state of consciousness allows spiritual energy to move through our emotional and physical bodies, creating a mind of fluidity. Our true nature is found within the reconnections to our essential self. Our essence grows and strengthens through the feeling qualities found in light, which transmutes an etheric pattern or design into our bodies. Once this design is established, we can feel the relationship we have to all of life.

As we relinquish more of our safety and comfort zones, we walk into joy. Joy and control cannot exist in the same space. The image we have tried to fulfill about our self changes as we relinquish control. Instead of projecting upon our selves and others, we support others and choose to be supported by those who want us to awaken to our highest vibration. We need to be prepared, no matter how painful it may be (and, in some cases, it will be painful), to say goodbye to people and situations that prevent us from fulfilling our most divine potential. From there, we must refuse to shift out of the joy and love that vibrates around us and through us. This is a central spiritual tenet.

Win the Battle of Control

Unfortunately, the battle of control burns behind all wars on this planet. Control begins in the body when we reject the parts of our self that carry spiritual strength; this strength is what is needed to resist the manipulative influence of others. We close down and push away the parts of our self that feel unwelcome, rejected, ignored, violated and not seen or heard. We push them into the deepest recesses of our self— into a dark cavern. Like master builders, we construct intricate structures to conceal and hide these aspects of our self. We work very hard to make sure no one hurts or insults these parts. We learn how to control. The harder we live up to someone else's expectations, or are degraded or maligned by others, the more we control. We want to be received for who we are, but instead, our hearts are emotionally bleeding. To reduce or numb the pain, we learn to control how much we share of our self and how much we receive from others. It takes tremendous energy to hide this vivacious, joyful, brilliant and loving self. It shaves years from our lives. We become controllers so we can shut our true selves down.

Every day, we must ask Spirit to help us expand our divine connection. When we live in Spirit, we can creatively approach each challenge presented to us. Love becomes the connecting link between our selves and others. The hardships of life lose their controlling power. Spirit asks and sometimes demands that we relearn the projections through which we define our selves.

Our chosen controls are built upon trying to manage two or more parts of ourselves that are in conflict—the heart's desire to love, and the mind's desire to block out love. However, we cannot live in two paradigms at once if we choose to grow spiritually and lead more purposeful lives. It's impossible. If our hearts are connected to light and our bellies are filled with hatred, pain and anger, we will live in a split consciousness. We break off from our most authentic nature if we are divided over such things as thinking about God while simultaneously fearing what it would feel like to be sexually connected to the God power within our bodies, or if we try to give ourselves fully to a partner but at the same time worry about being hurt in the same way as we were in past relationships. If we block our creative drive and re-direct our life to please or support the selfish desires of others, we will lose touch with our self. If we expect a person to fulfill our pictures of a relationship while we withhold our deepest love, we become split.

As we allow the light to embrace and fill us, the kingdom of heaven is reopened within us, just as Jesus said it would be. We focus in on our hearts and feel all that we are, including the unknown, and we experience oneness. The kingdom cannot remain separated and isolated from our consciousness any longer. Christ consciousness will come again to illuminate our inner and outer worlds. This is the prediction imbedded within the Holy Grail. This is the true meaning of the "Second Coming."

Creating Your Protective Sheath

To protect and heal our chakras, emotional and etheric bodies **from those who would seek to control, manipulate or use our energies**, or to bring another aspect of our soul back into our bodies, we create a sheath to harmonize and maintain a strong connection to the spiritual force.

Our souls resonate to beauty and need to be protected energetically. Most of us are walking around without that sheath. Controlling another person or being controlled is less possible when the sheath is safely restored. We have greater ease being centered in our hearts and body and can access the beauty of creation in our physical body.

To create the sheaths:

Sheath One: Begin 20 feet diagonally above your head. Visualize silver, then bronze at the outermost point of the oval shield you are about to create. As you move towards your body, create one color after another until you reach your heart center. Bring gold into the center of your heart. Use hues of every color to create each layer from the outside of the oval to the gold center.

Sheath Two: Visualize layers and layers of diamonds, emeralds, sapphires and rubies around your entire body.

Sheath Three: Visualize violet in the center of your heart. Extend the violet out around your body.

Sheath Four: Create a clockwise spiral that spins from the top of your head through the center of your body, then into the earth. Turn it into different colors. Complete as you turn the spiral into blue or gold light.

The sheath can be of any color or colors that you choose. As the colors reveal themselves to you, weave their energy around yourself.

Once we draw these sheaths around us, we can begin to heal the original wound caused by the long-ago destruction of these same sheaths. We will return to the place we occupied when our sheaths were intact, before our bodies and souls became separated. As your etheric body heals, spiritual energy can pour freely through your physical body.

Part IV

Mary Magdalene: Her Teachings Revealed

Chapter 14

The Legacy of Mary Magdalene

"Mary was the embodiment of the Cosmic Mother
—a human pure of spirit
and heart who could hold open the direct portal
into the Great Mother,
the Creatrix of all matter, of all time and space."
~ Tom Kenyon and Judi Sion

Mary was the woman called "the Magdalen," a Hebrew epithet meaning "tower" or "stronghold"—not "whore" or "prostitute," the common associations. A pillar of strength and conviction, Mary came from the sacred priestess lineage, an initiator and carrier of the cosmic seed of conscious awareness. She lived in accordance with her body, breath and spirit, and was the opening to heaven's gate.

A consecrated priestess in Greek was known as *hierodule*, a sacred woman. Mary belonged to this once strong tradition, which began in Atlantis but was dying out when she entered training. During her lifetime, Mary became symbolic of a misunderstood ancient way that not even Jesus could successfully reverse. Mary's gifts as a conduit of the divine feminine, once held in reverence, became identified with the word "prostitute," thus losing the dignity and blurring the roles of a temple priestess and a woman of the street.

Yet there is no doubt of Mary's status with Jesus himself. When Mary anointed Jesus in Bethany on the Mount of Olives outside of Jerusalem, she used a pound of spikenard, or "nard" upon his feet. The nard-filled jar comprised her entire dowry of perfume, meant to last her lifetime. In this moment, however, she chose to use it all in a single ritual on Jesus' feet. Why? The road to an answer presents itself in the Bible's Song of Songs: "For the King's banquet, my nard gives forth its fragrance." The passage goes on to state that spikenard is a symbol for the bride herself! Furthermore, in the fourth Gospel of the Gospel of John, it is written twice that the woman who anointed Jesus was Mary, the sister of Lazarus (John 11:2, 12:3).

Mary's Spiritual Origin and Mission

In times prior to Mary, the Goddess anointed a man through an ancient ritual of sex. She would invoke and become the Goddess herself, transforming her body and soul as the temple of divine light and power. Through their intercourse into light, the man would be anointed into spiritual awakening.

It was an honor and a sacrament to offer one's self in this manner. In Heliopolis or Baalbec, in what is now Syria, custom required every maiden to prostitute herself to a stranger at the temple of Astarte. Matrons as well as maids testified their devotion to the Goddess in this way. In Phoenician temples, women prostituted themselves in the service of religion, believing that by propitiating the Goddess, they would win her favor. It was actually a law of the Amorites that before marrying, a woman must for seven days sit by the main gate and engage in sexual relationships with chosen men. At Byblus, the people shaved their heads in the annual mourning for Adonis. Women who refused to sacrifice their hair had to avail themselves to strangers on a certain day of the festival; all money that they earned was consecrated to the Goddess. A Greek inscription found at Tralles in Lydia indicates that religious prostitution survived in that country as late as the second century A.D. In Armenia, the noblest families dedicated their daughters to the service of the goddess Anaitis in her temple of Acilisena, where women acted as prostitutes before they were given in marriage. In Cyprus, all women were obliged by custom to prostitute themselves to strangers at the sanctuary of the Goddess before marriage. This religious duty was performed in the service of the Great Mother Goddess whose name varied from place to place: Astarte, Aphrodite, Ishtar, among others.

In Babylon, every woman, whether rich or poor, submitted once in her life to the embraces of a stranger at the temple of Mylitta, and dedicated her wages to the Goddess.

In the pagan rites, the anointer would initiate her bridegroom through the sexual act. Their divine union would spread joy and abundance throughout the land. Through their sexual intimacy, they would build, grow and disperse life force to the earth and all individuals living upon the land, creating prosperity through an abundance of crops. In the ancient tales of Osiris and Isis, Tammuz and Ishtar celebrate the life force of nature and the resurrection and dying of crops through the symbolic and ritualistic death and then resurrection of the bridegroom.

Mary Magdalene came forth to Jesus as an already sacred woman—though examples of her actually offering herself sexually to others *do not exist in any Gospel, book or passage.* She sought initiation and training from the Christ. Difficult as it may have been for the other disciples, Mary was taught high-level spiritual disciplines by Jesus. Her previous training in sacred feminine healing enabled her to become his beloved. Much to the dismay of the other 11 disciples, Mary became the emanating light of the divine teachings and the carrier of the Holy Way. She not only carried the seed of God's light, but also embodied the union of the divine within her body. Mary radiated the essence of love.

After the crucifixion, Mary stepped into her role as physical and spiritual carrier of the Holy Grail. Mary became a teacher and healer in France while raising three children. Her teachings were to awaken the spiritual rays of divine light in the body. A profound healer, she carried on the prophetic powers of Jesus and assisted people in healing themselves. As a bridge between spiritual planes, she brought forth information to help return a person to his or her divine wholeness. Mary taught women to be carriers of the divine flame of love as mothers, healers and wives. She believed in each person, often to the point of helping them restore their belief in their own God powers. Mary did not see herself as a prophet or savior, but as a simple devotee of God.

Centuries later, her power and influence became the subject of scorn by the Church. The Greek word *harmatolos* (one who has transgressed spiritual law, as Jesus and Mary did by the way they conducted their relationship) was misinterpreted to mean "sinner" by Pope Gregory in 591 A.D., when he pegged Mary Magdalene as a prostitute. Yet, in all four Gospels, there exists no reference to Mary being a prostitute. The true nature of her mission *does* exist in plenty of other writings.

The Relationship of Jesus and Mary Magdalene

Jesus and Mary Magdalene built their relationship upon the knowledge that procreation was for renewing and empowering their union in God. Their relationship existed outside the religious norms of the day, honoring many of the social customs while remaining true only to those that maintained their holy and sacred union. Their promise to one another and the path they forged, through the love they shared and their tremendously magnetic spiritual energy, enabled God to be felt by all in the land—even by those who didn't directly cross their paths.

In the original Book of Mark, in a passage later omitted, Mary Magdalene stepped outside the house during a visit from Jesus and some disciples. It was a Jewish custom that only a husband could give permission for a woman to step inside or outside of the house while in his presence. Much to the confusion of the disciples, she did not step back into the house at *their* request. The Jesus-Mary relationship was sanctified in a union the disciples did not understand. The light of the holy couple's sacred connection went beyond what anyone could acknowledge or accept.

In the Order of the Essenes, couples evolved through initiations together. Certain practices and codes of honor were sustained in the relationship. To earn the external state of outer marriage, seven to ten years of sacred practice and observance were expected. The inner marriage or *hierosgamos*, the divine union of the inner feminine and masculine, was attained first. These practices included a daily integration of the forces of one's feminine and masculine energies. Sexuality was practiced as a means to commune in God. The practice of clearing one's mind and emotions, and deepening one's relationship to Source, was the foundation of relationship. Jesus cleared Mary of "the seven demons," the karmic and ancestral energies that burdened the seven chakras; it was the task and responsibility of any great healer to perform this work. After that initial body and soul clearing, she received higher and more refined vibrations. On the third day after the crucifixion, when she saw Jesus in his radiant form, Mary was clear enough to receive an initiatory teaching that could only be given when the master-teacher was out of the body. Of all the disciples, she alone received this initiation.

Jesus and Mary Magdalene were never described as a couple because they broke the rules of their Essene-Judaic order. They were married before completing seven years of required spiritual protocol, thus skipping outer levels of religious regimentation. In the Essene tradition, marriage was viewed as a spiritual discipline based more upon upholding rites of initiation than human love. Many Essenes were unmarried and instead practiced celibacy. Meanwhile, the Judaic tradition upheld the vows of marriage as a practice of moral integrity and responsibility for the couple's service to community and child rearing. Rabbis had to be married to enter the holiest parts of the Temple, and were considered incomplete or disobedient to God if unmarried.

Truly, Jesus and Mary walked their own spiritual path. Renegades to both Judaic and Essene customs, their journey was defined by deep love and friendship, rooted in the traditions of eastern spiritual consorts and sacred marriage for the purpose of reaching God together.

Mary's Higher Spiritual Initiations

Mary Magdalene had direct experience with the divine. Proselytizing had no place on her path of the sacred marriage. Her relationship with Source embraced divinity through the senses, the feeling world and the body. Like Mary the Mother, Mary possessed the gifts of "inner knowing," the developed abilities of "seeing" in the deepest way derived only from a profound spiritual connection with the soul and spirit.

Mary's higher spiritual initiations by Jesus prepared her to lead the path of the "Christed One" as the anointer and guide through darkness into light. Mary the Mother passed her teachings to Mary Magdalene and completed Mary Magdalene's trainings as a divine feminine link in spirit.

In 1896, the Gospel of Mary was found in an antique shop in Akhmin, Egypt and transported to the National Museum of Berlin. The rediscovery of the gospel resulted in a number of translations, the first in 1955. Translator Jean-Yves Leloup produced a version in 1997 that changed the Sahidic Coptic to French. Pages 1-6 and 11-14 were missing in the copy found in Egypt, making interpretation difficult. Purportedly written in the early part of the second century, it conveyed the teachings of Jesus that Mary Magdalene carried on throughout her life. It also contained many comments written about her by other disciples, among them:

> Then Andrew began to speak, and said to his brother:
>
> "Tell me, what do you think of these things she has been telling us?
>
> As for me, I do not believe
>
> That the Teacher would speak like this.
>
> These ideas are too different from those we have known."
>
> And Peter added:

"How is it possible that the Teacher talked in this manner, with a woman, about secrets of which we ourselves are ignorant?

Must we change our customs,

And listen to this woman?

Did he really choose her, and prefer her to us?"

(Gospel of Mary 17:9-20)

The Gospel of Phillip further defines and sanctifies Yeshua's (Jesus') love for Mary: "The Lord loved Mary more than all of the disciples, and often used to kiss her on the mouth. When the others saw how he loved Mary, they said 'Why do you love her more than you love us?' The Savior answered them in this way: 'How can it be that I do not love you as much as I love her'" (Gospel of Philip 59:9).

When a man and a woman truly love one another, there is a point of divine power and love between them that is created by their interchanges of respect, higher love, sex and trust. As the love deepens between them, this force becomes magnetic in nature and polarizes their emotional, spiritual, physical and etheric bodies, connecting them directly to God through their love. The more spiritual love they pour into their magnetism the greater their powers become individually and jointly.

This is the model of Jesus' and Mary's love and the gateway to the divine love that is possible for all of us.

The *Nous,* The Treasure: An Introduction

Jesus spoke of the in-between point between invisible and visible realities and between the soul and spirit as the window into infinity. Within the soul lives the gateway to creative expansion and vision that bridges the body and spirit. The higher emotions of love and joy strengthen that bridge. "There where is the *nous*, lies the treasure" (Gospel of Mary 10:16). By living in the *nous*, the center point where the creative and spiritual forces meet, we can experience the powers of God opening. Living in the *nous* can happen when the heart, soul, emotions and spirit are aligned in one's highest light and love. To live in this center is to live in the Holy Grail—the crux of Mary Magdalene's mission:

In the *Gospel of Mary,* Peter said to Mary:

"Sister, we know that the Teacher loved you

differently from other women.
Tell us whatever you remember
Of any word he told you
Which we have not yet heard."
Mary said to them:
"I will now speak to you
of that which has not been given to you to hear.
I had a vision of the Teacher,
And I said to him:
'Lord I see you now in this vision.
And he answered:
'You are blessed, for the sight of me does not disturb you.
There where is the nous, lies the treasure.'
Then I said to him:
'Lord, when someone meets you in a Moment of vision,
is it through the soul (psyche) that they see,
or is it through the Spirit (Pneuma)?'
The Teacher answered:
'It is neither through the soul nor the spirit,
but the nous between the two
which sees the vision.'"

By living in the *nous*, higher alignments in the body can occur and one can exist in the place where body, soul and spirit meet. When this happens, a feeling of *gnosis*, an all-knowing connection with all forces in the universe, is simultaneously sparked. The result is a holy sense of attunement, acceptance and peace.

Here, in the *nous,* resides the Holy Grail—Mary Magdalene's teachings.

Chapter 15

Mary Magdalene: From My Heart

The cup being offered
was finally accepted
and those who drink now know the taste of love.
~ Rumi

I invite you to travel through a tunnel of profound beauty and grace to understand what lies beyond your fears and limitation. There exists a land of the sacred heart where no woman or man stands alone. The doorway begins in your belly, the home to your feelings, power and sexuality. Most of you will want to give it away—until I show you how foolish this would be.

Here in your belly, you can remember who you are. Freed from repressing your true identity, the divine feminine will make her presence known to you. She will make you ache inside until you say "yes" to her. Many of you will numb the ache, but I promise she will re-emerge in different forms until you acknowledge her. Your senses must awaken to her smell, touch, voice, taste and sound. Her essence is meant to arouse you and drop your conceptions into the ocean of knowledge within you. Your intuition and knowingness will merge, enabling you to live in the union of your soul.

Each passing day, you dress yourself without realizing what it is you have covered up. Feel deeply enough, and you will find your light and power within the most dismal and ugly part of yourself. The voices in your head arguing to be right are only the ones abandoned and forgotten. In the split from your true self, your lost energies manifest as desperate voices. With no direction or acknowledgment of who they are, they will wrap ropes around your heart, enclosing you in their darkness.

Penetrate and fill your heart with the power of the One living within you. Join with compassionate resonance to hear the voices of your own creation. Each voice carries recognition of its true source ready to make contact with you. Even the darkest voice within you is connected to the true source of all life. In its pain, it turns away from the light and hides in the dark, waiting to be seen, felt and heard by your heart. The second doorway within your heart experiences truth while the wisdom in your belly unites in the heart's fire. Move this fire into the cave of your soul's passion—your throat, the portal and bridge of your higher and lower self.

From here, you can heal with and manifest the intelligence of the One by focusing your intention of integration and wholeness into the physical and non-physical realms. Become what you seek.

My master taught that within us is the kingdom of heaven, in which rays of light shine and radiate outward, forming new connections and creations every moment. We can become both the receptor and the creator of these streams of power. Every cell that is destroyed and created is a part of the living fabric interconnecting every strand of life. The more light we weave into the matrix of our self, the stronger our DNA becomes and the easier it is to let go of cords of the past. The secrets of birth and death are understood by becoming the full synthesis of every strand of creation that exists in our soul consciousness. No matter how ugly or deformed a part of our self may appear, when reconnected into the light, the full consciousness of this part becomes awakened and fully alive. The force of life flowing through the column of light within the center of our body vibrates stronger as it spirals deeper and wider into the river of creation.

Become magnificent in your creation. Remember each moment, each movement of your body and soul as it touches the flesh and light of the universe. Allow life to align to the highest octave through you.

We touch upon the octave of our soul by opening into union with the divine. Our hearts are the interpreters of this matrix. Its light and sound are the gateways into the universal design of oneness. We are here to become creators of life intelligence and power through merging our spiritual essence, soul and body into light—the highest consciousness of life.

Now is the time to transform darkness into light. Give voice to the limitless power of love.

Chapter 16

The Secret Teachings of Mary Magdalene

"And in that place I saw the fountain of the righteousness
Which was inexhaustible:
And around it were many fountains of wisdom
And all the thirsty drank of them,
And their dwellings were with the righteous and holy and elect."
~ The Book of Enoch

Mary Magdalene taught the deeper mysteries of life and of divine feminine power and how to use it appropriately, in service to spirit and humanity. She fulfilled her destiny to teach the secrets of resurrecting the force of life within the body and spirit, and to co-create with the Holy Spirit.

Known as the "anointer," she opened the centers of higher awareness within a person and understood the life force as the union of sexual and spiritual God powers. Her intuition and faith were as great as her partner's, if not stronger in certain areas. To Jesus, her partner as well as Messiah, she conveyed the understanding and devotion he needed to complete his mission.

Through an untold number of organized and spontaneous lessons, Mary conveyed the essence of the divine feminine as the heartbeat of spiritual union, the Holy Grail. For thousands of years, this power was enacted daily by women and men. The intuitive powers and healing rituals that maintained their connection with Source provided spiritual and energetic nourishment *(manna)* for their daily lives. They viewed circumstances within their families and communities from a perspective of wholeness. It was known that the divine body enlivened the mind at all times to live in a state of balance and integration.

As cultures moved away from living in divine union, they created religious, sexual, business and family dogmas to help them survive. The feminine perspective of transforming and merging light and darkness was no longer accepted. Viewing each day as a healing grace became a perception of the past. The need to survive prevailed over divine connection. The old ways of healing and union disappeared. Those who held onto their divine relationship were often poisoned, killed or exiled; their power was considered a threat to social governing forces.

The next wave of "spiritual" development followed: rationalizing and attempting to make intellectual sense of precepts that were beyond the mind's grasp. This now-dominant masculine perspective sought to explore spirit through the mind, diminishing the feminine perspective of living from a place of oneness in body, heart and soul. A disconnect between mind and body ensued, due to this separation of masculine and feminine forces.

Many ancient writers, philosophers and scientists—somewhat more protected from harm than ordinary citizens and much more inclined to take risks—were driven to keep alive the golden link between divine masculine and feminine consciousness. The following was translated from Lucius Apuleius' *Metamophoses* in 1566 and voices the mythical treasure of Isis, Queen of Heaven:

"Behold, Lucius I am come, thy weeping and prayers has moved me to succor thee. I am she that is the natural mother of all things, mistress and governess of all the elements, the initial progeny of worlds, chief of powers divine, Queen of heaven, the principal of the Gods celestial, the light of the goddesses: at my will the planets of the air, the wholesome winds of the Seas, and the silences of hell be disposed; my name, my divinity is adored throughout all the world in diverse manners, in variable customs and in many names, for the Phrygians call me Pessinuntica, the mother of the Gods: the Athenians call me Cecropian Artemis: the Cyprians, Paphian Aphrodite: the Candians, Dictyanna: the Sicilians, Stygian Proserpine: and the Eleusians call me Mother of the Corn. Some call me Juno, others Bellona of the Battles, and still others Hecate. Principally the Ethiopians which dwell in the Orient, and the Egyptians which are excellent in all kind of ancient doctrine, and by their proper ceremonies accustomed to worship me, do call me Queen Isis. Behold I am come to take pity of thy fortune and tribulation, behold I am present to favor and aid thee. Leave off thy weeping and lamentation, put away thy sorrow, for behold the healthful day which is ordained by my providence, therefore be ready to attend to my commandment."

Invitation to Your Higher Self

1) Sit towards the east. Pour water into a bowl. Light four candles for the four directions. Give thanks. Spread rose petals. Anoint your third eye with either sandlewood, frankincense, rose, patchouli, neroli or rosemary oil. Absorb the presence of the divine mother in your heart.

2) From 10-20 feet above your head, create a beam of laser light and love. Send this ray of light into the open shaft or column inside your body – what advanced yogis call the *sushumna,* the inner spine. Within this elevator shaft corridor, look for the part of your power that is in the dark and shine the laser beam towards the bottom of the corridor until you see her or him. Find out why she/he is in the dark. No matter how hidden or alone she/he is, remain with her/him. Tell her/him that you have come back for her/him. Ask why she/he has been in the dark and what she/he needs to live within you. Embrace the power, innocence, fear, or pain in their eyes.

3) Open your heart to her/him. Let them in. With a piercing gaze, look through their darkness until you see the light of who they are. Now, with a gentle gaze, perceive the outline of who they are as light. Hear, feel and absorb their essence. Invite them to share their knowledge with you. Listen, feel and receive.

   This is the light of our highest self. Sometimes, we find it in the darkest corner of the soul.

Re-Establishing Divine Union: Honoring the Power of the Elements

Within all of the ceremonies of the divine feminine is an honoring of relationship to the source of life. Women maintain a connection to their power by honoring their wombs, as Botticelli depicted in his paintings showing the ripeness of the divine feminine and her powers of fertility. Look at a ripe pomegranate after it is pulled apart; the fruit is one of the most luscious symbols of the divine feminine. Its seeds nourish and rejuvenate the body with nutrients and anti-oxidants that promote longer, healthier lives.

Virtually all female physical illnesses are manifestations of an imbalance in deep belly energies, signaling disconnection from the divine feminine. When we reconnect the currents that move the divine feminine through the body, health can be restored. When we can see from the realms of the invisible, transforming darkness into light, matter into spirit, we become empowered by the divine feminine. Enter the earth, become the air, transform negativity through flames of fire, merge into water and become the ethers, the void of the unknown.

Women are naturally connected to the power of the elements through the cyclical movement of their ovaries. Breathing life force into the deep belly maintains the connection to feminine power. Honor the power of how the feminine manifests in you. Allow her to expose you to reveal your fullest, most beautiful nakedness. Let her come to you; enter into her. Receive and give to her. Pour water for her. Plant seeds. Bathe her in milk and honey. As you eat her juicy fruits, take in her lightness. Wash her feet. Soak her in salts. Give her a pen and special notebook, and allow her to journal her voice through you. See through her eyes. Enter her world through the stars. Enter space. Touch diamonds and become her. Complete yourself by making her the central bodily force in your life.

Dissolving into the feminine unites us with her source. This is the act of love. We move and respond to the flow, power and force of love. We become one with life by transforming in her bliss, change and renewal. When we are immersed in her stream of deeper consciousness, we experience destruction not of life, but of falsehood, deception and ego. Just as Mary Magdalene professed two millennia ago, the secret teachings of the divine feminine are the guidelines to re-establishing her existence on this planet. She will fill you. She will never let you down.

When we forget the divine feminine, we forget ourselves. If we forget to visit the stars, we abandon the power in the dark void of creation. Her power is not meant to be used selfishly, but to unite with. Remaining separate creates greed, anger, lies and indulgence. Rather than celebrating her, we have made it more difficult for her to survive. Women were forced to abandon her. They betrayed their union with her to stay alive. Any woman found in union with her was killed or forcibly harmed. Unfortunately, women have now become accustomed to abandoning their own power. They run from their creative genius and sexually reject their partners to avoid healing their own feminine imbalances. As for men, they often find fault with partners who are connected to the divine feminine. Unless spiritually integrated, they interpret this power as something they do not possess—and thus are threatened by it.

We must end the madness present in our world. Remember your divine mother and bow to your heart, her heart, for she gives you life.

Opening to the Divine Trinity

Divine Feminine: Meditate and visualize a silver full moon. Bring the lunar light into your lower belly, solar plexus and heart. Turn her into a white pearl, and place the pearl within you.

Divine Masculine: Meditate on the sun and bring him into your solar plexus, navel and lower belly.

Holy Trinity: Focus into your third eye and invite your divine feminine and divine masculine selves to appear to you. Take them into your heart. Create divine union by inviting your inner child to sit with your divine inner male and female selves. They are the connection to Father and Mother God within your own soul.

Dissolving Walls in the Emotional Body

The emotional body is the bridge between the soul and the physical body. The state of our emotional body determines the spiritual health of the soul and physical bodies. Without this strong alignment, living in spiritual and physical union is virtually impossible. When a child's soul expression is blocked, the emotional body builds a protective wall for itself. This wall of energetic cement prevents us from feeling the true state of our hearts and keeps us separate from God power. The density of the wall is determined by the degree of mental or physical control a person has experienced or suffered. For most, the wall blocks the ability to experience deep intimacy and sexuality, as well as the ability to love one's self or others. As long as we keep pain as our master, we perpetuate relationship loss and health problems, and we remain attached to the cement wall. It serves to keep everyone at arms length, and it deadens the pain held behind the wall, preventing it from being ever heard or felt.

Some build walls to block out the chaos of emotional bodies so open these people are unable to differentiate where their own feelings begin and end. They use creative expression to define who they are because they are so connected to everything and everyone. However, they also lose their spiritual bodies and relationships with the divine. Others have no such external walls, but instead possess thick inner walls that mask their vulnerability, preventing anyone from getting too close. It is much easier to retreat from relationships that require complete intimacy, and choose to connect to others who also create walls that prevent a state of physical, emotional and spiritual oneness. For these people—the vast majority, I might add—pain, suffering, gossip, lack and illness remain their consistent bonds to life. Their walls create stubbornness, resentment, judgment, fear and self-righteousness, and compartmentalize the emotions, along with the mind, body and soul. When these walls are kept in place, they foster a false sense of control, but engage the ego full-time. Our outer persona may not appear ego-driven, but it takes so much work to keep the parts of our self in contained inner spaces that the mind can become exhausted and easily overwhelmed until spirit begins to shake up the wall. Most of us do not even know the wall exists until someone comes along who loves us so much or so desires to know us at the deepest level that we ourselves begin to question why we can't meet her or his level of communication, depth and intimacy. Then we peer inside ourselves, and we recognize the reason—the wall.

Our cement walls lead to physical conditions that can develop into debilitating or life threatening diseases such as strokes, heart attacks and cancer. A healthy emotional body is connected to all of the chakras and receives sustenance from these energetic centers. The wall blocks our chakras, and as such deprives us of this sustenance. The body responds in a host of damaging ways: addiction, obsession, rigid thinking, escapism and denial. Many negative emotions percolate, including hurt, anger, grief, sadness and fear. Once the walls between the bodies crumble, however, joy can infuse our being and our energetic centers can return to their vibrant state.

Love dissolves the wall. Once we choose to no longer use daily events as a distraction to being in the moment, we find the opportunity to breath into the cement, love the wall and tell it we no longer need it. As soon as we choose love as our master, we begin to love our self.

Dissolving Emotional Walls

1. Come into your body and feel without judgment.
2. Practice receiving another person completely by listening more and talking less about yourself.
3. Observe how and why you block receiving from your heart and from another's heart.
4. Observe how you separate your mind, body and emotions from fully receiving and giving. Pay attention to how you attempt to maintain a comfort zone of ease and non-conflict.
5. Why and how did you create any wall that might exist within you?
6. Question if you're ready to remove the wall.
7. Identify the wall as an extension of ego in your body. Ask if it is ready to serve you in another way.
8. Identify the role of this wall—not only how it has protected you from others who attempted to steal or control your full power, but also how you have isolated and held onto your greater power.
9. Connect the light in your heart to the light in your ascended self, ten feet above your head. Send a ray of pure light, in any color, into the walls. Dissolve these walls with any level of intensity or flow that you choose.
10. Perceive the energy of what existed in the box. From the depth of your heart, accept the magnitude of what now exists.

The Way of Divine Union

Feelings and heart-felt thoughts open the etheric body. Joy, light, self-acceptance and gratitude continue opening the body to perceptions and expressions of sound, color and vibration. The etheric body reverberates the expressions of beauty and movement, and expands as one solidifies his or her intention to connect with greater love. When the etheric body is opened, health and vitality spiral and fill the physical, emotional and mental bodies. Sound translates God current into the etheric body as ripples of magnetic energy. Color mends holes, rips and tears in the etheric body that were caused by negative thoughts, dense vibrations and psychic attacks. The etheric body is a much finer, more sensitive template, or double, of the emotional body. Once the etheric and emotional bodies are functioning in unison, we are able to project great energy into our thoughts, circulate healing energy and magnify our creative forces. The natural aftermath of this increase in energy is the manifestation of our greatest goals and desires, provided they contain a spiritual component meant to serve and help others as well as our selves.

The chakras are portals of spinning light that connect the etheric, emotional, physical and spiritual bodies. The more clear they are, the more access we have to their currents of power and energy. When our consciousness is connected all the way into each chakra, there is no room for anyone else's energetic cords to penetrate into our energy field. If our consciousness is merged with the divine, we are also woven into the divine; we become channels of this energy. We must free our self from any ego-conscious identity to divinity, then combine this state of awareness with the true identity of self—spirit. By living in spirit, the flow of God, we co-create with God while understanding we are not the Source of All That Is. Our physical bodies become vehicles for containing spirit and the sweetness of spirit may fill us. Unless we empty ourselves of all negativity, plus selfish desires and needs, we are unable to fill our inner containers with pure spirit, which is truly God's medicine. As soon as we classify who we think we are in spirit, we lose connection with our divine identity.

Clearing the Chakras

Staying connected in all of our chakras at the same time, keeps us centered in our spiritual power.

Begin with the first chakra, located at the base of your spine. Ask what color it needs to be cleared. Bring in that color and spin it in a clockwise spiral. Carry the spiral upward, through the core shaft of light in the center of your spine, to the second chakra. Ask what color it needs to be cleared. Bring the color into the spiral and spin it. Take it deeper into the chakra until you reach the center of the spiral. Move through the navel, solar plexus, center of the breast bone, heart center, throat center, third eye and crown chakra, repeating the visualization of the spiral and the invitation to clear the chakras. Press the spiral all the way down through all of the chakras to the first chakra, then let go and allow the energy to rise through the central spine.

Repeat this exercise 12 times.

The Purpose of Our Spiritual Power

We are on an eternal mission: to return to the center of God from the periphery, which is where we sit when we confuse personal power with God power. Our spiritual power opens and develops as we merge into Source and release the need for our mental body to control and run the show. Spiritual power grows stronger as the chakras are aligned and the central core shaft of light in the spine is unobstructed. Moving blue light through the central core shaft of light serves as a tremendous clearing force. The more spiritual power we have coursing through us, the clearer our brain functions. Without spiritual current, our brain functions at less than half of its potential.

There are as many neurons in the brain as there are galaxies. Emotional, mental and spiritual currents run through neurons at approximately 200 miles per hour. The body magnetizes these spiritual forces and higher mind powers as we accept and receive currents of light. As the brain receives spiritual currents, it continues to create new neurons throughout one's lifetime. The brain can be trained to maintain information and send messages to the body and soul when it knows how to transpose light frequencies into feeling levels. Connecting feelings to light alters the mind from survivalist thinking to acts of love and universal thinking.

The central core shaft of light through the spine is a highway for light and power to engage. The chakras need to be thought of as portals into the main highway of expansion and manifestation. For example, the more our third eye unites with our heart chakra and sacral chakra, the stronger our connection in spirit will be. The messages from our sacral chakra are then able to increase in clarity, making the spiritual eye become even clearer. We only begin to see clearly from our spiritual eye when our sexual, power and creative issues are removed from within our sacral chakra. Once the sacral chakra is balanced, then our chakras are able to be bridged into a connected highway where energies build and interconnect, and where we are able to refine our spiritual power. The faculties of the higher mind, brain, emotional and soul body increase as the rays of light of all seven principal chakras integrate. Our personal power can thus integrate with our soul, and we can rise up into states of illumination with which we become familiar as spiritual power.

Creating Life from Spiritual Connection

When we practice connecting into spiritual consciousness every day, we begin to notice patterns of nature that reflect our spiritual state. We notice how we engage in daily routines that range from brushing our hair to choosing our clothes, bathing and conversing with others.

Our simplest actions take on new meaning as we feel, recognize, remember, delight and build upon the images, sounds and sensations that come to us. The pores of our skin, vital organs, brain, eyes, ears and nose vibrate to the deeper senses of the spirit. Expansion, contraction and union with spirit become a dance of our hearts and souls as they merge to experience the next moment.

The gateway to the divine is located at the point where spirit meets the body. The Holy Grail awaits you there. The temple of the body is illuminated and penetrated by this gold light of universal spirit.

The regular practice of oneness through dance, writing, breathing and energy exercises, meditation, painting, composing and the expressive arts enable us to develop a relationship with the Holy Grail. By aligning with our desire to merge our self with the divine, and magnify the power of being in union with spirit, we catapult the dive into the greatness of spirit. The soul remembers its destiny—to bring us into union with the divine. We become magnetized. Then we, too, remember what it was like to be united with spirit.

When this happens, we birth our new self, and we are likewise birthed into the kingdom of heaven within. This is the deeper meaning of the phrase "born again," and also the message Jesus tried to convey by being baptized (dipped into union) in the waters of the Jordan (spirit).

Initiating A Woman's Power: Birthing Life

Let's go back 2,000 to 4,000 years. At the moment of conception, the mother invites a new soul to begin life within her womb. Her preparation for pregnancy has been part of her training in the womanly arts. She's abstained from sex for six to eighteen months to develop the ability to see the energy currents within her own body and live in them. She has transformed into a source of power and knowingness. She can see, feel and be in communion with the earth as it reflects within her body. Her well-trained body serves as a mirror and container for the fullness of nature that surrounds her. She can draw the elements—earth, water, air, fire and ether—inside herself to use for healing, regeneration of health and transformation of the body, soul and spirit. She knows the uses of the roots, stems and leaves of surrounding plants by simply holding the plant and feeling its vibratory essence run through her hands, into her heart.

Now, she uses this training while a child is developing within herself. She can feel the essence of the child's heart and soul and speak to it. She is consciously guiding the development of the mind, body, soul connection of the child. The child's birth becomes a spiritual initiation to show her how to move with ease into the inner planes to meet the soul, and bring it down into her body.

Being in the life giving force during the birth experience is a joyful celebration in which the child's soul meets the physical and subtle bodies. The power opened in the woman through childbirth is honored and revered by the mother's community of people. Each woman has to witness her own decisions and actions as extensions of herself, while becoming one in the divine. There's no "fall from grace," because the laws of union are followed. Each woman becomes a law unto herself. She is attuned to experiencing spirit in her body without fear. She grows into one who knows, a true bearer of light. By sitting in reverence with the divine, she knows who she is and the truth that will be upheld throughout her life. Childbirth teaches a woman to keep the doorways to spirit open. This ability also enables her to become a healer. She can utilize this skill to travel into the inner worlds to see the causes of illness in body, mind and soul.

Her role as mother is to maintain the child's connection to the higher levels of spirit until it becomes possible for the maturing child to stay focused on the divine connection on her or his own. A mother's community further takes on the responsibility for mirroring the power of the child. As the child reaches puberty, his or her heart is open and divinely connected to his or her greater self, thanks in part to an ongoing relationship with nature.

The role of the parents in creating a physical body in which a soul can take up residence is supported and respected. The child is acknowledged as a gift to honor and adore, a soul to shepherd. Never is it seen as a possession of the parents. God extends a deep blessing to the parents to care for each child. The role of parenting is considered a learning exercise to practice seeing the uniqueness of each soul, and to refrain from breaking the will of an innocent.

Women in the community who choose not to bring children into the world know their path is to cradle the vibration of power within their bodies and live as harbingers and guiding lights for others. Their connection into Source is as strong as women who experience childbirth, however their training is of a different sort. They carry deep wisdom, sitting for long hours in seclusion and interchanging their powers with the forces of nature until they become conduits for the divine. Their own personalities merge into the essence of their spiritual power. These women are the pillars of the community and are held in the highest honor. They also welcome mature women, who have raised their families, into higher service and training.

Nothing has changed towards motherhood or parenting in the spiritual realm. It's a much different story on earth now, however. It's time to return to this sacred teaching that Mary Magdalene carried.

Healing

Years ago, illness was considered an unpleasant but necessary burning away of karma. Healers knew how to clear the causal and mental bodies to remove the root causes of illness. All thoughts, traumas, repressed emotions, spiritual betrayals and violations of an ancestral lineage were cleared and or harmonized in the body, creating health and family peace. When cleared, past life beliefs opened the soul and mind into balance. When united, a healer's heart and third eye viewed the invisible workings of the soul and body from the perspective of spirit. The healer thus assisted a person's soul travels into the invisible realms of light and sound. By aligning a person to their vibration, the healing mind was able to remember deep peace, and experience its unique soul purpose.

As the pieces of self were restored to oneness, illness and disharmony were healed and the true relationship with the divine was restored. Once returned to life through light, the soul became its highest expression, choosing not to destroy self or others, but to create abundance and freedom instead.

The Hidden Holy Truth

We have direct connection to Source. We are born in alignment with the divine, and the issues that arise for us are meant to help us reconnect our power to Source once again. Living out our patterns without conscious recognition of what is driving our soul is like swimming against a mighty current for no reason. By coming to know the forces that activate our soul, body and spirit, we are able to live from union and direct our lives from conscious creation. By merely connecting the forces of our divine masculine and feminine energies in our psyche, body and soul we activate our spiritual power.

When these forces are reconnected we realize we are a sacred geometrical design of light. Our consciousness lives divinely interconnected with a larger web of life that offers health, peace, compassion and oneness.

The Holy Grail is not an ancestral bloodline from a divine lineage but an initiatory design of holy interaction. Its design always existed and will forever exist. How to enter its power is what has remained the secret. Through codes of light existing within the matrix of the body (entry doors or power points), the connection into the Holy Grail's design can be accessed.

By activating and becoming one with the design of the Holy Grail, beauty, light, power, sexuality and love unite in the chalice of divine wisdom.

The Power Points

There are portals of power within our bodies that connect the etheric, emotional, physical, soul and mental bodies. When these bodies are connected, it is possible to be centered in our core power. Power points activate the channels of higher mind, love and spiritual power. Energy currents connect these portals of God consciousness in the body and form geometric configurations. When these points are connected, they ignite "star consciousness" in the body. Streams of knowledge, realization and potent expressions of mind, soul and spirit blaze through our bodies. This sacred geometry is the energetic language of the divine consciousness state, a sacred cosmic structure of oneness and eternal love. The patterns start with our physical place in the scheme of things; according to ancient Indian *rishis*, human beings are almost exactly halfway in size between the smallest subatomic particle and the largest galaxy. From here, great works of art, writing, music, filmmaking, social and financial systems, empowered positive relationships and genuine inspiration are birthed. Just by connecting the dots of our inner constellations, we are able to ascend into higher states of consciousness. By focusing our attention first, then bringing light into the points, we enter the gateways into the divine.

As our inner bodies are reconnected into the source of light, we become a star system of sorts and can experience divine motion. Here, we enter the *nous*, the place where all energies interconnect. Here is the center of the universe, the center of our hearts, where time stands still. By living in the *nous*, we transcend the realms of duality and find the gateways into the Holy Grail. These gateways are portals of light that sustain spiritual power in all of the bodies. Just by breathing into them simultaneously, the currents of light are activated.

Living in the *nous* is one of the most treasured secrets of the Holy Grail. There are levels of its experience such as: physical body/athletic peak performance; mental body fluidity, stamina and interconnectedness; and creative-spiritual peak performance. The first code to accessing the power bridging mind-body-spirit is to clear the emotional and causal layers. The second code is to connect the soul's purpose and one's existence. The third code is to align one's sexuality and pineal/pituitary centers. The fourth code is to align The Temple point that awakens the body as a chalice of embodiment for the heart.

When we transcend the peak connection points in the physical, mental or etheric/creative body, living in the *nous* becomes a potent possibility. The *nous* feeds the peak performance points of the other bodies. A dancer or yogini can hold their balance longer, an athlete enjoys greater endurance, the scientist bridges many theories simultaneously, the windsurfer flows with greater harmony with the currents and the financial planner plays in broader possibilities.

The *nous* is the balance point where all realities spin and touch. Center your feelings, mind, creativity and physical energies in between your navel and solar plexus. Live in this fulcrum. Let the spokes of your highest soul purpose express into the world. From the *nous*, you can manifest your life without pain or struggle. No longer will you be battling the forces of negativity and control.

The *Nous Codes*

First *Nous* Code: Clearing the Emotional and Causal Layers

A. Breathe gold light into a triangle with its top peak in the center of your collarbone, directly below the bone. The base points are on the insides of both arms, directly in the middle.
B. Breathe blue light into a diamond with its top peak in the center of your collarbone, at the base of the "v" below your throat chakra. Extend two rays to both sides of your rib cage, to their bottom most point, then bring both into the center point of your pubic bone. Fill the diamond with blue light.
C. Send gold light on a clockwise spiral into the center of your navel. Travel on an inner cord through the back of your navel via your third eye until the journey ends. See what image is there and bring it back into the gold light in your navel.

Second *Nous* Code: Soul Purpose and Existence

Bring gold light into the hollow valley directly above the point of the sternum. If you place your third finger of your right hand in your solar plexus and let it slide up and over the bump into a hollow, you are in the point. Raise your third finger up higher by one inch into another notch, or valley. Breathe deeply into both points. Maintain a simultaneous focus sending and sealing light into these points, plus the second chakra and third eye.

Third *Nous* Code: Sexual and Higher Center Alignment

Males: Bring focused light inside the base of the your penis. Females: Focus your light into the cavern of your vagina known as your G-spot. Focus light imbued with love into these points of power. Create an energetic figure 8 of light from these sexual points, through your heart center, into the center of your head between your third eye and crown chakra, down the back of your head, through your heart center, and back into your genital points. Repeat the cycle 8x.

Fourth *Nous* Code: The Temple

Place your focus in your heart center and send a diagonal ray of light into your spine between your navel and solar plexus. This is the Temple Point. Now, from this point send a ray of light into your solar plexus, into your heart center and back into the Temple point. Fill this triangle with vibrant light from your heart.

The Holy Grail Mystery, often called the Mystery of the Divine Feminine, is the art and science of reconnecting the energy currents in the body to the divine currents of the Universal One. Preparation to receive the power in these energy currents requires only two things: to live from the heart and to be willing to know one's soul. The masculine and feminine aspects of our soul connect to these divine currents in their own unique ways; this is what makes us individuals. We are each a distinctive star of light, made up of swirling forces of known and unknown light and darkness. The pleasures of the spirit and body are manifestations and expressions of this holy union. No one can give the communion of soul with God; rather, it is found within the perfect design of our aligned heart, body and soul. We must use our power, love and focus to reunite our spiritual forces, simultaneously becoming empowered by this deep reconnection and divine union.

The Holy Grail's Power Centers

Spirit is the medicine that reunites all life. The mystery of all life is found in spirit, which is found within our own bodies. Spirit destroys illusion, reunites the consciousness, body and heart into love and ignites what has been lost or shut down over time. It is the carrier of the power of God, flowing through our blood, chakra centers, organs, brain, soul and energy circuitry. This is the way of the Holy Grail.

A. Blood

The life force spins through blood, magnetically speaking cell to cell. Each thought is translated into vitality and nourishment. Our blood has relationships with our bones and transmits our abilities to create, destroy and surrender into life. Passion, the joy and intense expression for union, speaks through the fire of our blood. Power, action, life-creating, bold serenity creates new blood cells. They pulse through our hearts and bodies, carrying our anticipation for life and reminding us of the excitements and challenges of loving and growing. The symbolism of drinking blood, the wine of the

Holy Grail, is in actuality our enactment of ingesting the universal forces that connect our heart and soul to the divine. We become filled; we radiate the ongoing and eternal flames of creation. We purify our blood to carry light and release any dark beliefs and thoughts passed to us by our ancestry. Through direct communion with our body, by sending it joyous thoughts of abundance, light and vision, we create our blood to be a river of the life we want.

B. Brain

The centers to our inner sky, oceans, canyons, valleys and mountains open through our brain and body. Speaking back and forth between brain and body, circuitries feel and transmit spiritual energy to nurture and feed the inner self. This energy is what pushes us forward to solve problems, build, sculpt, write and create beauty in our lives.

When the higher centers in the brain open, we see the inner stars of the astral body. Sound, color, vibration, images, rhythm and scent speak to the brain. When we connect heart love and belly power with the gateways of the brain, light flows effortlessly. Create two rays of light from the heart chakra, and crisscross them in the heart, throat, back of the skull, third eye and crown chakra. Allow the rays to cascade like a fountain from the top of the head, to then flow back down into the heart center.

C. Other Vital Organs

The liver is the general of the body and needs to be maintained, since it regulates all physical function. Imbalance creates anger and impatience, and symptoms that can include infertility, low energy, hormonal problems, allergies, skin problems, cancer and more. The liver and its accompanying organs require clean blood; these organs include the gall bladder (breaks down fats), spleen (cleans blood), lungs (filter air), heart (pumps blood), kidneys (filter impurities) and pancreas (processes sugars and proteins). All of these organs benefit from consistent servings of steamed and raw green vegetables. Mustard greens, chard, kale, spinach, chlorella, spirulina, barley grass, wheat grass, broccoli, asparagus and parsley, among others, build and clear the blood. Green food is rich in chlorophyll, which is almost identical in molecular configuration to hemoglobin in the blood. The life force of the blood carries the divine health of a person throughout a lifetime. The blood carries the spiritual spark of eternal memory, emotional clarity and divine wisdom. When our blood is clear of negative thought forms, it is easier to maintain union with God.

Awakening Your Power Points

1. Apply mild pressure with the third fingers of both hands right above your pubic bone, and breathe blue light into this point.
2. Apply mild pressure with the third fingers of both hands above and below in the center of your lips.
3. Hold the pubic bone point with your third finger of your right hand. Press the top labia point, then the lower labia point with your left hand. Feel the energy move between the points.
4. Bring a diagonal ray of light up to the back of your head, from your pubic bone into the back of your skull (medulla). Breathe into the back of your head.
5. Hold the third finger of your left hand in the center and under the occipital ridge. Hold the point and breathe.
6. Hold the third fingers of both hands inside the indentation between your upper jawbone and the little knob of flesh of where your ear meets your face. Breathe.
7. Place the middle finger of your right hand into your navel and the middle finger of your left hand on your spine directly across from your navel. Breathe light from your navel into your middle back, expanding the middle back. The navel is the portal between the light body and your soul body. This is where energy is stored; it is a doorway into the emotional body.

Masculine-Feminine Integration Points

A. Place the 3rd fingers of each hand directly under the center of each breast, under the nipples. Breathe into the points. Hold for two minutes. Feel for the integration of the masculine and feminine energies.

B. Move the thumb of your right hand onto the bony bump on the outside of your wrist. Slide your thumb down into the hollow and press. This point nurses old wounds and releases emotions caused by exhaustion and sadness. Breathe into your heart center.

C. Draw a line from your nipples into the center of your chest. Press into a hollow with your middle finger of your right hand. Breathe. Press the middle finger of your left hand two inches above this point. Feel for tenderness. Breathe into both points at once.

Gateways and Healing Points of the Organs

Spiritual Gateways of the Brain

1. Star Gate
Apply pressure with two fingers into the point 1-1/2 inches above your hairline. Feel for an indentation. Stimulate it for two minutes.

2. Stairway to Heaven
Meditate and focus light in the medulla (occipital ridge). Feel for the indentation under the occipital ridge and press your second and third fingers of both hands into this spot and bring in light. Move the light from the occipital ridge over the top of the head while touching eight points from the ridge to the forehead with two fingers of each hand. Move your fingers in two diagonal lines down from this spot and press. Place the thumbs of both hands under the medulla and reach the rest of the fingers up to the top of the head. Breathe.

3. Window of Light
Focus within the third eye, two inches inside the forehead, and visualize a window opening to sunlight. Bring the light into your entire body. Feel it as a river of light streaming into your third eye. Become this light.

4. Finding Home
Visualize a blue star in your third eye. Gaze into the gold light within the center of the star.

5. River of Life
Connect your third eye with the portal in the medulla (back of the skull).

Emotional Gateways of the Brain

A. The Bridge
Using your index finger and thumb, fold your upper left ear together. Draw a straight line up the side of your head with your finger, and stop approximately two inches before reaching the top of your head. Apply pressure into this point with your middle finger. Then go to the top of your head and apply pressure. Move down approximately two inches to the right side and apply pressure. Return to the top of the head. All of these

points help with depression and uncertainty, and assist in the quest for new beginnings.

B. Sitting in The Sun

Bring your mental focus into your solar plexus. Fill your solar plexus with golden-yellow light. Gaze up through the top of your head, watching, receiving and feeling light from above your head flowing down into you. Breathe the light into your body and balance your brain.

C. In the Valley

Place both thumbs under the occipital ridge behind your head. Slide your thumbs over the ridge into the indentation. Hold your thumbs in the indentation and spread your fingers over your skull. Close your eyes and breathe into the valley beneath your thumbs. Shift your focus to being in the valley. Breathe into the back of your skull.

D. Releasing the Past

Place your thumbs under the brow bone of your eyebrows inside the bridge of your nose. Close your eyes and breathe into this spot.

Lung Healing Points

1. Removing Mind Limitations

Focus on a point opposite your lungs, in the middle of your spine. As you breathe into this point, imagine you are inhaling into large wings on your upper back.

2. Expanding Mind and Soul

Move the index and middle fingers of your right hand under your collarbone, to the endpoint where your collarbone meets your shoulder. Press into the indentation under the bone. Use your left hand to repeat on the other side. Relax into the point.

3. Reconnecting Body and Soul

Place the third finger of your right hand beneath the rib cage, at a point directly above your solar plexus. Slide your finger up one inch, into the small hollow. Breathe in blue light. This point is very powerful. When opened, it will give profound results.

Stomach/Spleen/ Pancreas Healing Point

Etheric and Soul Body Weaver: Place the third finger of your right hand in your navel and your thumb in your solar plexus. Let your second finger move onto your skin. Ask your body what color this point needs to be in order to restore harmony. Mentally transmit that color. Close your eyes and place your second and third fingers on your spine directly across from where your second finger is located. Create a mental figure eight between these two points in the color your body requested.

Liver Healing Points

A. Mind and Body Opener to Universal Archetypes

Press your thumb into the extending tip on the outside of your anklebone. Slide your thumb all the way down to the back of the ankle, towards the Achilles tendon, and press into the crevice. Hold the point, close your eyes and breathe.

B. Grounding

Bring the second finger of your left hand between the big and second toes of your left foot. Apply pressure as you dig your finger into the top of your foot about one inch from the top. Feel for a crevice and hold the point for at least one minute. Expect it to be tender. Repeat this step, using the second finger of your right hand on your right foot.

Heart Healing Point

1. Heart Regulator

Press the thumb of your right hand into the "valley" between the second finger and thumb of your left hand. Hold for one minute.

2. Heart Restorer

Move the second finger of your right hand along the pinky on your left hand. Press into the indentation on the left side of your pinky knuckle. Hold. Reverse hands.

Kidney Healing Point

Feeding the Brain: Press your thumbs behind both knees and hold. This removes obstructions from the eyes and opens inner vision.

Mysteries of the Holy Grail: Practices

The divine feminine mysteries are the interplay between the energies of the soul and the universe. Over the course of history, these powers have been misused and abused, which is why they went underground. They have the ability not only to transform your life, but the lives of those around you and the world.

The divine state of love begins to open in the body after the emotional body is realigned with the soul, the soul is aligned with the heart, and the heart is aligned with spirit in the body. Love is the state of consciousness that is awakened when God meets the body in a state of union.

Union in the divine has no beginning and no end. Soul is always connected to its eternal self, the divine mother who is perpetually creating life. If we end a lifetime with our third eye and heart unified in God, we create the chance to return to this planet in a body aligned in spirit. We are always connected into spirit, but our real challenge is how to stay connected and still relate to the world around us. By maintaining our connection to love, we stay connected to our source. Anything less than love creates our downfall.

The following spiritual practices prepare the Holy Grail aspirant to receive the finer tuned initiations of spiritual alchemy, the illuminating transformation of awakening consciousness into existence. They create a foundation for mind and body to assimilate higher spiritual truths.

Practice #1: The Spiritual-Physical Power Points

Alignment 1: Align heaven and earth by pulling up core energies of light from the earth into the belly, navel and heart.

Alignment 2: Place your focus first under the tailbone. Simultaneously add the focus of the base of the skull (medulla) and then the heart center.

Alignment 3: Place your focus in the base of the skull (medulla), third eye and solar plexus.

Alignment 4: Place your focus in the center of the core shaft of light in the solar plexus. Travel up the shaft to the back of the heart center, then loop down into the lower belly (second chakra).

Alignment 5: Place your focus in the center of the pubic bone, and send two diagonal rays of light upwards.

Alignment 6: Place your focus 10 feet above your head, and send two diagonal rays of light down the sides of your body into the earth

Alignment 7: Place your focus 10 feet above your head, and send a beam of white light down the center of your body.

Alignment 8: Create two overlapping triangles to form a Shield of David. The base of one triangle runs through the lower belly (second chakra). Its tip reaches into the heart chakra. The horizontal line of the second triangle runs through the solar plexus. Its tip touches the center of the pubic bone. Fill the triangle with blue light.

Alignment 9: Create Shields of David from the under the tailbone (first chakra), through all the chakras and into the crown chakra.

Alignment 10: Place your focus in the center column of overlapping Shields of David from the first chakra to the crown chakra. Pull blue light up from the center of the earth into the column of light running through the Shields of David.

Practice #2: A Visual Activation

1. While sitting with your focus in your solar plexus, gaze upwards 10 feet above your head and ask your higher self to descend closer to you.

2. Visualize traveling 10 feet above your head, join with your higher self and look down into your body.

3. Look for fear in your body.

4. Ask the fear you find to create an image of its appearance.

5. Ask what color it needs to heal.

6. Send that color. Surround and fill the image with the color.

7. Send fear the inner message that you recognize that it hasn't been allowed to be its true self.

8. Look into the fear and ask it to show you its true self.

9. From 10 feet above your head, peel off the thought form or projection that originally created the fear.

10. Send the projection into white light.

Practice #3: Awakening into Movement

By shifting the attention from your mind into your body, you alter your consciousness and make it possible to experience greater awareness. Through movement of consciousness comes movement into being. As you connect your body with a greater sense of being, your thinking shifts. Your emotions also shift into a higher frequency and integrate with your soul. As your body opens, it aligns to its deeper soul messages and reconnects all of its splits and dichotomies. It becomes whole. A greater dance can now begin:

1. Rub your hands together creating heat and friction.

2. Face your palms together in front of your heart center.

3. Place your palms slightly apart from one another.

4. Move your palms together and apart so they never touch. Feel the energy between your palms.

5. Draw the energy apart in your hands as though you are stretching taffy. Push the palms together again.

6. Focus into the center of the energy held between your hands.

7. Reach your hands towards the earth and pull light up from the earth into your body.

8. From 10 feet above your head look down into an open column of light in your body.

9. Seek the image of a child wanting to be seen.

10. Invite him/her into your body and open to receive him/her.

11. Ask him/her what he/she has come to do in this lifetime.

12. Make room in your pelvis, down through your pubic bone into your tailbone.

13. Ask him/her what you need to receive to give him/her permission to exist.

14. Focus your breath into your tailbone, inside the pubic bone, then into your lower belly. Send rays of light in a circle all around your body.

15. Connect the rays of light into a round, oval circle or auric field around your body.

16. Feel the energetic force of the circle around you, and breathe into it. Stretch to receive it, and feel it surrounding you.

17. Move into the streams and currents of energy inside your self, and move your body into the flow.

18. Explore your body's arches, curves, angles and circles.

19. Find three unique bodily movements; express them, then repeat them.

20. Bring into your movements the elements of fire, then earth, water and air.

22. Describe your movements in writing and/or drawing. Repeat them daily.

Practice #4: Writing To Remember

The divine inner feminine must be called back into our souls. Call to her from your heart. As you open your heart to her, write her responses. Ask her at what age she went away. Ask her what she needs to come back. Which parent rejected her? Write about your ancestral and parental beliefs about the divine feminine. Breathe into the parts of your body where your feminine does not presently live. Write about those parts. Invite her to raise her voice, so that you can hear her words to write them down. Write in her voice. See what facets of her you have not wanted. Bring light into these parts and ask why they are shut down. Make it safe for these aspects of your feminine self to fully enliven your body. Let her speak to you and teach you. As you write, take her in all the way.

The divine inner masculine waits patiently. Ask him to come to you. Ask him to tell you about his highest purpose on the planet. Write what he says. Let him show you his passions and commitments. Write in his voice. Feel him. See what he is wearing and what his voice sounds like. Ask him to show you what he has been doing for the past centuries or millenniums. Ask him to reveal all of your inner masculine energies. See how they control, withhold energy and hide. Look through these parts until you see their full light. Write their feelings, hopes and desires. Let them write back and forth to one other until they are aligned to your divine inner masculine.

Invite your inner divine masculine and feminine to dialogue together. Ask them what they need from one another to live together and serve their highest vision. Let them speak through your writing. Invite them to exchange their energies with one another so they can feel fully seen and received. Let them celebrate the power of their Holy Grail as it is activated in your body—bringing to you the union of heart, soul and universal alignment.

Part V

Jesus:
The Initiator of Light

Chapter 17

Yeshua of Nazereth, the Messiah

"The Torah teaches us not only to hear the language of Light, but to humbly receive and use the language of light to probe and understand the higher spheres of the heavens and the Shekinah dimensions of the Father's garment of which the Earth is a part."
~ The Book of Enoch, Key 206:18-29

In Hebrew, *Yeshua* means "freedom" and *Nazara* means "truth." *Messiah* means "the anointed one" or "one who gives limits." Thus, the one from Nazareth is the truth, the liberator, and the giver of limits.

In a time of political turbulence and religious control, the mission of Yeshua, or Jesus, was to eradicate principles of injustice. Wherever he went, he exposed the hypocrisies that prevented spiritual growth. In Saying 43 in the Gospel of Thomas, it is written that "[his] disciples asked him: Who are you to say these things to us? Jesus replied: 'Don't you recognize who I am from what I say to you? You have become like those who like the tree but loathe its fruit, or they who like the fruit but loathe the tree.'"

Jesus' intention was to maintain wholeness, not to choose one viewpoint over an other. He pushed people to look at how they built their inner homes. He saw, in too many instances, how their minds rejected spiritual power—so he encouraged them to reverse that practice. "Show me the stone that the builders rejected. It is the cornerstone" (Gospel of Thomas: Saying 66, quoting Psalms 118:22)

Jesus was known at birth as Immanuel, "God with us" (Matthew 1:23). To other cultures, he was called Iesous (Greece; the modern spelling came from Ancient Greek and Aramaic, not Hebrew), Issa (Buddhists, Muslims, and Hindus), Jesu (Aramaic), Yuzu (Persia). He was instructed in India by many great yogis and teachers, including one now known as the Master Babaji. Born to a mother who knew her role in regards to his greater mission, his spiritual training began at age four. Stunning the rabbis of his time with his knowledge, the child was seen as the way-shower. His mission was not made clear to him until ten years after he disappeared from the Biblical radar—and after he'd received extensive training in advanced meditative practices, visualization and initiations to directly connect him further into the Godhead. Teaching that faith was the art of receiving and love was the art of giving, Jesus brought the highest vibration of creation to the simplest of levels.

Divine relationship was an aspect of God union in which Jesus lived. Phillip, the third apostle and the one known to communicate the Master's direct messages, initiated an Ethiopian royal official into his Master's teachings by baptism. To this day, there are crosses in Ethiopia bearing a man and a woman in deep embrace in the center of the cross (Jesus and Mary Magdalene, symbolizing the union of divine masculine and feminine). Such divine union with God, consummated through the love of a man and woman, was beautifully exemplified through Jesus' deep understanding and chronicled in a number of Philip's writings:

> "The embrace of the Lover and the Beloved
> Belongs to the mystery of the Union;
> And only those who have become the same as them can see them."
>
> —*The Gospel of Phillip, pg 84, plate 130*

> "If a plant has not been planted by my Father who is in heaven, it will be uprooted.
> Those who were separated will reunite and become fertilized.
> All those who practice the sacred embrace (koiton) will kindle the light;
> They will not beget as people do
> In ordinary marriages, which take place in darkness."
>
> —*The Gospel of Philip, pg 87, plate 133*

"The fire that burns by night flares up, and then is gone;
But the mystery of that embrace is never extinguished;
It happens in that light of day which knows no sunset.
If someone experiences Trust and Consciousness in the heart of the embrace,
They become a child of light.
If someone does not receive these,
It is because they remain attached to what they know;
When they cease to be attached, they will be able to receive them
Whoever receives this light in nakedness will no longer be recognizable;
None will be able to make them sad or miserable,
Whether they are in this world, or have left it.
They already know the truth in images.
For them, this world has become another world,
And this Temple Space (Aeon) is fullness (pleroma)
They are who they are. They are one.
Neither shadow nor night can hide them."

—The Gospel of Philip, pg 88, plate 134

Born An Avatar

Russian journalist Nicolas Notovitch collected 244 verses from the scrolls at Himis about Jesus' life and work. An encapsulation of the earliest details:

Jesus was born in 7 B.C. to Mary the Mother, the daughter of Joachim and his wife Hanna. Mary's cousin, Elizabeth, was married to Zechariah, a high priest, who arranged for Joseph and Mary to be married. Years earlier, an angel appeared before Joachim, a wealthy farmer of Nazareth, after he had prayed to God to bless him with a child. Shortly after, Hanna was visited by an angel, who confirmed that she would give birth. Hanna made a vow that she would take the child for service in the Temple, as a gift to God. As per her promise, her daughter, Mary, was placed under the care of the priest at age three; there she remained until age twelve, undergoing trainings of the sacred mother-father God union. At fourteen, she gave birth to Jesus with the respected architect and high priest Joseph. Mary birthed four sons: James, Joses, Judah and Simon. She also purportedly mothered two daughters, whose names are not known.

The three wise men who appeared at Jesus' birth from the East were Buddhist priests looking for the predicted *tulku,* the Bodhisattva or future Buddha. Having learned from their astrological studies and spiritual studies that an Enlightened One had been born in Judea, they reached Jerusalem. True to their custom, they would reappear at some future time to take the young person for intensive training.

Between 6-4 B.C., Joseph took Mary, his wife, and the infant Jesus to Mataria, an Essene monastery in Egypt. There, they found refuge from Herod's suppression of Galilee. According to Apocryphal works, Mataria was one of three Essene communities; the others were Wadi-el-Natrun and Al-Moharraq. The 4,000 strong Essene brotherhood dressed in white robes, practiced the laws of Moses, were committed vegetarians and did not believe in animal sacrifice. Amidst this order of spiritual initiates who embraced non-violence and moral integrity, Jesus was first exposed to the life of contemplation and meditation. Known as profound healers who worked with color, music, stones, herbs and energy healing, Jesus' "extended family" knew how to remove evil spirits, cleanse the auric field and chakras, heal the soul and body, and balance the mind and spirit. The Essenes were carriers of Holy Grail Healing. Between his parent's training and the time spent in community with master teachers, Jesus' healing powers began to develop.

At age four, Jesus began his rabbinical schooling. Soon, he was recognized as an exceptional child who could read and retain information instantaneously. By the time of his Bar Mitzvah, he had surpassed the formal training available from the rabbis in Nazareth. Even though Jesus was proficient in the Torah, Psalms, Prophets and the Old Testament, he sought the deeper knowledge of the East. He chose to leave Israel when he realized that unless he departed he would soon be married off to one of many wealthy families who wanted him as a future son-in-law. According to the Jewish scriptures, celibacy was not allowed; an unmarried man was not respected as a teacher. His Bar Mitzvah (literally, "son of the commandment") was a rite of passage into his new life.

Travels to India and the East

Sufi mystic, Fida Hassnain of Kashmir spent most of his life researching rare documents about the life of Jesus. In his book, *The Historical Search for Jesus*, he shares the kernels of Jesus' trainings, sermons and destiny. Tibetan scrolls found in 1925 stated Jesus was thirteen years old when he left for India. In the *Natha Namaval,* an Indian Sutra, it is written that Jesus, Isha Natha, arrived in India by age fourteen. He lived and studied ancient Vedic texts at the temple of Jagannath at Puri in Orissa.

When he arrived in Kapilavastu, Nepal after six years of study in Jagannath, India, Jesus was taken in by Buddhist monks. He attained mastery in the Sutras, the Vinayas and the Abhidharma. The following was written in the Tibetan scrolls:

"We stand today upon a crest of time. Six times ago a master was born who gave glory and light to man. And now a master sage stands here. This Hebrew prophet is a rising star of wisdom. He brings to us knowledge of God. All the world will hear his words, will heed his words and glorify his name."

While Jesus studied at the temple in Jagannath, he also traveled to Juggernaut, Rajagriha and Varanasi (Benares). It was in Varanasi that he gave his first sermon to the people before God: "They that deprive their brothers of divine happiness shall themselves be deprived of it. Help the poor, assist the weak, harm no one, do not covet what you do not have and what you see in the possession of another."

In Juggernaut, Jesus' life was threatened for teaching the Holy Scriptures (the Vedas) to a lower caste called the Shudras. He became embroiled in a conflict with the Brahmins and Kshatriyas (the priestly and warrior castes). He left Juggernaut by night and went to the foothills of the Himalayas in southern Nepal, the birthplace of Gautama Buddha, where he lived for the next six years.

Ancient Buddhist manuscripts discovered in India, in a Ladakh monastery, tell a remarkable story of Saint Issa (Jesus). Nicolas Notovitch first found the manuscripts in 1883 near Ladakh. In 1887, Notovitch published *The Unknown Life of Christ,* which was later re-published in New York in 1890 as *The Life of Saint Issa.* While living at the monastery, Notovitch was shown the biography of Issa by the head Lama, who brought him two large bound volumes. The scrolls were originally written in Pali, which later were translated into Tibetan; copies were preserved in various Buddhist monasteries. The head Lama said: "The name Issa is held in great esteem by Buddhists, but little is known about him save by the chief Lamas, who have read scrolls relating to his life."

In the introduction of *The Unknown Life of Christ*, Notovitch shares a conversation with an unnamed Catholic Cardinal, who told him, "The Vatican Library possesses 63 complete and incomplete manuscripts in various oriental languages about the life of Issa in the East which have been brought to Rome by missionaries from India, China, Egypt and the Middle East."

The Vatican has made them unavailable to the world.

In 1922 Swami Abhedananda, born in 1860 and a disciple of the great master Ramakrishna, went to Ladakh and was told that the account of the life of St. Issa was true and was shown a copy of an original manuscript lodged in Lhasa, Tibet. He reached the Himis monastery on October 4, 1922, and discovered a manuscript of the unknown life of Jesus the Christ, previously chronicled by Notovitch. With the help of a senior lama, he obtained a translated copy of the important portions of the life of Jesus, and incorporated it into his book *Kashmir O Tibbate*.

In 1928, Professor Nicolai Roerich led an expedition through central Asia to Ladakh and Kashmir. In his book, *The Heart of Asia,* he records that he visited Himis and was shown a number of scrolls. By that time, all documents and manuscripts about Christ were kept in the darkest part of the monastery's storerooms. By 1974, the lamas of Himis admitted there had been serious losses suffered at the hands of thieving foreigners.

The Church eventually denied the existence of a Russian by the name of Nicolas Notovitch or of the existence of a Buddhist monastery named Himis. The scrolls were eventually stolen, taken or confiscated, with no trace of their whereabouts. It is believed the original revelations of Notovitch were a threat to the Church.

What about the U.S. Supreme Court Justice? William O. Douglas—one of the great arbiters of justice based on freedom of speech and expression—traveled to Himis, the legendary monastery in Ladakh in 1951. He later wrote in his book, *Beyond the High Himalayas,* about the legend of Jesus coming to Ladakh and becoming known as Saint Issa.

Jesus Returns to Israel

As spirit moved his life forward, Jesus knew it was time to return to his place of birth. His own initiation process was not yet complete, but he had mastered the first ten levels of higher consciousness necessary to become a clear instrument for God. He was sent to the West to serve spirit by his teacher in the Himalayas. His mission: To convey the inner works of God and to steer people back from basing their lives around outside distractions.

Hassnain, in *The Historical Search for Jesus*, elaborated on Jesus' travels through Persia and other countries during the teacher's return trip to Israel: "He told them to perceive God with their hearts and not with their eyes. He advised them not to deceive any one, to abstain from debauchery and to try to attain supreme bliss by purification of the soul."

The priests were threatened and fearful of him and forbade people to listen to his talks. In answer to the priests' questions, he replied: "I preach no new God but our celestial Father, who existed before the beginning and will exist until after the end."

Upon Jesus' return to Israel, he found the Israelites filled with despair due to sufferings inflicted upon them by their Roman rulers and intransigent rabbis who often sided with the Caesars. Jesus told them to have faith in God; they swarmed in multitudes to hear his words. He removed dark forces throughout Galilee and restored many people to health. The Holy Grail of divine wisdom, which he contained within his being, was greatly desired by the Israelites.

Jesus spoke to an overcrowded Palestine, Hassnain writes in *The Historical Search for Jesus*, where, unlike his past, the Jews were earning a meager living as manual laborers. Once, there was a time when they had been rulers of the country, but now their position was no better than as slaves or as subjects of the Romans. Jesus said: "Enter into your temple, into your heart; illuminate it with good thoughts, with patience and unshakeable faith in your Father. Do that which is agreeable to God, for in doing good to your fellow men, you perform a ceremony that embellishes the temple wherein abideth Him who has created you."

The experiences Jesus had in the East during his spiritual trainings deepened his sacred union with the divine feminine. He was taught meditation practices that initiated the currents of feminine and masculine divine energies and empowered him to live in their union. It felt natural to him to receive female followers and help women feel honored, because he'd integrated the divine feminine. He understood how to keep the flame of the divine inner feminine active and moving in the body.

Thus, he became the first spiritual leader since the days of goddess worship to advocate greater roles and voices for women. During this time, women were not allowed to read from the Torah in public or study under a rabbi, yet Jesus gave his female followers all of the opportunities to spiritually advance under his guidance, just as he did men. He revered the essence of each person's soul. He taught that as their "original sin" was healed—the split of their divine inner masculine and feminine, their inner Adam and Eve—that their souls could then be guided to return into full spiritual and physical wholeness.

Jesus' humanness and deep compassion for his spiritual brothers and sisters made him the teacher and liberator of the soul. If his message of making all human beings equal (which they are in the eyes of God) would be taken to heart and combined with his passion to remove false power and replace it with true power, ***our present world situation would be reversed.***

Jesus often visited Bethany to see Mary Magdalene, who became one of his disciples. From being trained in the east, Jesus was prepared and spiritually attuned to having a partner who was the divine feminine reflection—Shakti—to his divine masculine energies—Shiva. Their bond exemplified the highest spiritual and sexual union, a relationship that was later erased from history.

Jesus' great-uncle, Joseph of Arimathaea, a counselor to the Jewish Sanhedrin, was also an Essene and a merchant trader. He sailed regularly with his fleet of ships to the British Isles. Between 26-27 A.D., Jesus accompanied Joseph to Glastonbury to experience the culture and universities of the Druids, and revisit Cornwall, where he had traveled as a child with Joseph on one of many visits to his mother's family. From Cornwall, he returned to Jerusalem to begin his mission. Joseph treated Jesus as a son and would soon be called to save Jesus' life.

Jesus' Central Mission

Jesus welcomed all souls desiring the holy adventure of divine union. His intention was never to begin a new religion; even in AD 27, there were more than enough. His true motivation was to integrate and present, in both common language (outer teachings) and parables (inner teachings), ancient wisdoms that revealed direct union with God.

Everywhere Jesus looked, he saw separation of the heart, soul and mind and wanted to give the keys to finding oneness in the self. Jesus vested his energy in providing people with direct tools by which to center themselves in Source. His vision of a church was more of a city where people from every tribe, culture and tongue could gather to find the terrain of their souls. Like his mother, Mary, he wanted to see differences healed and for people to live in peace among one each other. He loved mankind.

As with many of the new souls being born into the world today, Jesus entered the world pure and whole to restore the balance between the powers of dark and light. In the Gospel of Philip it is written, "I have come to make the lower realities like the higher realities, and the outer realities like the inner realities. I have come to unite them in this Temple Space, where they reveal themselves through images and symbols." The Apostle went on to explain that "Those who say that there is someone in the sky are mistaken, for He who has appeared has come from the depths, and He who owns the hidden things is beyond all the opposites. It is right to say that the inner and the outer are one; what appears to be outside the outer does not exist; it is the outer darkness."

Jesus' larger mission was to reunite the tribes of Israel. The ancient tribal symbol, the Star or Shield of David, can be traced back to early India and the Middle East as a symbol of divine union. The upward-pointing triangle signifies the divine feminine lifting earth up to heaven; the descending point is the divine masculine bringing heaven into earth. In the middle lies the meeting of heaven and earth, corresponding to the heart chakra.

As for the apostles, they had no doubt about the background or status of the man whose teachings they later carried to the world. They referred to him as "Master" in a time and place where spiritual leaders were called "Lord" or "Rabbi." "Master" is a yogic term of ultimate honor to the guru, spoken by his disciples. The designation still remains in some versions of the Bible, though traditional editions like the King James have replaced "Master" with "Lord."

Jesus did not make promises for the future. He rejected the concept of a Future Kingdom—an expectation Christians have nonetheless advanced in churches, political forums and on battlefields for two thousand years, at the cost of many millions of lives.

The Master wanted people to take responsibility for their actions and thoughts and to self-actualize. He fought against blindly following the rules of others who had not begun to face their own souls. If on earth today, he would stand in defiance of the present dogmas of the Church. He spoke of disengaging from what is false in one's self and returning to the original essence of light, where everything begins and ends. After all, what one finds after tremendous inner work is what has always existed in the beginning—purity, wholeness and union with the Divine. In *The Historical Search for Jesus*, Hassnain reminds us that the Master said, "I and my Father are one," reminding everyone of their divine link to Source. The disciples are said to have asked Jesus, "'Tell us about our end. What will it be?' Jesus replied: 'Have you found the beginning so that you now seek the end? The place of the beginning will be the place of the end. Blessed is anyone who will stand up in the beginning and thereby know the end and never die.'"

Jesus stood firmly behind his beliefs that all men were equal in the eyes of God. "God the Father establishes no difference between his children; who are equally dear to him." Jesus challenged the caste system, Hassnain writes, stood up for the poor and confronted false priests who subjugated the people.

The Crucifixion: A Different Outcome

At the time of the crucifixion, a special cross was made for Jesus at the request of the Sanhedrin. Joseph of Arimathea made sure that in front of the cross, a short stake was attached on which Jesus could place his upper body weight while being tied. The Gospel of John tells the story of Joseph of Arimathea meeting with Pontius Pilate in Palestine to have permission to take Jesus' body from the cross; in Joseph's mind, he was attempting to arrange a different outcome to the crucifixion.

Jesus' reverberating words from the cross: "Elo i, Elo i Lama sabach-thani!" when retained in its original Hebrew means: "God, God how thou has glorified me!" In Hebrew 'elo i elo i' translates as 'elausia' which means: "There is no God save Elohim." Both Krishna and Buddha recited "Elia" when being opposed or attacked physically or psychically. Jesus was *harnessing the power* of God, not turning away from his life-long connection—but for what activity? The accepted translation in two Gospels: "My God, my God, why hast thou forsaken me?" couldn't be further from the truth. Jesus' native tongue was Aramaic and Hebrew, and the accepted version is a Greek interpretation of Jesus' words.

There are yogis who can slow their heartbeat almost to a vanishing point, sometimes taking a breath only once every minute. Jesus had this ability. According to the Spanish Orthodox Church, Jesus also made a certain circular motion of the headknown in advanced yogic circles as a high-level *kriya* that can lift one into *nirbikalpa samadhi*, or complete physical and karmic liberation from the tethers of the body and world. This is largely corroborated by an ancient holy text, the *Natha Nama Vali*, the Sutra of the Nath Yogis:

"After crucifixion, or perhaps even before it, Isha Natha (Jesus) entered Samadhi (Nabikalpa) or profound trance (beyond human consciousness), by means of yoga. One of his gurus, Chetan Natha, happened to be in profound meditation in the lower regions of the Himalayas. In a vision he saw the tortures that Isha Natha was undergoing. His response to what he saw was so strong that great storms of thunder and lightning quaked the earth. Chetan Natha made his body lighter than air and passed over to the land of Israel, and woke Isha from his Samadhi while he was in the tomb."

Still, when one of Pilate's guards was asked if Jesus had died, he said "Yes." Pontius Pilate then gave permission for Jesus' body to be given to Joseph of Arimathea. Nicodemus, a secret disciple of Jesus, and other Essene friends met in secret council to devise ways to save Jesus. According to the Essene version of the crucifixion and its aftermath, Nicodemus said to Joseph: "As sure is my knowledge of life and nature, so sure is it possible to save him."

The Essene version goes on to state that Joseph and Nicodemus gently untied Jesus' hands and took out the spikes with great care. Jesus was taken into the private sepulcher prepared by Joseph. After the stone door had been sealed, the Master's friends and family entered a secret passageway and went to work. Nicodemus had brought along long pieces of byssus. He spread a powerful Essene healing ointment made of precious herbs and spices into the cloth and wound it about Jesus' body with the help of Mary the Mother and Mary Magdalene. Then they placed balsam in both the nail-pierced hands. As a healer, Nicodemus believed it was best not to cover over the wound in Jesus' side, knowing the flow of blood and water would be beneficial in the renewing of his life.

The *Gospel of Luke* speaks of the spices and ointments Joseph of Arimathaea brought to Nicodemus for use on Jesus. The ointment was known as *marham-i-rusul*, the "ointment of the prophets." It encourages the formation of fresh tissue, and helps increase circulation and recovery from numbness. The twelve ingredients in the ointment, as first recorded in the *Greek Pharmacopoeia,* included: white wax, the Ayurvedic herbs gun gugal and aristoelchia longa, galbanum (of Persian origin), plumbi oxidum (a Tibetan herb), myrrh, sub acetate of copper, gum ammonicum, pine resin, olibanum (frankincense), aloes and olive oil.

When Christ rose again, he rose in the physical as well as the spiritual body, as two scriptures made clear: "Behold my hands and my feet, that it is myself; handle me and see; for a spirit hath not flesh and bones, as you see me have" (Luke 24:39). Also, "And I rose up and am with them; I will speak by their mouth. I did not perish, though they devised it against me" (Songs of Solomon).

Thirty-five years after the crucifixion, James, the brother of Jesus, was executed by the Romans. Jerusalem was stormed and the Temple was burned down while 11,000 people died of starvation, fulfilling Jesus' predictions. Meanwhile, Jesus presided over a monastery in Srinagar as Yuzu Asaph (father and prophet of the Children of Israel), as he was known in Kashmir; he'd spent fifteen previous years teaching all over the East. Mary the Mother had passed in Kashmir, and Mary Magdalene raised their daughter, Sarah, in France, where Mary became known as the Black Madonna. Jesus and Mary's two sons were raised in Cornwall, England with an Essene community. All of this well-documented history would later be torn into bits and concealed to preserve the central Church myths of Jesus the Only Begotten Son of God, Mary the Virgin Mother, and Mary Magdalene the Prostitute.

Divine Exaltation: It is not I

Like every great teacher, Jesus taught that the kingdom of heaven was within the self. He knew the gateways and cracked open the resistance points for those ready to embody union in God. Those ready to be his equals—James, his brother, Phillip, Mary Magdalene, Thomas and Matthew—were pushed forward with grace.

Jesus knew the forces of life as himself: moon/sun, yin/yang, dark/light, gravity, breath/body, sex/God, and elementals (earth, fire, water, ether and air), all of which served as inspirations to live in divine order. When he experienced holy union with God and powerfully resurrected his spirit fully into his body, he completely merged into God —one unto himself. His powers of physical resurrection gave him 48 more years of life after the crucifixion in the Himalayan mountains, in particular the beauty of Srinagar, Kashmir. He also etherically and physically instructed souls that later manifested as great masters in their own right: Catherine of Siena, Michelangelo, William Blake, Hildegard von Bingen, Teresa of Avila, St. Francis, St. Claire, Lahiri Mahasaya, Ramana Maharshi, Mary Eddy Baker, Paramhansa Yogananda, Rudolf Steiner, Shammiz Tabriz, Mahatma Gandhi, Hazrat Inayat Khan and many other great Tibetan and Sufi masters. These original teachings of direct spiritual connection into Source come through the lineages of Shivaism, Kriya Yoga, Shaba Yoga, Bhakti Yoga and Sufism.

In Khanyar Srinagar exists the tomb of Rozabel, "the sacred tomb of Kashmir." Many believe it to be where the prophet Yuzu Asaph, known to the West as Jesus of Nazareth, is buried. Stone slabs with the traces of raised wound marks, with one foot slightly deformed, were found in the chamber. After significant testing, it is clear that the imprinted man's feet had the stigmata wounds of a crucifixion—left foot over the right foot, with one nail hole perfectly positioned in both feet as though a single nail pinned both feet to a cross.

Chapter 18

I am Jesus: The Kashmiri Transmission

Those who think they know falter and those who know they do not know are given the keys to the kingdom.
~ Jesus

The mountains are clear and snow-capped. Today, I listen to my inner silence; the sheep are in my company. Their bells spark each moment of my heart as I walk through these welcoming green valleys. I have grown accustomed to my way here. The people have adopted me as their own, and it is here, near where I came as a young man, that I can continue the ways of my teacher. He comes to me often and tells me that in his next sojourn on this plane he will return and stay in physical form for hundreds of years. He will be known as Mahavatar Babaji. We have become one, he and I. In our breath, in our hearts we are one. I see him in my mind's eye in his remote dwelling high in the mountains of the Himalaya.

I sense that my years are limited now. I have written the Precepts passed to me by my teachers and know I have faithfully written down what God wishes of me. It is of my heart that the fears imparted by those who "do not have the ears to hear" are forever cleansed. Fear covers the gateways to true power within.

It is only a matter of time that the peoples of this planet will comprehend the lies spun to keep them controlled in my name. No religion speaks of what I came here to do. It cannot, for freedom is never born from controls or dogma. Freedom is born by remembering your divine birthright as a spark of light, creation and Source. Then, by dissolving the limiting beliefs keeping you from that freedom, the passion to reunite the light of your feminine-masculine soul is reopened, blessing your life with the ray to immerse in God forever. The roar of the sea becomes music in your flesh. The light of your heart expands and touches the infinite as you live in union with the divine creator.

Trust that you know yourself. Now, freed from the emotions created by allowing others to live through you, the grace of your spirit guides your life. Be willing to lift above everything that suppresses your spirit. Imbue every moment of your past and present with the love inside your heart. Never allow anyone to tell you that you cannot do something. The power of God that lives within you can manifest the passions of your soul. The feminine power of God is the creative force able to lift any negative fear, illness or misconception.

Why did I come here? The ways of the old had grown dim. There was very little time left before the forces of evil would enter into the minds of man and diminish the path of union many had passed from one generation to the next. I had been prepared for seven lifetimes to walk this path of initiation. Many holy ceremonies and sacred understandings held the secrets of how plant, animal, mineral, elemental kingdom, soul and spirit of mankind are interconnected. The body, soul and spirit are interrelated; the knowledge of maintaining this connection forms the ancient secrets.

As we learn to hold greater spiritual force in the body, the closer we draw to becoming one with the source of life. This inner force field builds the container that holds the Holy Grail. It is the feminine power within the body. Only by destroying her can the existence of the Holy Grail be prevented. In her absence, only darkness can rule. The body, when acknowledged as a holy vessel of life force and conscious union, is one with God. No one can destroy the real temple of God when the soul, body and spirit are united.

I will live unified in spirit as a connecting rod to the many who desire union. I will never forget any soul who crosses into the inner plane where I reside. It is easy to find me. Enter the golden-yellow gates and find passage to me by your desire to love your true self over self-judgment, rejection, or betrayal. Fully receive the love I offer as the same love residing within you. Become the christed light of gold heavenly hues transforming your body, soul and spirit. Know we are never apart. I will always be with you. No one will be left out of the ultimate meeting with the divine self. Everyone eventually longs for union and chooses to dissolve their own pain and need for separation. In this time of immense darkness exists the discovery and gift found in the union of love and power. From darkness into light we can return into oneness that is our true destiny. Now is the time.

This is the power I came to rebirth in the heart.

The lamp of trust has grown dim. As men and women turn away from the joyous union within their souls and hearts, bondage to the outline of their lives are tightly held in place. In the flower of the heart lives the breath uniting mother-father God. In each moment, the essence of who we are shines like the morning light. It interchanges with every molecule in creation. We are the masculine life-giving energy of Father God nourishing the creative forces of the feminine Mother God in the awakening consciousness of love.

The gold light of your consciousness will take you into the truth. Here you will always have access to the realms of eternal love and power. Know you are here to heal the separations of your mind, body and soul. Remember the stories of your breakthroughs and triumphs with spirit. Let them guide your journeys from darkness into light. Each day of your life is meant to be an awakening into the light of God within you. Welcome the darkness as the teacher of surrender. It is here only to test your passion and desire to reach the light. Become the flame of transmutation. Let its fire unite God and your body.

May love always rule your heart.

Chapter 19

The Secret Teachings of Jesus

"All initiates in pre-Christian times had experienced out-of-body initiation and had then returned to the physical body able to give an account that was actually their own direct experience of the spiritual worlds. This was the kind of initiations undergone by Buddha, Moses and others. But in Jesus, a being came to earth who could see the higher worlds while remaining in a physical body."
~ Rudolf Steiner

We all have the potential to become living Gods. We have the potential to bring love and the energy of the universe together, and not keep them separate, which is false power. We have the opportunity to unite our life force with God force, so that it roars through our being like a vibrant river, clearing everything on its course. *The power is already within us.* By learning to master the energy currents of the life force, we can fill the chalice within our body and thus feed our soul eternally. This will do nothing less than reunite the energies between the brain and body, reconnect spirit and alleviate suffering. The world can then change.

The greatest adjustment will take place in the mind, which has been miscast for two millennia as the center of our physical universe. As the mind surrenders into the divine, the soul is realized in its pure expression. The mind discovers its true place. It is meant to serve spirit, not itself. The mind is disciplined by teaching it to surrender and serve the soul. The body is meant to be listened to and honored, and to become one with the soul and the voice of God, or spirit. Its feelings, passions, truths and knowledge are the expressions of our light and darkness reconnected. When allowed to exist they awaken the mind. The body is not controlled by the mind, as many think. The soul learns to trust the intelligence of the body-mind, allowing the ego part of the mind to dissolve. The emotional need to stay attached to old safety nets and self-protection lift as the soul recognizes it is no longer being controlled. When the mind lets go the body can be reconnected into light. Light fills the consciousness with joy, existence and eventually with eternal bliss.

If the body surrenders to the mind instead of the soul, the power of the feminine is unable to be fully realized. The feminine power fuels the body and soul and the masculine power delivers the message, or accomplishes the task at hand. Notice how most of our political and religious leaders teach us to separate love and power. "Love is what you give your spouse and kids; power is the measure of one's control over home, community, environment, society and/or the world," they say. We're socially (and, in some cases, family) conditioned to crave the power of the mind while yearning for the love of the heart. It is only by bringing together the power and the love of God in your body and heart that you will know the power of your true self.

It is the right time in humanity's story on earth to lift the controls we have so carefully designed to keep our powers contained and stored. The contrast of light and dark has not been this severe since the days of Atlantis; the only way to overcome the challenges of this time is to reunite and realign them into Universal Intelligence, or God. The rays of God and the currents of our body align to reflect the physical mysteries of the universe—axial rotation, gravity, contraction and expansion, polar opposites, duality and light circumference. We again become the inner empty space of the center of creation.

Once reconnected, we feel united with the universe and its magnetic power. As a co-participant working from the center of creation—mirrored in our body as the center of the cell of life—we create and exist within the forces that hold and sustain matter and spirit together. Our actions can either draw us closer to living in this center or pull us further apart. As we activate the magnetic current within our body, we come closer to living in spiritual law. Our physical body can assimilate the prana (life force energy) and be sustained by its molecules.

Then our emotional body, sustained by beauty, joy and love, can express its true nature. Magnetized to the will of God, our mental body surrenders and allows spiritual power to fill it. Our etheric body becomes a weave of golden light and shields us, protecting and invigorating our other bodies with light patterns that foster higher vision, thought, health and serenity. We become part of the tapestry of creation.

To live in the center of creation requires the mind's fullest attention and a heart consciousness that dwells in the divine. This alignment makes it possible to achieve oneness with the order of the universe and live in balance with spiritual law.

Understanding Spiritual Law

Spiritual laws encompass the universe and its creation. When they're followed, our physical and spiritual bodies form a harmonious latticework, a snowflake of perfection and beauty. The mind creates a union with spirit when soul is strong and united. The body can experience union with spirit when the mind knows its true master. The heart becomes one with spirit when the mind and body have ceased their battle.

We become connected to spiritual law, the grand tapestry of life force and creative energies, by ending our separation to our inner self and the life around us. We recognize our connection to the plants, trees, animal kingdoms, planets and elements, and experience our self as part of universal design. Spiritual law flows while man-made laws are static. The figure eight is a symbol that shows how heaven and earth are woven together, duality is bridged and the esoteric and physical are integrated. If we apply the figure eight to all aspects of our life, we can merge our divine and physical needs.

A true spiritual teacher comes to fulfill the law, not change it. She represents the way of uniting physical life with all divine forces. She does not impose her way on others but rather shows how to reconnect to Source. She holds the keys to unlock the doors to direct connection. She embraces all who want to end their separation. She knows everything is inside of you and gives you the courage to face the challenge. When aligned in universal oneness, we become magnetized to such expressions as freedom, charity, grace and honor. The joy of giving unconditionally when consumed within the limitless state of our soul's freedom creates the grace to honor others and life itself.

The highest law is of the heart. Spirit and matter cannot be split. Spirit and the flesh cannot be separated. If we separate from the outcome of our actions, we are living in spiritually static man-made laws. The laws of spirit are the heart's highest truth; spiritually, they are ever-flowing and ever-growing. By integrating spiritual and physical law, we are abiding by the forces that ultimately run our eternal self.

The 12 Steps of Spiritual Law

1. If you misuse your personal power to access the power of creation, you will lose your ability to create your life in accordance with God.
2. Practice silence.
3. Practice stillness.
4. Remember emptiness
5. Live in the space where the divine and human meet.
6. In the single flame of the third eye, come to know the soul in its completion.
7. Know thyself through the clarity of your divine body temple.
8. Birth thyself, through the tunnel of your darkness, into the gateways of light.
9. Do not take from another what they have attained through Father-Mother Divine.
10. Allow life in others to grow and take root as it will.
11. Give back to the wellspring of life by sustaining your own current.
12. Honor each life as though it were your own.

Instruction from the Cosmic Planes

As you become aware of yourself as a being who abides by spiritual law, your consciousness will open beyond the physical plane. For some, the gates open slowly; for others, they break open with great force. Many spiritual aspirants receive a lot of astral and etheric blessings when they're starting out, then the gates close. Don't be concerned; as one meditation master pointed out, this is often God's way of "teasing" a soul to see how badly she or he wants the gifts of the kingdom of Heaven.

As we move more deeply into the 21st century, the astral and physical planes are drawing closer together, making it impossible to ignore intuition, higher intention, soul purpose and feeling. We're beginning a new age of transparency and direct relationship with Source, fueled by a higher spiritual vibration than the previous age of reason and assisted (with priests, imams, rabbis and ministers as go-betweens) relationship with Source. Those who continue to separate feelings into corners, will find it increasingly impossible to avoid major consequences in health, money matters, relationships and livelihood. The earth mother and heavenly father are struggling to reunite. Their union will culminate in restoring peace onto this planet, no matter how long it takes.

Beyond the worlds of duality, there are spiritual planes of higher frequency. Here, the movement of energy is rapid, color-filled and imbued with light. Thoughts travel instantaneously, healing occurs prolifically, and death is a shift in perception coupled with a merging into a higher state of consciousness. The hearts of the doubter, the fearful and the arrogant are mirrored back through the crystal-clear image of the cosmic planes. They are given the opportunity to embrace the very power they have feared and denied.

Through the crown chakra, you can draw down the powers of transformation and transmute the limited and disassociated perspectives of how you turn against yourself. By receiving the moving, vibrant current of God force, you have the ability to transform limitation. This current works at a faster speed than the mind can travel on its own. When the current is limited to the mind alone, imbalance exists. Some call it ADD/ADHD; others describe it as disconnected, non-consistent or confused thinking.

The solution is to connect the current into the body-mind and receive integration of mind and spirit, a wondrous transformation. Try this simple exercise: Draw fire up from the center of the earth and move it inside your tailbone and into your lower belly. Cast aside all doubt and uncertainty. Toss all the ways you turn against yourself into the fire. Feel these old ways transform, *alchemize* into new creative powers that bridge your mind, soul and heart. Their beauty, strength and purpose are created by receiving and moving into vibrant currents of God force.

Spiritual Law Gateways

Practice moving these energy currents in your body. They will enable you to open yourself to receive and practice Universal Law:

Energetic Figure 8's

1. Place your focus inside the base of the tailbone.
2. Move a ray of blue light in a diagonal towards the solar plexus, around the top of the head, behind the skull, back to the solar

plexus, around the lower belly and through the genitals into the tailbone. Repeat.

3. Move a ray of blue light from under the tailbone, through the genitals and lower belly. Draw the ray diagonally through the solar plexus, upper back, through the back of the skull, forward to the third eye and back through the solar plexus until you return to the tailbone.

As Above, So Below- Meeting in the Center

A. Bring your focus into your solar plexus. Fill it with gold light. Sit in the center of the gold light. Look up and observe white light pouring into you. Bring this light into your entire being. Breathe it in.

B. Allow the light to move all the way into the earth. Pull it back into your solar plexus.

C. Breathe into the sides of your body.

D. Extend two rays of light from either side of your body, through your heart center, arms and hands.

E. Bring your attention into a sphere of gold light, uniting and filling your heart center and solar plexus. Continue to fill the sphere with white and gold light.

F. Center your attention into the gold sphere while sending a beam of light through the crown chakra, a beam into the center of the earth and horizontally through the heart, arms and hands.

G. Draw in gold light from above your crown chakra, as well as from the ray of light in the earth. Bring gold light through your hands and pull it into your sphere.

The New Commandments

The original Ten Commandments are the foundation for living in integrity with self and others. These laws, written and handed down during Moses' time, gave the Hebrews the guidance to rediscover their inner home. Greed threatened their existence, and their gifts through communion with Source were no longer revered.

Now, three thousand years later, ten new commandments offer the way to heal our separation from God. They help to heal the causal and emotional patterns that cause all disease in the bodies, while also addressing soul causes of physical and spiritual disconnection, self betrayal, abandonment and rejection.

I. You will not live through another.
II. You will not take or use another's energies.
III. You will not attach anything to self.
IV. You will not abandon self to please another.
V. You will not go into the dark void to harness its power for use against another.
VI. You will not think of self as the power of God, but rather as a co-creator.
VII. You will not leave the voice, truth and spirit of the heart.
VIII. You will not separate the oneness of the divine inner masculine and feminine nature.
IX. You will not turn against Mother-Father God.
X. You will not choose fear over love.

Clearing

We must clear old beliefs that were created when we divided our minds, hearts and souls into fragments in order to cope and survive in the world. Our soul enters this world already in an evolutionary process, with its own perception of what energies and powers require development in order to further evolve. Our life mission is to unite with these energies and powers, and express them in the way we live. Without maintaining a clear connection to our mission, we lose our self. Our mission comprises the steps necessary to complete our soul's journey.

When we take on the religions, belief systems and dogmas of our family without first being given the opportunity to know our self, we are derailed from our mission. Trust in your own vision and take on the courage to return to your original energies. Become the pulse of what moves you into action.

Become your self by remembering yourself. Allow the light of your brightest ray to shine forth into the inner temple, the body of your soul. See where darkness has settled and hardened, and shine the light of your power onto the lost expressions of your holy self. Resurrect the parts of your self that have forgotten what they are. See and feel who is crying, shouting and screaming inside, and listen to their call. Come home to your self and do not run away. Stay with your self until you shine as a star from within and can blaze like a galaxy of a billion stars.

Responsibility

Develop the ability to respond to the inner callings of your higher mind and soul, and you will find the portal through the seals of your chakras. Respond to their promptings to touch spirit. Do not become distracted or pulled by the screaming voices of the hungry dark. Our hungry voices manifest through actions such as over-eating, talking too much, seeking sympathy, attachment to our creature comforts, etc. These cause us to live in separation from the joy of creation. Responsibility brings fulfillment, not from taking power from others, but from filling one's cup with constant attention on the greater reward and purpose of a particular task, thought or feeling — connection to the One. Whatever arises to bring you closer to your true self must be transformed through the fires of your own God self.

The Light That Is Your Birthright

Every change that you're called to make in life is designed to honor the light within you. When your life is no longer working for you, seek your heart's desire and follow its messages. You were born with a spark of light that lives within you, ready to be ignited. It calls you through dreams, visions and feelings, to stimulate a desire to be closer to universal wholeness. When you ignore the callings, you ignore the higher purpose of your existence. Sometimes the light will call, and your mind will ignore the love behind all of your desperations. You want others to hear you and acknowledge your pain. If they do not, you may either catapult into a battle outside of yourself or assume the inner pain of past memories and hurts.

Trust the light that burns in the center of every thought and feeling. Connect it to the center of your heart; there, you will be given the answers to your next steps. Spirit always provides the answers to the most difficult problems.

The Power of Will

Our will is the union of truth, power and intention. It is connected to the solar plexus and navel chakras, the most important centers for healing and reconnecting into the spiritual dimensions. How we use our will creates or destroys our relationships to others and all life energies. There are three primary acts of will: how we command our energy with others, with life and with our soul.

If our will is out of balance, we push our way onto others. We think we can see what is right for others, and we become very opinionated—a by-product of an overzealous ego. However, if we remain in our own God centers in the body, we do not lash out, or seek to change or disempower others. The challenge of the God path is to stay connected in one's own centers and to practice living in that connection every moment. Separating daily work and spiritual flow is the most common way of distorting and sabotaging one's path. Maintaining a balance between work and spirit brings joy.

Whether we are in a deep intimate relationship with another human being or with our self, we are constantly in relationship with the divine. How we treat another person speaks of the extent of our larger relationship with divinity. If we leave our sacred connection to the divine, we often abandon or betray the trust of others. We stay aligned with the divine by right intention and right use of the will. When we leave our solar plexus, lower belly, heart or third eye connections, we misuse our will. We think we are helping others, whether it be a loved one or acquaintance, but we are actually stepping into self separation so that we can meet their separated self. Consequently, we steal vital life force from our own self. It is more challenging to master the laws of will while in relationship with our self, but the final test is how we apply those laws while in relationship with another.

The personal will can remain enmeshed in its ancestral, karmic and genetic beliefs, or it can journey into its own identity by merging into spirit. Many of us shoulder family issues and karmic battles at birth or at some point in childhood. This choice distracts or distorts us from reaching our life goals, and dilutes the power to use will properly to remain focused on our soul missions. The soul evolves into higher states of light when it leaves behind the attitudes of the lower will—holding on (clinging), manipulating, deceiving, owning, attaching and controlling. A person who is seeking the light can slow down or detour their own process, destroy positive relationships or sabotage their creative and spiritual integration by letting someone who is in the dark grasp or clutch onto them. Using one's will to venture into the dark to rescue another does not work on a soul level. It might bring comfort to a mind filled with past regrets and guilt, but a person languishing in the dark can only emerge through their own longing to be released from their own pain. When a person chooses emotional and soul level pain, they are using their will in the negative and will always pull another into their delusion without hesitation.

To work in the light and honor one's own will means we must say "no" to willfully denying our higher truth in order to serve another. The higher truth is a matter of mastering the ability to hold eternal love's vibration. Do not move into the dark to show your love; this is false use of will. Eternal love goes beyond our own need to be received. When we are born to parents whose consciousness is unawakened at our conception and/or birth, we are prone to becoming addicted to emotionally bringing others from darkness into light. It becomes our first and primary act of survival and compels us to sacrifice our light for those in the dark. Until we break that pattern, we are tested over and over again, often destroying our own equilibrium or a relationship that, once lost, we regret or ache to restore. The urge to carry people from the dark can become an obsession until we learn to let everyone remain where they are and trust the power created from living in divine connection to our own God light. This shift makes it possible to live in the right use of our will.

The will develops through lifetimes of facing one's soul desires. The warrior spirit, for instance, blocks out all needs on a physical and emotional level in order to develop will. Warriors enter a state of self-sustenance by cutting off their inner needs and serving others. They sometimes hit a spiritual wall by using their will to sustain the hurt and self-abuse they create. Their shadow side is decadence and the misuse of money and power, which is caused by the same denial of spiritual needs. All forms of extremes, from creating dramas to aggressive behaviors, are experienced until the soul uses will to bring greater beauty and creative light into his or her life. The goal is to love one's self while loving another, and to live in balance.

Another example of the soul's evolution is the artist's will. The vision or sense of hearing drives the soul to manifest the inner creation. A spark fuels the will to overcome all obstacles and stay with the process until the song or word is written, the stone is carved, the movement executed, the film shot or canvas filled. These same desires, when applied to finding God or honoring one's soul vision, bridges personal will with universal will. Universal will is the natural cycle of creation's ebb and flow, contraction and expansion. The ideas enter (the inhalation); the creation is born (exhalation). The will begins to transcend its lower self by identifying with totemic forms of its spirit self, whether it be an eagle, bear, dolphin, light ray, mystic, goddess, flower, breath, color, musical phrase or gemstone.

The shadow side of the artist's will shifts the powers of creativity into either a highly intellectual zone with no feeling, or withholds the inner feelings of the creation out of fear the expression will be stifled, taken away or rejected by others. The latter situation has resulted in the shattered existences of more than a few artists over the years; there are plenty of famous artists in every generation who suffered this fate. A stifled artist's attachment to a safe identity keeps him or her in a comfort zone, and excludes him or her from the ability to receive, channel or embody spiritual power in his or her works or lives.

Balance Your Will

Exercise 1

1. From ten feet above your head send a ray of pure white light down into your navel.
2. Feel within to see whose energies are occupying your navel.
3. Ask the energies why they are there, and what they want.
4. Tell them they can no longer be there and must depart.
5. Ask your body what color it needs to clear this energy.
6. Send the energy into your navel and unhook the others' energy, returning it to their body and then sending it into the earth below and the light above their body.
7. Ask your body what color it needs to fill your navel. Send it into your navel everyday for two weeks or until healed.
8. Each day, scan your navel area for darkness and light. Remain aware of how you connect with people who are caught in addictions and dramas of life that never seem to cease. Make the choice to let go of your addiction to giving your energies to the dark. Bring your own life force completely into the light. Try to release the subconscious desires to keep friends, family and parents who remain psychically alive at the expense of your own psychic health.

Exercise 2

1. Focus your mind down into your navel.
2. Breathe into your navel area.
3. Send light into your navel area.
4. Intensify and focus the light into your navel. Expand it into a full circle with strong intention.
5. Release your attention.
6. Let the energy soar upward into your solar plexus. Push it back into your navel and once again release them into your solar plexus.
7. Finally, send the energies into the earth's center.

When your issues of self-existence are cleared, your soul feels a "green light" to proceed towards living in union with its will. We can then begin to grow new cords into both the earth and heaven and establish the right use of will.

The Power of Your Intention

Intention is how we focus our power to accomplish the alignments, relationships and connections we want. If we want to experience the highest spiritual state of christed or illuminated consciousness, we place our intention upon that goal and focus our actions and thoughts through the feeling of that consciousness. We open and shift into another level of experiencing everyday life. If we want to realize our greatest potential in a skill or trade, we do not settle for our present perceptions. Instead, we learn to leave our comfort zone and reach into the unknown, where we'll find the essence of our thought, feeling or connection. Spirit works with connection; the intellect works with observation, understanding and insight; and feeling works with integration, oneness and expression. All are portals into oneness. As soon as we shift into an intention that embraces our desire to feel at-one-ment on any level, we will manifest what we desire for our soul mission.

The intention of sacred relationship encompasses holding space, honoring the other and loving with wholeness. When we treat the other as a sacred being, deserving of all that God has to give, we are breaking engrained patterns of abuse and dishonor. Our intention of creating sacred communion with another raises us into (w)holiness—whole acceptance, respect and love.

Holding space is the ability to open one's heart while remaining present and connected to one's self. The intention of putting aside one's own emotions and attitudes while being present gives the other the wonderful sense of feeling completely received, heard and seen—the three greatest needs of all human beings. Through the fulfillment of these needs, the potential for anger, pain and resentment are minimized. The experiences of openness, joy and love blossom. Even in difficult situations, where issues of power and future needs are involved, individuals feel supported to enter the spiritual zone of unconditional creation and unlimited possibilities.

A circle created with the intention of holding truth for another and one's self provides a container for the emotions. It helps to dissolve fears connected with opening one's heart. Relationship with another is really a reflection of how we are in relationship to all life. In deep, loving relationships, we're pushed to open to life. If we remain in our comfort zones, we miss the larger opportunity of the relationship.

When the intention in a relationship is to fearlessly hold the space for another person's feelings and truth while anchored in one's own self, the power of love is multiplied. Life interacts with the elements at all times; by allowing another to interact with his or her own elements while you maintain a spiritual space, you allow for simultaneous growth on many levels.

If the tree is alive within us, our roots and branches receive the nutrients needed to feed our emotions and soul. If we separate from those roots, we may end up alienating or controlling our significant other—who only wants to open and express more of who she or he is. The more we acknowledge the original source of our emotions, the easier it is to live in our hearts and act from integration and integrity, rather than react to displaced or denied emotions and watch them spill into buckets of misunderstood feelings. Every emotion is a doorway to living in Source. If we take every emotion into our deepest heart, we'll find resolution and healing within. Emotions also consist of the pain and suffering we experience when we leave, betray or reject our self. When someone really loves us, they support us in finding the way back to our true nature.

When you create a circle of light in which to sit in with a beloved, whether your lover, partner, sibling, son or daughter, remember to summon all the forces of life energy. These forces sustain, renew, transform and allow the soul to die and be reborn into itself. When a relationship is able to assist another to surrender and experience rebirth through a circle of love, the greatest miracles occur. Every outer candle holds the light of truth for the other. As the light of inner beauty and love are awakened, allow the candle of your heart to illuminate the space of acceptance.

The intention of the soul is to become its full creative and life-giving self. It always wants to feel a part of the universal plan. When a person violates this natural intention, his or her mind becomes dark, tormented. They usually seek to appear to be the most important in a given situation, the one needed to fulfill the life of a person, corporation—or nation.

As you unfold, realize and live the evolving story of your soul's intention, realize your highest truth. Your free will allows you to come closer and closer to your source in God by navigating how you are going to serve. You have the power to build the foundational structure of your life with light so your intentions are manifested. Let go of false intentions and learn to shift into your soul's intention of truth.

Part VI

Mahavatar Babaji: The Enlightener

Chapter 20

Babaji: Teacher of the Master Jesus

The way of divine union begins with the activation
of the physical and etheric currents of the body.
These currents seek to unite universal forces
of light and energy dwelling within the cells of all life.

A man who was well versed in religious scriptures once came to Mahavatar Babaji and wanted to know the significance of the "cosmic body of God." Babaji, who rarely spoke and characteristically kept his silence, continued to sit quietly. But after a while he said: "Close your eyes and worship God for some time, and then open your eyes."

The man did as he was instructed. He meditated on God for a while, then opened his eyes. As he looked around, he saw Babaji everywhere. Not only that, but every single object on which he trained his eyes became Babaji. Then the great Himalayan master said quietly: "No one can really define God by reading the scriptures."

Babaji's mission in India has been to assist prophets in fulfilling their individual calling. He has given yoga initiation to Shankara, ancient founder of the Swami Order, Lahiri Mahasaya, the carrier of Kriya Yoga, to Kabir, famous medieval saint and countless others.

Mahavatar Babaji speaks a mixture of many languages including Nepali, Hindi and Kurmachal. Whenever conversing with someone from a particular region in India, he speaks fluently to them in their own native language. No one knows when he was born or where. He mastered all the known siddhas (Yogic powers) and occasionally performs miracles in a natural way. Most people are drawn to him because of the bliss they experience in his presence.

Between 1861 and 1924, Babaji appeared in many places in Northern India. Known by a range of names in various regions, people didn't realize they were referring to the same person until a man named Mahendra Brahmachari had a vision of him in 1949. For the next thirty-five years, he traveled all over India, collecting stories about encounters with Babaji. He published these in India under the title *Punya Smriti,* using the pen name Guru Charnasrit.

It is known that when you move into a prayerful or meditative state and utter Babaji's name with complete reverence, you will receive an instant spiritual blessing. If you pray sincerely from the heart, you may receive a visitation from him.

Babaji is called "the deathless yogi." He has ascended into the immortal body, moving seamlessly between the physical and etheric worlds, never to physically die. He assists individuals as well as saints, sages, prophets and masters who are physically helping their followers, community, country and Mother Earth. He is in the East, working for the benefit of all beings. Babaji's spiritual dedication and promise is to always be here, until all beings are enlightened.

The deathless guru appears to be no more than twenty-five. Fair-skinned, of medium build and height, Babaji's beautiful, strong body radiates a perceptible glow. His tender eyes are dark and calm, and his long, lustrous hair is copper-colored. It is a strange fact that Babaji bears an extraordinary physical resemblance to his disciple Lahiri Mahasaya. The similarity is so striking that, in his later years, Lahiri Mahasaya might have passed as the father of the youthful-looking Babaji. Before taking his present incarnation, Babaji lived a succession of lifetimes as Adi Nath Shiva, Kal Agni Nath, Dakshin Murti and Gorksha Nath.

Babaji's teachings initiate divine union in the physical body. In this vital manner, his work aligns directly with that of Christ, Mary Magdalene and the Holy Grail, and is to be considered a major inner teacher available to us today.

Throughout his reign of service as an Avatar (enlightened teacher and way-shower) for over 1,800 years in his present body, he has helped to enlighten the teachers called to disseminate the vital spiritual truths and practices for our time. As a master teacher for Christ in his former incarnation, Babaji discovered Christ's true light in the world

—an initiate who, like himself, was dedicated to transforming the battle of dark and light into a New Dawn, which is the phase on our planet after this time of fear and separation.

Both Babaji and Christ teach the entry points, or portals and alignments necessary for complete spiritual realization. They both initiate the original vibration of creation and choose to empower the full divine feminine-masculine spark of each soul. Dogma is insignificant to them both, but self-discipline, devotion and healing for the sake of one's self, others and the world advances their mission to raise people into enlightenment and freedom. They are both master yogis.

By bringing light into the chakra centers and through the central core channel in the spine, Babaji's *Way of the White Swan* activates God force in all of our physical, mental, emotional, spiritual and etheric gateways. The *Way of the White Swan* works with the two main currents in the body. The first pranic current, the *ida,* flows on the left (feminine, lunar) side of the spine, from the coccyx to the third eye. The descending apana current, or *pingala,* flows on the right (masculine, solar) side of the spine from the third eye to the coccyx. Babaji named this ancient practice Kriya Yoga; in his former incarnation, he taught the *ida* and *pingala* current movements pre-Christ. Kriya is also known in ancient texts as Kevali Pranayama and Kevali Kumbhaka. The true pranayama transcends the necessity for puraka (inhalation) and rechaka (exhalation).

When the eyes and will are focused in the third eye, the circulation of life breath up and down the spine creates a magnetic pull between the two poles, generating a strong current in the *Sushumna,* or central spine. This current is the highway for the evolution of consciousness. When fully activated, it opens the "wings of the swan," the ventricles in the brain, and exposes the body and mind to tremendous amounts of spiritual light and energy. As awareness expands into the lateral ventricles, the "wings of the swan" generate flight into cosmic consciousness.

When done with deep devotion and concentration, each round of Kriya—which takes about 30 seconds—burns away one year of accumulated karmic seeds, or *samskaras,* from the etheric spine. If meditation is the pathway to God, then Kriya is a comparative superhighway. Kriya is capable of bringing its most devoted adherents to complete soul liberation in a single lifetime. The practice is so sacred that, to this day, the technique is taught and given only after one has prepared the inner spine to receive the supercharged currents that regular Kriya practice generates. It is believed that Jesus taught his closest disciples—including Mary Magdalene—this sacred practice, which he learned during his years of study in the Himalaya.

Now Babaji brings forth new practices to assist in the spiritual renaissance occurring on this planet. Among them are The Holy Grail

Energy Elixirs, shown in this book for the advancement of his original work.

Through the co-operative work of the Elohim, Mary the Mother, Mary Magdalene, Babaji and Christ, the time is now to bring in these divine higher teachings.

Mahavatar Babaji is of the highest light of the Elohim, a group of Celestrial Beings who have stationed themselves as guides for this planet and planets in other galaxies—both physical and etheric—on which spiritual beings reside. They are teachers, guides and initiators to individuals who have shown their dedication to bridging the dimensions of darkness into light and the path of reaching oneness. The Elohim have been guiding humanity since its beginning and work with many ascended masters to direct the details of our spiritual evolution. They bring in the next step for humanity's spiritual growth.

The New Universal Laws

A new code of spiritual law is manifesting on this planet. The Teachings of the Holy Grail continue to progress and expand the original teachings that were practiced in silence and given orally by attained masters—then taken deep underground during the Dark Ages.

As the spiritual flames of transformation course through our spine and infinite cells, our soul awakening can merge with the union of God forces. This penetrating purification unifies our astral, etheric and physical bodies. Emerging from an age of separation, the mind is called to the meeting point where spirit meets the body. This point of expansion breaks governing forces of fear.

How we create our life is of vital significance. Become fully responsible for what energies and thought forms you connect to. The longer we continue to avoid learning to reconnect and settle the mind, clear the emotional and soul blockages repeating themselves from lifetime to lifetime, the longer we remain in denial.

The New Universal Laws empower from a place of light. It is impossible to move into the new paradigm when the cords of our pain and attachment are in the control seat. It takes full commitment to move through our own grandiosities and uncover the energies to which our true self is aligned.

We are being given the illusions of freedom through unlimited credit lines, global Internet access, ultra-fast computers, readily available fuel products, etc., yet we are being directed by these same market forces to hand over our freedom. They can do this because we're not sufficiently trained in the powers of the spirit and soul. If we did have the training, we would rebuke, with no more effort than a wave of the hand, those who try so unscrupulously to wield power over us. These illusions prevent many from seeing the new freedom.

What can you do to practice new universal law? Imagine no part of your self out of sync; everything within you is in agreement. If there is dissent or unrest it is spoken about and conscious interchange occurs. Connect to beauty and open to all levels of beauty within you. Listen to every nuance of disturbance within yourself and respect it. Pay attention to each inner dissent and its needs and requests. Be willing to discover your deepest truth under the disturbance and follow it back into your true self. Journey through the emotion into your light. End the separation between love and fear. Take responsibility for how you have created splits of consciousness to maintain your unrest or disturbance. BE. Soak your past facades, fears and limitations in a luxurious, liberating bath of universal light, boundless energy and eternal love. Absorb the love completely and allow it to shift whatever you are holding onto right now.

Move deeply into your heart. Feel the pain caused by separating your mind and heart. Pain is the teacher of the heart to propel you forward. Many fear the pain in their soul, yet in actuality, it is a gateway home, a path to Oneness—the state where separations melt into the I am One. Become one with self, heart, universe, spiritual ancestors, earth, body and spirit. Quietly chant *ELOHIM ELOHIM NAMA*. Become one with the peace of your heart.

I am Babaji: A Transmission

A new pattern of awakening is aligning itself in our bodies. We can no longer look at ourselves as physical beings separate from cosmic energies. Beyond being conscious human beings, we are enlightening receptors of dynamic life-giving forces. The authenticity of each soul surpasses any mental declarations or affirmations of personal power. We must see our self as unique expressions of the One and connected in all of our bodies to spirit. Within spirit's individuation exists the rod of strength and universal power. Standing in this column of light, we live connected to our eternal home.

Our bodies are temples of beauty. As we look through the opening archways of our self, we experience a never-ending terrain of bliss. By expressing sacredness, respect and willingness to wait for the door to open into ever-awaiting love, we come closer to the meeting with divine self. I will mirror the endless universe of eternity as we become one. For I am the gateway into eternal silence. Each time you send a ray of light to me, I will come closer to you until our hearts are one in undivided space and time. There is no separation between us; the God in you activates each time you come closer to me and I to you.

The ideas sleeping in your soul awaken as the barriers surrounding your true existence fall away. All that will be left are the creations you have previously committed to complete and the promises you first made when you recognized that you were God's spark of eternal love. Anything that does not carry a vibration of love only burns up your love and wastes it. It is important to learn to recognize the illusions of love. It will help you to not be fooled by those who cloak themselves in love but are only imitators of the divine. Uniting with love and living in its presence is the highest divine mission you will have.

The subtle and physical bodies unite in rays of light; in the center exists a matrix of love. Within this meeting point is your unique presence, where nothing else exists. As you come to know yourself by this eternal meeting point of love, you are connected into the worlds of light. You simultaneously enter the wellspring of life within you and around you. The moment you recognize your true identity as being one who is a connector of life force with the rest of the universe, and a continuously lit lamp bulb, you begin to realize that you are capable of anything and everything.

As you enter into the ascended form of your etheric, spiritual and physical bodies, you will find yourself. Here, you will find me, always waiting for your return.

Chapter 21

The Secret Teachings of Babaji

Only light is worth attaining.
All darkness is only a shadow of our first breath.
Return to the center of light within. Within the movement of God's divine forces exists the portal into life beyond the body.

We live in the center of universal forces that serve as an axis to creation. When we become knowledgeable and familiar with the universal forces inside our body and soul, we transform into the energetic and elemental forces from which we are created. By properly preparing and entering the doorway into the unmanifested, the divine feminine, we are able to ignite the spark that exists in the core of the molecular configuration within our consciousness.

The awakening of the spine's inner channels prepares the body for ascension into a multi-dimensional realm. Here the chakras transform into geometric energy generators that connect the alpha and the omega—the beginning and the end. The chakras become castles of higher consciousness, primed to maintain a strength and presence of creation energy. The original creation of light becomes reactivated in our consciousness, imbuing us with healing power.

The next level of Babaji's teachings prepares the aspirant to live in the center of who they are—their original spiritual blueprint—fully empowered and connected. The colors within our cosmic bodies become one with the universal design of our christed self. The missing link in our molecular structure is reconnected through the union of our spiritual energies and the originating christed light present in the universe. We become one with the balanced energies of the universe, while at the same time, our energies help balance the universe. We reach into the heart of darkness with the sole purpose of contacting and igniting the moment of liberation: God awakened in the body. Freedom awakes us. Touching into the heart of life leaves us breathless and enlivened beyond what our mind or body can imagine as possible. This union allows us to live with greater ease during these globally trying times.

An initiation into the presence and connection to Babaji is available through the Holy Grail Teachings.

Warm Up Exercises

Morning Glory: Pull the energies up from the earth with both hands, up through your feet, legs, pelvis, through the center of your body, throat center and third eye. As the energy is pulled up through the crown chakra with your hands, as it opens and pours down around you, use your hands to push it all the way back down into the earth.

Neck Releaser: Stand with your feet parallel and under your pelvis. Hang over, bending your body toward the ground, fingers touching the ground. Breathe in as you bend your knees slightly, then exhale while straightening your knees without locking them. Relax your neck muscles as you press your fingers and/or palms into the ground.

Squat: Drop into a squatting, half-sitting position, keeping your feet in a parallel position while keeping your heels on the ground. Use a book under your feet if you cannot place your heels on the ground. Clasp your hands together and bring your thumbs to your third eye. Rock gently back and forth on your feet, from front to back. Bring your hands behind your neck and stretch your neck down until your chin is on your chest. Breathe into your tailbone and then up your spine.

Solar Plexus Opener: Ball your hands into fists and "walk" your knuckles up your spine, one vertebra at a time. Bring your shoulder blades together, chin up and look up.

Downward Dog: Stretch your back and keep it flat as you press your heels and hands into the ground. Bring your chin into your chest, then reach your chin forward, then back into your chest.

The Holy Grail Energy Elixirs

The physical, emotional, etheric, mental and spiritual bodies are reconnected and aligned by these Energy Elixirs. They reconstruct your soul's original spiritual blueprint in union with Source. Practice each exercise for two weeks before adding in a new Elixir.

Spiritual Grounding: Create a beam of white light from above the head and send it through the torso, pelvis, legs and feet, and into the center of the earth. Travel into pure white light in the center of the earth and pull it back up through the feet, legs, belly (second chakra) and solar plexus.

Cleansing Light: From twenty to thirty feet above your head, send a beam of blue light through your body and into the earth.

Energy Balancer: Create an energy connection by placing your right thumb on your navel and your left thumb on your third eye. Hold these points and feel the energy moving between them. Generate figure-eight loops through the chakras, beginning at the tailbone, then traveling up the back, to your navel, solar plexus, heart center, throat, third eye and crown. Then repeat the exercise, traveling down your back.

Chakra Spiral: Spiral up through all the chakras to the crown. Let the ensuing energy flow down either side of the spine to your tailbone. Expand the spiral behind your neck, skull and crown chakra, and into your third eye.

Chakra Loop: Visualize a flame of fire from underneath your tailbone to right below the navel. Pull it like a piece of elastic into the tailbone and pubic bone. Raise it up into a loop three times. Pull it up from the pubic bone and into the second chakra. Push it down into the pubic bone three times. Loop the energy from the pubic bone to the solar plexus, then to the heart, throat, third eye and crown chakra, each time pulling it up with greater momentum and power. Proceed to the second chakra and pull it into a loop through each chakra, moving upwards. Repeat the looping circuits from the navel, solar plexus, heart, throat center and third eye.

Heart and Soul Diamonds: Bring a ray of gold light up from the earth into your heart center. Spin it clockwise in a spiral, creating a sphere of gold light in your heart. Create a second sphere of gold light directly above your heart and spin it clockwise. Create four rays of gold light from the heart and reach them upwards. Connect two of the rays into the sphere above the heart and two rays into the third eye. Spin them clockwise. Now, from the sphere above your heart create two rays of gold light and extend them downward to meet two of the rays moving up from the heart and create a diamond. Create a sphere of gold light in your third eye and spin it clockwise. Then, create two rays of light from your third eye and send them down to meet two of the rays moving up from the heart center and create another diamond. Slowly begin to spin the two diamonds into light and sit with this experience for as long as you want.

Next, create a sphere of gold light in your solar plexus and begin to spin it clockwise. Create three rays of gold light and send them downwards. Create a sphere of light into your second chakra and spin it clockwise. Create three rays of gold light and send them upwards to meet the three gold rays coming down from the solar plexus. Connect the rays into a 3-D diamond and slowly begin to spin the diamond. Invite colors to flow from your third eye into the diamond. Place yourself in the center of the diamond, into the shaft of light within the center of your body.

Now, create another 3-D diamond beginning from the solar plexus and send it into the earth. Feel yourself moving with the rotation of the earth. Place yourself in this larger diamond and be in its center so that you feel in the center of the movement. You are still within the motion.

Earth Vision: Bring your focus into your navel and fill it with light. Create a ray of light from your navel into your third eye. Hold the connection between the two points. From your third eye, project your vision so that you are looking down upon the earth from a high vantage perspective. Send a ray of light down into the center of the earth. Feel and see the streams, rivers, oceans, wind, mountains, valleys and fire deep within the earth. Bring their essence into you, absorbing their power. Perceive and feel what your role has been with the earth over time, and what you are specifically being asked to do here in this lifetime. Ask for clarification on your possible pitfalls, and what to be aware of so you can accomplish your mission.

Bring yourself fully into your body and connect even more deeply into your third eye and navel circuit. Begin in your navel and create a figure eight down into the center of the earth, then bring the loop back up into your navel, looping it above your head and then back into your navel. Repeat eight times. Fill the resulting container within your body with any color you choose.

Sexual/Physical Union: Place your focus in your tailbone. Create two rays of light centered in the core shaft inside your tailbone. One ray begins on the left and the other ray begins on the right. Crisscross the two rays through your base chakra, expanding them to the inside of the core shaft of light, then back into the second chakra. Move the rays upwards simultaneously crisscrossing them through your navel, solar plexus, heart center, throat center, third eye and crown. This is the caduceus, the double helix, the complete intermingling of two energetic bodies, symbolized by two intersecting snakes. At the crown center bring your energetic caduceus up like a geyser and then send it down both sides of your spine back down to your tailbone. Move the caduceus slowly then increase the momentum. Repeat 12 times.

Create two rays of light from either side of your base tailbone center and repeat the practice 12 times. Create four rays from either side and repeat 16 times.

Complete the exercise by focusing upon blue light in your third eye. Hold the gaze for as long as you can.

Empowerment: Send a ray of light down through your body into the earth. Create a diamond of energy in the earth; as you pull it up into your body, begin to spin the diamond clockwise. Keep the diamond spinning. From above your head, send a beam of light down into the open elevator shaft corridor in your body. Look for a part of you that appears very small but actually is a giant of power and light. Ask him/her to share with you the knowledge he/she has been carrying throughout time.

Double Diamond: From your third eye, create a diamond within the earth's center. Fill it with white light. Now, with your third eye, create a second diamond in the center of the earth. Fill it with gold light. Begin to spin the center white-light diamond, then the outer diamond. Sit between the two diamonds as they spin. Create two pyramids, overlaying one atop the other on the inside column of light within your spine. Begin at your first chakra, then create a double pyramid in each chakra as you move up the core shaft of light. Begin to spin the pyramids and place your focus in the center of the core shaft of light. Hold this focus for 15 minutes.

DNA Elixir: Create a diamond of gold light from your third eye into the earth, Feel yourself submerged into the earth. Create a strand of blue diamond shapes from the center of the earth up into your navel. Create six strands of gold light from the base of the blue diamonds, three on either side of the diamonds and crisscross them in wide sweeps up the diamond strand to your navel. Now create three more strands of blue diamonds creating a total of four strands. Undulate the crisscross from the center of the earth up the four strands of diamonds around each chakra center to the top of the head. Repeat this 20 times. Then begin to spiral the six strands of gold light rapidly around the diamonds until you experience them spinning all together very quickly. The energies will begin to pour over the top of your higher centers, at which time have them flow down into the earth. Repeat the rapid spiral spin up the center of your core shaft and be in the center. End with creating a gold orb or sphere of light around your entire auric field about six feet around that is impenetrable to energies at a lower vibration than that of the gold light.

Spheres of Light: Create a sphere of light in both palms of your hands. Let them grow in strength and size. Send a ray of light from each sphere deep into the center of the earth. Create a diamond shape in the earth's center and connect its highest point to your third eye. Add another diamond shape near your first one within the earth and feel your connection to it from your third eye. Fill both diamonds with light. Next, place your focus on your palms. Using the light of the spheres you initially created in your palms, create a geometric shape inside the two diamond shapes and place yourself in the center of this shape. Be in the core shaft of energy within your spine. Become one with the geometric design. Spin the two diamond shapes around your core.

Fire of the Earth: Create a triangle of light in your second chakra. Send a beam of light into molten fire in the center of the earth. Slowly move the fire up into gold triangles of light, starting from the shaft of core energy in your pubic bone and advancing through all of your chakras. Move the fire up the center of the chakras through these gold triangles, stacked one atop the other, until you reach the third eye. From the third eye, create a large triangle that goes below your feet into the center of the earth. Fill it with gold light, then open it into a pyramid within your mind's eye.

Lighting the Heart: Begin by rubbing the palms of your hands together rapidly until there is friction and heat. Slowly bring your palms apart, feeling the existing energy and warmth. Pull your palms apart and back in very slowly, like you are pulling taffy, and feel the magnetic energy. Place your palms in front of your heart center and send this energy into your heart. Create a triangle in your heart center and turn it into a pyramid of any color. Begin to build four pyramids around your heart center. Sit focused in the center of the pyramids and create a wide base and foundation that begins and goes beyond the body.

Higher Self Configuration: Create a beam of light from above your head and bring it down through the central column of light into your body. Breathe into your lower belly and create a spiral that moves clockwise in your navel and second chakra, then descends into the center of the earth. Bring the fire of the earth up into your feet, legs and lower belly and into the column of light inside your tailbone. Raise the energy into your middle back. Push it back down, then pull it up and back down like you're pulling on elastic. Generate a loop of energy from the tailbone to the solar plexus, then back down to the tailbone. Move up to the heart center, and return to the tailbone. Repeat these loops 12 times. Now, take a loop of gold light and draw it from the tailbone up into the throat center. Repeat 24 times.

Bring your attention to the column of light in the navel area. Extend spokes of light out from the navel into a sphere or bubble of light. Breathe into your navel. As you breathe, the spokes get stronger. As you inhale, draw the spokes of light inward towards your navel and extend the spokes of light outward as you exhale. Draw the energy back into the core of your navel. Create a loop of gold light from your navel up the core shaft of light into your third eye. Loop the energy effortlessly 12 times.

From your third eye, visualize a gold geometric configuration of light above your head. Begin to move it clockwise, very slowly. Let it be filled with different hues. Slowly begin to move it down into your whole body. Allow the geometric points to touch your body as it settles in. Eventually bring it to your feet. Feel it expanding throughout your entire body.

Petals of Light: Bring purplish-blue light into your navel and ripple it up along your inner spine, through the back of the skull, third eye and then back down to your navel. Repeat 12 times. Ripple the circuit through the inner column of light in the spine into your solar plexus. Repeat 12 times. Undulate the circuit from your pubic bone through the inner column of light back to the pubic bone. Repeat 12 times. Create three layers of white light-like petals on either side of your body from your pubic bone to your shoulders. Use your breath to bring them to fullest blossom. With your breath, draw them up to the base of your skull and envision them spreading outward like wings of light. Inhale and open the petals of light; exhale all the way into your core column of light. As you breathe, allow yourself to become invisible and dissolve into the petals of light. Bring your focus into your second chakra and third eye, deep within the core column of light.

Heavenly Octave: Begin in the navel area in the core column of light. Bring a ray of gold light up through the shaft, behind the skull and through the crown chakra. Loop the gold light above the head and bring it down through the third eye, into the heart center and into the navel. Repeat 12 times. Now bring the circuit into the solar plexus instead of the navel. Repeat 12 times. As you bring the circuit into the solar plexus, loop it through the heart center and continue through the center of the spine, through the crown chakra, above the head and back down to the solar plexus. Repeat 12 times. From the heart center, create a gold loop and then a full figure-eight loop through the navel in the core column of light, down the tailbone, through the genitals and up through the navel into the heart center. Repeat 12 times. Create a sphere of moving energy in your heart center and place your focus within its center. Create five ovals of energy that spin around the center of that sphere. Stay in the center of the sphere as the ovals spin around it.

Solid Ground: Breathe indigo blue/purplish light into the collarbone. Focus your attention within the center of your collarbone. Create and send two rays of indigo blue/purplish light into your kidneys and lower back. Send a ray of this light into your second chakra and then back up into the center point of the collarbone beneath the throat center. Loop energy from that point up through the skull to the third eye and back into that point. Send two rays of indigo blue/purplish light deep into the center of the earth. From the center of the earth, create rays of indigo blue/purplish light and bring them up through your feet. Create the same number of rays to ascend upward through your feet and legs on both sides, whether four, six, eight, ten or twelve rays. Crisscross these rays through all of your chakra centers. Let the rays of light overflow from the top of your head, around and through your body, and down to the center of the earth. Connect your heart to the center of the earth. Repeat this exercise 12 times.

Lighting the Way: Create a beam of blue light from above your head and send it deep into the earth, Spiral it clockwise. Draw the energy up from the center of the earth and spiral it up through your feet and legs into your second chakra. Create four triangles that overlay one another, and breathe light into them until they shift into a bright color. Slowly spiral this bright color clockwise into the second chakra. Move it through your central core shaft, and through your navel, solar plexus, heart, throat, third eye and crown chakra. Push the spiral back down through the chakra centers, finally dispersing the energies into the earth. Repeat the exercise12 times. Now practice the exercise by moving the energy up from the earth and passing it through the second chakra, rather than stopping to create the triangles. Bring the energy spiral up from the earth and through all the chakras to the top of your head. Push the energies down through your body, as though you are pressing down on a top, then draw the energies back up. Each time you press down, you are moving the energies faster and faster.

Gold Star: From 20 feet above your head, bring in white light through your core shaft of light and connect it deep into the center of the earth. Bring the light up from the earth and into the core shaft of light inside your tailbone. Create the base of a triangle of light from the tailbone and extend its tip to the solar plexus, with the navel in the center of the triangle. Breathe into the triangle and take in its light. Next, create a second triangle of light with its base in the navel and its tip in the heart center. Breathe into the triangle and absorb its light. Create a third triangle with its base in the solar plexus and its tip in the throat chakra. Bring gold light up from the earth into the three triangles: tailbone to solar plexus; navel to heart chakra; solar plexus to throat chakra. Feel the alignment of the triangles. Extend eight rays of light above your shoulders and head (two each from the tailbone, navel, solar plexus and heart chakra) to a gold star that surrounds your body. Allow the gold light from this star to bathe your body.

Heavenly Earth: Begin by creating a blue star of light and placing it into a sphere in the center of the earth. Move it clockwise within the center of the earth. Draw its rays of light into your second chakra and create a second blue star so that both stars are connected to each other. Create a shaft of light between your second chakra and the center of the earth that will allow hundreds of stars of light to move between these two points. Bring your attention into the star in the center of the earth and pull up its power into your second chakra, navel and solar plexus. Now, pull blue light from your second chakra through your throat center and into your third eye. Send your focus back into your throat chakra, and create a blue star of light there. Allow the rays of this star to emanate 360 degrees around your throat chakra. Connect the rays of the star in your throat chakra to a gold star above your head and pull the light from this gold star into you. Gently guide the gold star's light into your heart center.

Breaking Through: Create a gold star of light in the center of the earth. Pull its energy through four rays of light up through the core shaft of light into your solar plexus. Push the energy back down through the rays into the gold star within the earth, widening and increasing the light rays'power. Create a four-pointed diamond inside your solar plexus as you pull back up these four rays to create a second diamond. Expand the second diamond beyond the perimeters of your body. Begin to spiral the diamond clockwise and bring your focus into the center of the diamond and into your heart chakra, and into the power points right above your solar plexus and sternum in your breastbone. Remain with this connection for 10 to15 minutes. To complete, breathe into your navel inside the core shaft of light and move the energy up through the neck, back of the skull, third eye and back down through your pubic bone and into your perineum and tailbone.

Part VII

Living In Source

Chapter 22

Holy Grail Principles

"I often wonder if religion is the enemy of God. It's almost like religion is what happens when the Spirit has left the building."
—Bono, U2 lead singer/humanitarian

Drinking of the Holy Grail is the gift of attaining a state of alignment with God power. The body transforms into the chalice. The heart becomes the harbinger, the pointer of the way; as the generator of creation, the soul becomes one with Source.

Without a chalice, it is impossible to hold the immense spiritual and energetic power of total attunement. Inlaid with precious gems of light and received when drinking of the Grail, the chalice can only be given when the soul relinquishes its own agenda with power and realizes it is a co-creator with power, not the source of power.

Life is a series of events that test how we use the power we are given. If our chalices are filled with love, we are less likely to succumb to the darkness of lack and emptiness within. The key to living in power is to not allow anything to get in the way between you and your divine whole power. The present moment is an invitation to remember your connection to the power that lives in each part of your body, soul, heart and love. Nothing is stronger than love, and only a deep focus like the eyes of one who gazes at her or his beloved can remove illusion.

These power-centering exercises help us to maintain a constant state of focus and connection with Source.

Power Centering I

1. Revolve a purplish-blue circle counter-clockwise until it becomes a spiral in front of your third eye. Revolve 21 times.
2. Visualize and place a violet stone in your navel and invite archangels and angels to enter this power center. Remove anyone else's energies from this center, and balance it.
3. Chant Om Nama Shivaya 28 times while placing your attention in your heart center. This is the *mahamudra,* the "great" mudra; it creates attunement with the vibration of Source.
4. Bring your attention into your third eye, then down into your navel. Energetically connect the sites together.
5. Practice staying in this connection.

Power Centering II

1. Bring your attention behind your knees and spiral your focus up to your navel.
2. Gather the light of a large diamond in your navel.
3. Send a ray of light directly into your heart chakra.
4. Maintain your focus in your navel and heart chakra simultaneously.
5. Resonate their connection from within the light of your heart.

Power Centering III

1. Chant *Aum* four times.
2. Place your focus behind the bridge of your nose.
3. Bring in blue light and allow it to expand into your third eye.
4. Allow rays of light to move down into your body and around you.

Power Centering IV

1. Place your attention diagonally up and back from your third eye.
2. From this point, create a Star of David (two overlaying triangles). The highest point is above your head, and the lowest point is centered around the base of your tailbone.

3. Infuse the Star with a color that naturally comes to you.
4. Breathe into the Star, and fill your spine with its energy.

Power Centering V

1. Focus your attention on the top of your pubic bone.
2. Create a spiral of white light infused with color in a clockwise circle.
3. Move the light in a rippling motion through the core of your body into your throat.
4. Relax and tilt your head back. Breathe into your throat.
5. Bring your head back to normal and sound *"AH"* 3 times, bringing it deeper into your belly with each sound. Repeat.

Power Centering VI

1. Bring pink light into your second chakra and use your breath to send it into your back.
2. Create an energy loop of consecutive loops of changing colors up through the center of your body and out the top of your head.
3. Circulate it down the front of your body to your genitals and back up to your second chakra.

Power Centering VII

1. Visualize streams of color running up your body then down your body.
2. Feel for energetic dips, dents, holes and rough spots.
3. Allow these streams of color to move into and fill these spots.

The Rush of Gratitude

Gratitude rushes through the core of our body, washing it clear of hidden debris. As love magnetizes itself through the union of our heart, spirit, sexuality and light, we polarize our self to the forces within us that magnify our desire to become the river of life. Our body increases in vibration as the walls of separation dissolve between our soul essence and spirit. The colors within us magnify, aligning the roots of our existence with our spirit that seeks oneness with the divine. Stagnation ceases. Golden branches that extend from the solid core of intelligence within our matrix of love reverberate with waves of creative union from the divine.

We know our self as the source of life current flowing through living creation. There is no doubt. We sparkle in an endless eternal shower. We help it rain. The rain saturates the membranes of our cells. We drink with mouths open to the sky. Our roots suck in the nutrients. We smile again. It has been a long drought, a long journey through emptiness. Now, there is nothing blocking the shower. This is the gift. The space opens. Silver, pink, orange, magenta, hues of blue into yellow and gold melt into pure white light. Their watercolor rays enter the core shaft of light in our body. We become the most rooted of trees, spinning radiant strands of creation from heaven to earth and back again. We breathe deeply. The space becomes larger. We merge and no longer need to think of drinking. We are saturated. The wellspring is filled. We dip our chalice and drink. This nectar refreshes us. No longer is there a way to stop drinking, for we have become the chalice, the goblet, the Holy Grail.

The Principles

Here are the 27 Holy Grail Principles. Follow and remember them. They will carry you into complete union with the divine. God will take on a new meaning. You will live beyond concepts and beyond separation of your mind, body and spirit.

1. Be willing to move through the dark to reach the light.
2. Align the chakras to live in your power.
3. Keep your third eye and second chakra connected.
4. Bring gold (christed) energy into your body.
5. Clear your chakras to create inner space for your God power to live within.
6. Restore the connection in your navel to your soul's innate, original power.
7. Bridge your purified heart, soul and God to access your true power.
8. Reconnect the parts of your soul and keep them connected.
9. Honor the trinity of your inner mother-father-child representing the divine creative principle.
10. Integrate the divine feminine and masculine energies of your soul.
11. Ignite the power of God in your body by integrating the divine feminine and masculine.
12. Keep the core column of light in your spine (that connects your spiritual and physical energies) activated.
13. Maintain spiritual union with your emotional body—the bridge between the soul and physical body.
14. Surrender your mind to your soul.

15. Open the gateway to heaven by reconnecting the energies in the back of your head (medulla) with your third eye.
16. Reconnect your solar plexus and the center of the earth to bridge your divine masculine and feminine energies.
17. Honor your heart chakra center as the gateway into the divine.
18. Enjoy sex as a prayer of opening to God in your body.
19. Ignite the light of love in every cell of your body through sex.
20. Live in the center, where all of the bodies meet.
21. Create long-term health by sustaining vibrational balance in your body.
22. Care for your body as the temple of God.
23. Spirit is the nectar of God dwelling as nourishment for the body, heart and soul.
24. Purify your spiritual and physical bodies so the power of the divine is able to recharge your circuits.
25. Maintain the movement of energy in your bodies as the way to connect to divine consciousness.
26. Live in the center of the cell where stillness exists, connecting all of the bodies into oneness.
27. Live in your divine essence. Utilize it as a conscious link to help restore cultural, political and creative vibrance and integrity.

Chapter 23

Holy Grail Healing

"I simply believe that some part of the human Self is not subject to the laws of time and space."
~ Carl Jung

Mary the Mother first appeared next to me when I was working with my client, Sarah, many years ago. I heard a voice say to me, "Please step aside, I have something to show you." I took two steps to my right and Mary transmitted her energy through my body while *speaking* a spiritual language through my hands and third eye. In that moment, the ability to clear and remove the originating energy behind all healing issues—whether emotional, soul, causal or etheric—was heightened within me. Sarah received double the benefits of a normal session that day, and the psychic scars from two past abortions were healed.

A few years prior, Jesus would come into my evening meditations. I felt seen and listened to as I shared my desire to be fully healed and to also be able to fully help others heal. We had many discourses during this time. I had many questions needing to be answered that would later become the foundation for Holy Grail Healing. Three years later, while living on the North Fork of Long Island, Jesus downloaded the full philosophical system of Spirit Gateways.

Soon after, I was sent by spirit to live in Manhattan for four years of clearing, healing and aligning the energy fields of many creative, powerful and prominent New Yorkers. It was here that I witnessed the full magnitude of how, why and where in the body that darkness and light merged or split. Health, relationship, political and corporate solutions were discovered and healed on deep individual levels.

A dear friend of mine introduced me to a picture of Babaji. I already had a special and sacred connection to Paramhansa Yogananda when he appeared in my bedroom with a personal message two weeks after my second daughter was born many years earlier. To my total amazement, I realized that Babaji was the being who had been appearing in my meditations when I folded myself into a sitting lotus position—for over 15 years. This discovery led to my receptivity and my ability to open fully to his guidance and download healing and spiritual practices that are designed to awaken and sustain the new paradigm of light in the body, soul, spirit and on the planet.

Another client, Alex, and I began working together after he had already experienced two years of hopelessness and despair, while writing suicidal letters to his family. He could barely function and was constantly depressed. He was on three medications to keep him afloat and was told by psychiatrists about his incurable condition; it was described in confusing, difficult-to-understand terminology. Within three weeks of practicing the Holy Grail Energy Elixirs together and reconnecting the parts of his soul from which he had separated, Alex began experiencing a complete turnaround. Within three months, he was healed and fully functioning in the world again, to the joy and amazement of family and friends.

As I continue to recover and restore all the parts of my own divine feminine and masculine self, implement and integrate this light and power, Holy Grail Healing continues to unfold and assist those individuals ready for divine masculine-feminine union.

Holy Grail Healing: Definition

Holy Grail Healing reconnects, clears and aligns all of the bodies —emotional, physical, spiritual, emotional and mental. The soul is reconnected while the chakras and subtle bodies are cleared and aligned. All parts of the soul are reconnected and reunited into the true self. When this happens, a person experiences "ancient memory"—a spiritual identity rather than a fabricated identity.

As the heart and soul unite, physical and emotional healing begins. Clearing the chakras and the energy grid of embedded past experiences heals ancestral and karmic imprints. As memory of the true self increases, the beliefs it has about surviving in the physical world can be released, freeing the soul from genetic attitudes and illness. The mind is liberated when the soul reunites in the body and reconnects to the universal current of spirit, the omnipotent power of God.

Holy Grail Healing unites dark and light, the known and the unknown, the inner divine feminine and masculine, the higher self and lower self and soul and body. The essence of self comes alive in the center of spirit opening the feeling, sensing and knowing self to work in consort.

The Holy Grail is the ever-present consciousness of divine nectar that lives in the center of creation—the point of contact where spirit meets the body. Here the energies of soul that meet the body, both feminine and masculine live in union. The feminine and masculine energies transform darkness into light and raw creative power into expression.

Healing reunites us to the passion within our soul. When engaged with the body and heart, the soul ignites the sensual and joyous link to spirit. Without the connection to spirit, it is of the flesh alone. When we reunite all the bodies we are able to fully enter the worlds of God. Aligned in Source we become a manifestation of the power and light of the Holy Grail. This responsibility is the gateway into serving God and is a delicate balance between heaven and earth and knowing the Creator as a co-creator. The ability to do this comes from clearing the emotional and causal bodies, living in the oneness of soul and living as a giver and receiver within spirit. As we become one in spirit we live in the center of its currents, a pulsation of expanding and contracting energies that exists in all life. We are tested by the will of God to strengthen our ability to receive greater current. The more current we can hold the more empowered we are just by letting go. The power is the link between God and our self and here is where its right use steps in. The only way to God realization is by actively clearing and aligning our emotional, causal, physical and spiritual bodies. Drugs by-pass the clearing and take you into an induced connection to spirit. Food preservatives and junk foods block the currents in the physical body. Both alcohol and drugs separate the mental, emotional and physical body sheaths. If the lower bodies remain separated and disconnected, it becomes impossible for the completion of the soul's karma in the body. The patterns originally created by our soul's separation from mind and spirit will not be healed. When the soul-body connections are made through one's own effort instead of through an outside substance, the results last lifetimes instead of a few hours or days.

A split soul is unable to communicate and live as a sacred, whole being. A split soul lives in separation from its feminine and masculine energies. The mind is separate from the body, the body separate from the soul and the soul separate from spirit. This is the condition of our present world culture; it was also the condition during the time of Jesus, Mary Magdalene and Mary the Mother.

Aspects of our soul separate from the body or hide within it because they feel they do not exist or have the right to exist. We are shown by example to stomp out our true nature. Others want control; they encourage you to relinquish your power or reject your self because you are a threat to their existence. We are taught from birth to reject and leave our existence. We grow up believing that our whole, complete self is too much. Our souls reach complete union when we are reconnected to each aspect of our power. Our ideas, creative expressions and desires become the grounding rod into manifesting the existence of our God self. By abandoning and devaluing our own unique expressions and desires, we sabotage the power of our own existence. When we leave our center of existence, we abandon the Holy Grail. We leave our existence and become emotionally split by taking on our parents' emotions, feeling everyone else's emotions and stuffing our own. We control our emotions yet want everyone else to feel ours. Consequently, we become over emotional or cut off from our feeling self.

The emotional body is meant to be a bridge between the soul and the physical bodies. When it is denied its purpose, it becomes an empty hole that, unless filled, festers into a breeding ground for disease. The hole causes emotional pain that translates into physical and mental pain. The emotional body is developed through the energetic imbalance or balance of the solar plexus, navel, second chakra and perineum-tailbone-genital areas. When these centers are energetically connected and aligned, they allow for harmonious and continuous flow of the spiritual energies that feed and empower the body. This is our goal.

Holy Grail Healing reunites the feelings, vision, thoughts, purpose, movements and gifts of mind, body and soul. We begin living in a continual healing state. This state of existence bridges heart, spirit, soul and God. We know our self as a divine expression of our union. We live in the center of our existence that is grounded in the Creator. Our heart becomes the chamber door to knowing our self as divinely connected.

Holy Grail Healing Techniques originate from direct connection into Source. Rewiring our mind body connection into our true frequency where soul meets spirit opens us to our healing potential. Clearing the chakras of childhood wounds and ancestral projections give us back the connection to our real feelings. Energetic cords are released from the body as the clearing occurs, allowing for the progression of our spiritual development. True desires, gifts, soul mission, insights and empowerments emerge from the deepest self. The causal body, the opened memory body, reveals its joys and sorrows and gives us the opportunity to recreate our life based upon who we really are, instead of basing our life upon the hurts of the past. Then, by reconnecting the parts of our soul, we are able to remember the true essence living within.

How do we accomplish such healing? The third eye and higher centers that are directly connected to our higher, eternal self are opened, providing clear vision and insight to all parts of our psyche and soul. Through the powers of our higher mind—intention, will and focus—we can integrate through our own spiritual power the parts of our self that need to be reclaimed and healed to wholeness; the journey of self and God- realization may then begin. Living in this healing state helps us stay strong while walking the path to God. Our lives become direct expressions of our deepest personal and universal truths.

Holy Grail Healing restores direct connection to the kingdom of God within the body. The body as a temple houses the power of God. It also:

- Integrates the powers of the divine masculine and feminine.
- Reconnects the body, soul and psyche.
- Clears, aligns and integrates the five bodies (emotional, spiritual, etheric, mental and physical) of ancestral, hereditary and genetic patterns.
- Removes displaced energies.
- Returns the body to wholeness through healing separation.
- Opens the creative and spiritual channels to serve God.
- Builds the life force between the spiritual and physical bodies.
- Integrates love and power.

Holy Grail Healing Principles

Principle One: All of the chakras "see," "feel" and "hear" at very subtle levels. When the attention of your awakened self is placed inside the energy portal of each chakra, power is opened. The soul can see, hear and feel the spirit within matter through focused awareness. This process transforms the emotional and etheric energies, creating spiritual strength and clarity.

Its Misuse: The individual senses another person's unhealed feelings and controls them through one of his or her chakras. This is found in all relationships, ranging from marriage partners and mother-child trappings, to doctor/healer/patient relationships.

Principle Two: The power of the united mind and spirit opens the gateway to creating from the context of vision, integrity and evolutionary purpose.

Its Misuse: The mind over powers the consciousness of spirit, and illusion sets in. Political and religious leaders, teachers and others can have a glimpse of a higher power and hook their own mind matrix into it, losing all sense of true spiritual reality.

Principle Three: The hands give and receive divine life force. This empowers a healer to pull out disease-causing energies and restore balance and harmony through giving or channeling the divine life force ray.

Its Misuse: The information pulled out is taken on and misinterpreted by the healer, who then projects his or her own unhealed material onto the patient.

Principle Four: Once the spirit within is discovered, it must be aligned to the principle of oneness. The spirit of the self does not exist separately from the consciousness of the God Source—the union of masculine and feminine power.

Its Misuse: We think our visions, ideas and expressions are divinely guided, rather than recognizing them as imbalances of our spirit which may become expressions of personal dogma and fear.

Principle Five: We are meant to live in the center of the matrix of creation. We sit in the center of the lotus flower, within a snowflake, within the helix of a molecule. The atoms of matter are connected within us. We are the beginning and the end, complete unto our self. As the nucleus of the molecule, we are connected into divine origin. Our minds no longer can interfere with direct access to cosmic oneness. All of our actions come from love, even if they appear bold, intense and determined. We are linked into a central force, the control board governing the breath, our heartbeat and the roots of eternal existence. We truly own nothing, because we belong to the universe and are co-workers in making it the place of beauty we love and cherish. By living in the center of the nucleus, we are connected to all the energies of the universe, ignited and vibrant in our body.

Its Misuse: We claim we can make the best decision about a situation without the help of anyone else. We perceive our positions in the center of the universe as being more important than the people around us. We have lost the vision for freedom based upon collective joy; instead, we dump our dogmas on everyone around us. The Christ knew he was not better than anyone else. He had learned through the test of discrimination that the power of the Christ matrix was *non-ownership* of the word of God. Misuse of this principle creates destruction and breakdown both physically and mentally, and enslaves souls who do not know how to climb higher on their own.

Principle Six: Live in the center of your heart, where the known meets the unknown. Enter each moment as an opportunity for sacred union with the whole. Honor every person from this holiness, yet hold in your heart the truth of where each person has abandoned the love in their own hearts—to their true self—causing attachment to money, greed, dogma, anger, pain, etc. Honor their split, yet acknowledge them as whole. Give to life from the fulfillment received by living sacred oneness, whether it is financial, emotional or spiritual. Live from your highest place of perception and attainment. May your mind serve you as you live in the fulcrum point of duality, swinging neither too far right or left, up or down. Live in the center of creation, the heart of authentic power.

Its Misuse: You find yourself judging other's shortcomings, deciding on how others should live, and/or refusing to open to your own creative power. You keep your chakras working separately, and listen only to the voice within yourself that produces a feeling of security and control.

Preparation for the Holy Grail Healings

Before practicing the Holy Grail Healings, do the following exercise daily for one week:

Bring your focus and breath into your pubic bone and fill it with blue light. From inside your pubic bone, create the top loop of a figure eight in your second chakra. Then finish the formation of the figure eight by creating the lower loop in your tailbone. Repeat this 12 times. Send the energy deep into the earth, then return the energy through your feet into your lower belly and breathe.

Focus blue light into the core shaft of light inside the pubic bone. Pull it up into your belly and push it back down into your genitals. Continue to pull it up and push it down, creating a magnetic power.

Take it at your own pace as you push the blue light energy down into the earth's center, pull it up into your genitals and lower belly and then push it down back into the earth. Do this 12 times.

Holy Grail Healing #1
Soul's Existence

The existence we seek comes through food, fashion choices, friends and work. Security and survival run our lives.

There's another way to learn to feel, see and know the joy and love of our true existence: by entering our authentic light and reintegrating the parts of our self that live in the dark. Without transforming what is dormant into life force, our lives become projections of fear, death, sorrow and pain. We can find a greater existence through exchange with the powers of transformation, becoming expressions of the divine.

To find the light of healing, travel in your consciousness twenty feet above your head. Create a beam of pure white laser light, and shine it down into an elevator shaft corridor in your body. Shine it into the sides and to the bottom of the elevator shaft corridor. Look for the part of yourself that has felt as though she/he has never been allowed to exist. Shine the light gently onto her/him and view the side of her/his head and hair, as though you are behind a movie camera. Move your vision to the front until you can see where she/he is sitting or standing. Send a message that you want to make contact with her/him, then ask her/him what she/he needs you to know about her/him. Stay in dialogue and be sure to express that you are back for good and not going anywhere. Ask how you can be there for her/him and what she/he needs from you to trust you. Keep the connection as long as you can, then practice it everyday. Receiving the existence of this forgotten part reconnects you to your true nature.

Holy Grail Healing #2
Finding the Expression of Our Divine Nature

Within the union of our divine feminine and masculine selves exists a spring of energy that runs and motivates our soul. In your divine masculine self, you can and probably will find a master builder, or a hiding composer, a gardener or a being who empowers life. Inside your divine feminine may live a healing goddess of light, a life-giving energizer that births souls, writers, spirit interpreters or animal communicators. Get to know who you are.

Repeat the practice of focusing light from twenty feet above your head. Look to see an inner aspect of your male self, then female self who has not yet been allowed full expression. Find out who both are by asking them questions like, "What have you been doing all of this time?" or "What is it that you are here to give?" See what they're wearing, what they're doing and what they look like. Through your heart, feel their presence and be with it fully.

Another way to uncover your divine feminine and masculine selves is to enter an inward place. Visualize your self walking to an open meadow, forest or beach and setting a circle of stones large enough to build a fire in the middle. Sit by the circle and call forth an ancient female or male part of yourself. See him/her walking towards you and observe what he/she is wearing. When they arrive at the circle, ask him/her what message he/she has to give you, what his/her role has been throughout time and what he/she needs you to know about him/her. Introduce your divine masculine to your divine feminine. Invite them to ask how each can best support the other. Remain open to their responses and check with them everyday, encouraging them to listen to one another and receive each other's presence and energies.

Holy Grail Healing #3
Purifying the Emotional Body

The elements of fire, earth, water and air cleanse, build and strengthen the emotional body. By learning to move the elements through the emotional and physical bodies, the power to clear the etheric field is achieved. This helps to heighten the vibration of the body, preventing disease and uniting spirit in the body.

Air

Through the breath, the air element opens the emotional body. It brings life force into the body, removing impurities and rebuilding tired internal organs. The subtle bodies are connected through the air element. A couple of exercises:

1. Reawakening the Forgotten Sounds: Resonate the sound *ee* in the back of the skull. Focus a ray of light into the third eye resonating the sound of *hum*. Inwardly "sing" the sound *hi* into the heart. Send the sound *oo* through the core shaft of light inside the solar plexus, navel, pubic bone and up and around two inches above the tailbone. Resonate the sound *hum* up through your core column of light inside your spine. Inhale light into your entire body and on the exhale, fill your body with the sound of *hum*.

2. Breathe in essential oils such as eucalyptus, pine, cedarwood, geranium, rose, lemongrass, rosemary, vanilla, orange or bergamot to balance your mind and body.

Water

The water element clears old memories and stagnant energies, and harmonizes the electromagnetic fields in the body. It recharges the auric field by balancing the negative and positive ions. The water element creates a flowing movement, keeping the body and mind clear. It also activates the energies of regeneration.

1. Visualize a waterfall of beautiful colored flowing rays of light that wash over your body from above your head, through your body and into the earth.
2. Submerge your body in a bathtub filled with sea salts and essential oils such as rose, geranium, ylang-ylang and lavender.
3. Move to the internal rhythms of water flowing around and through you.

Fire

1. Stand in an open-stride position with feet positioned parallel.
2. Keep your knees over the center of your feet. Place your hands over your lower belly. Breathe in through your nose and pull the breath into your belly. Exhale the breath completely and say "HA." Repeat.

3. Stand in a parallel position, feet forward, with a distance of two wrists between your feet. Bring your arms in front of you, and crisscross them as fast as you can. After four repetitions, open them to the side. Rise onto the balls of your feet and say "HA." Emote the sound deeply from the base of your belly. Repeat.
4. Stand in a parallel position with your knees gently bent or sit in a meditative position. Send your focus into the molten fire at the center of the earth. Pull light from the center of the earth, up through your legs, under and through your tailbone to right above your pubic bone. Begin to draw up the energies. Pull them like taffy from your pubic bone into your navel area, then push them back to your tailbone. Draw them up again, visualizing them as flames of fire. Let the flames grow in size and power. Throw any emotions, difficulties or worries into these flames, and let them burn. These flames purify and clear the emotional body.

Earth

1. Stand with parallel feet, two fists apart. With gently bent knees, pull energy up from the earth and pull it through all of your chakras with your hands and arms including the top of your head. Open your arms to the side and push and clear energy down into the earth with your hands. Inhale your breath as you pull the energy up through your body and exhale your breath as you push the energies down into the earth. Repeat.
2. Sit in a meditative position and breathe into your belly two or three times. Bring your focus into your tailbone. As you inhale, bring the breath up the left side of the spine, drawing it into your third eye. On the exhale, send the breath down the right side of your spine back into the base of your spine. Take three breaths into the base of your spine, exhaling out your mouth.
3. Breathe into the center of your palms. This is the center of an inner sanctuary uniting your heart and the earth. Press your thumb into the center of your palm. Relax.

Holy Grail Healing #4
Chakra Clearing

1. Bring your attention ten to twenty feet above your head. Create a beam of light and shine it down into an open elevator shaft within you. Look to the base of the elevator shaft corridor and look to see whose energies are apparent in your first chakra—your mother, ex-boyfriend, employer and so on. Bring in blue light and spin the light clockwise, gently unhooking their energy. As you unhook each person's energy, send it back to the core self within the person's inner shaft of light. Send the person's energy down through her/his body into the earth and connect her/him to the light above her/his head. Go through each chakra center and repeat.
2. Bring in white light from the top of your head and send it in to your third eye. Send it down in to your heart chakra and loop the light through your upper chest, up and around back into your third eye. Repeat.
3. Place your attention in your third eye and create a loop of clear white light out from the body and down into the spot directly above your pubic bone. Bring the light up inside your spine, through the center of your neck, through the back of your skull and diagonally through your head into your third eye.

4. Stand with feet parallel, a hip's width apart. Let your knees be soft and relaxed. Crisscross your wrists over your pubic bone. Breathe into your first chakra and exhale as you open your arms to either side. Breathe in and crisscross your wrists over your navel, opening your arms to the side while exhaling. Repeat the crisscross and inhalation-exhalation breath up through your solar plexus, heart center, throat chakra, third eye and crown chakra and above your head, clearing the chakra centers above your head. When complete, open your arms to the side, bringing them down by your side. Repeat the sequence three or four times.

Holy Grail Healing #5
Connecting the Etheric and Physical Bodies

The etheric body holds the imprint of the emotional, causal (memory) body, spiritual and physical body. Seeds of every plant have a protective covering. Our protective covering is the etheric body; when aligned to the elements of nature, it moves harmoniously with the universe. As the etheric body expands, it can receive greater spiritual current. Energy is the language of the etheric body. When it is clear, we experience vibrant health, focused intention and spiritual openness. Sacred geometry mirrors the alignment found in the universe. Our divine self contains within it a sacred geometry uniting all of the bodies.

1. The diamond is the symbol of the soul's completion. Place your attention in your third eye and shoot a ray of light diagonally down in front of your heart center. Send a ray of light into your solar plexus and into the center of your spine. Send a ray of light diagonally behind your heart center and complete the diamond by sending a ray from behind your heart center up into your third eye. Project rays of color through the diamond design. Repeat.

2. Place your attention in your solar plexus and send two rays of light down your legs into the earth. Visually connect them to a point in the center of the earth, creating a diamond. From the center of the earth, spiral the light in a clockwise direction. Rapidly move it through the center of your body and into your third eye. Let the light open the window of your third eye.

3. From 20 feet above your head, look down into your body and see a grid. Look for any black spots and move them into the center of your spine. Observe their dissolution within the open space in the central column of light. Spin the spiral from your

third eye down the central core column counterclockwise, deeply through your lower belly, into the center of the earth.

4. To rebuild and maintain the strength of your etheric body, place your focus in your heart. While staying connected in your heart, shift your attention 20 feet outside of your body. From the outside in, visualize one color after the next beginning with bronze, silver and copper. Keep asking what colors you should use to build your etheric shield until you reach gold in the center of your heart: yellow, green, blues, red, orange, aqua, turquoise, white, lavender, light lemon, light pink. Breathe gold into your heart and spread pink around it. Feel the sheath of color around your body while weaving a new sheath in your heart by spinning these multiple colored threads into a tapestry around you.

Holy Grail Healing #6
Integration

Anxiety attacks, depression, rages, lifelessness, sexual difficulties, sadness and procrastination are caused by separation between soul, spirit and the body. Integrating the bodies aligns the powers of the divine masculine-feminine. You will feel stronger, more confident, grounded and focused.

1. Bring your focus into your solar plexus chakra. Feel yourself sitting in your solar plexus. Now look up through the elevator shaft corridor through the top of your crown chakra and watch golden white light pour down upon you while you sit in your solar plexus.

2. Breathe light into your solar plexus. Focus your energy into your lower belly, solar plexus, heart and third eye at the same time. Breathe into all four points at the same time. Close your eyes and see them linked up. Take a moment during the day to visually align them.

3. Create a figure eight from your navel down the front of your body, through your pubic bone, under your genitals, around and up under your tailbone, diagonally through your solar plexus and heart center, into your upper back and diagonally down into your solar plexus. Repeat. Bring the upper loop of the figure eight into your throat chakra three times, then up into your third eye three times, still going through the solar plexus. Repeat.

4. Close your eyes and envision, through your third eye, a scene with someone you know or a situation in which you are involved. While remaining connected in your third eye, connect your focus into your navel and in your first chakra (perineum and up inside the tail bone). View from the integration of all three points of power and ask for the highest healing for this situation.

Holy Grail Healing #7
Removing Emotional Wounds

1. From 20 feet above your head, create a laser beam of love and shine it down into the elevator shaft corridor inside your body. Shine the light to the bottom of the corridor and look for the part of yourself that was violated, disrespected or abused. Ask him/her to show him/her self to you and look to see how old he or she is. Trust you are viewing a part of yourself that was given the message that he/she could not exist, and was completely abandoned. Give your love to this part and invite him/her to enter all parts of your body. Ask him/her where in your body he/she wants to live. Invite him/her to take up as much room as he/she wants.

2. Sit in quiet solitude and breathe into your belly. Move your breath up the center of the column through your spine to your third eye. Move your breath down to your heart center, then up to your third eye. Repeat several times. Now, breathe into the energy around your entire body, expanding it all around you. On the exhalation, push out all of the negative emotional charge, closing all the pores of your skin. Repeat. Then, pull the energy up from inside your pubic bone and behind the tailbone through your spine, heart and throat center into your third eye. Feel the light in your third eye and move any old emotional wounding up to your third eye. Unleash the light and love within your heart and direct it to this wound, then send the light down through your body to the divine Mother of all Life within the center of the earth.

Holy Grail Healing #8
Restoring God Flow in the Body

Most of us are disconnected from God flow in our body at birth or shortly thereafter because of energies pulling at us to exist for a parent;

we were not given permission to live for our self. We end up outside of our God connection and praying to it, rather than living within it and receiving the karmic trials and gifts of our own existence.

1. Breathe into your navel area and pull in light. Move the light diagonally up the back of your heart center and behind your skull, over your head, down through your throat and heart centers and back into your navel area. Send the energy down the back of your legs and pull it up through your feet, ankles, knees, up through your genitals and back, and into the center of the column of light inside your navel area. Repeat.
2. Reverse the figure eight and move the energy from the navel center two or three inches behind the navel, up through your heart center and third eye, down the back of your skull, through your middle back and into your womb or pelvis, down the front of your legs, deep into the earth through your feet and up through your feet, into your tailbone. Complete this loop of energy in the area of your navel.
3. Travel 20 to 30 feet above your head into pure white light. Create a beam of light, a laser light beam of love, and shine it down into the elevator shaft corridor inside your body. Look for the part of yourself that is silent. Offer to listen to this part of yourself and keep shining the light on her/him. See her/him come alive from your beam of love. Listen to her/him by feeling and seeing the light and love either evident or hiding beneath a dark shadow. Bring her/him into your pelvis, sexual organs, navel and heart center, and invite her/him to spread out through your arms and into your body. Feel the currents of energy consciousness move through you, and sense the expansion of consciousness into the moment.

Holy Grail Healing #9
Color Healing

Blue

The blue ray clears ancestral and karmic cording. Blue brings the peace that pours through the body after family attachments and relationship entanglements are lifted. Focus blue light into the interior of the navel. Spiral it deep inside the navel and move it outwards in a cone shape. Allow the movement of the spiral to relax and center you as it circles wider. Pull blue into the core of your spine. It will heal your parasympathetic and sympathetic nervous systems. Hold the blue spiral within the space of your navel and your spine. Visually place your self into a sturdy and powerful tree. Send your blue light deeply through your pelvis, through your feet into the earth and back up through your heart. The power focused in the tree is the strength of your will.

Yellow

Yellow activates your will to merge with your divine purpose. Its shining light activates the sun within your body. Shift your emotional focus into your will and realign to the core universal consciousness within you. Yellow builds the etheric sheath of your soul, the expression of your will.

Visualize yellow pouring into your solar plexus and open to it, flooding your body in its light.

Red

Invite red, the life force, to move up from the earth through your thighs and into your genitals. Feel its fire of warmth and energy move through your blood and travel into your heart. When the fire is strong in your belly, it can feed your heart and bring health, vitality and clarity. Pull red from the earth as a triangle. The point is on top, in your solar plexus; stretching down are two red rays of power.

From above your head, draw down two rays of blue light so that they meet at a point below the red triangle. When the blue "V" and the upside down red "V" are placed one upon another they create a diamond. Breathe into this diamond shape and merge the red and blue into a purple diamond that fills your body.

Purple

Purple awakens the presence of your true self. Merging gold and purple integrates etheric and spiritual energies. Allow purple to fill your third eye, then connect it into your belly. Hold the connection. Allow it to fill you. Visualize a gold column of light stretching through the center of your spine. Breathe purple light into the golden column.

Green

Green resonates with the ray of the heart that integrates body and soul. Health in the body is created and maintained by green. The molecular levels resonate to green and stay in their natural spin. Visualize three spiral rings moving up through your pelvis to your solar plexus. Channel green up into the heart and into the higher centers—the throat chakra, back of the skull, third eye and crown chakra. Stand in the center of the spirals and feel them spiral around you with momentum. Have them spin faster so other rays of color are felt or seen. Your physical body is balanced to its original rhythm and molecular speed, creating vitality.

Orange

The power of awakened God force lives in orange. When united in spirit, the higher self emanates orange. The second chakra must be cleared and opened for the physical currents to transcend into spirit. Breathe orange into the soles of your feet, genitals and navel; draw the color four feet from above your head. Feel a shaft of orange light ignite these power spots and expand the awareness to the sides of your body, under your feet and up through your heart into your arms and hands. Breathe orange light into your palms.

Holy Grail Healing #10
Living In the Center

The emotional, etheric, spiritual, causal and physical bodies connect into the center of consciousness. Here the seed of consciousness unites the body, mind and soul. When we reside in the center of the nucleus, we live in the heart of God energy. Our mind, spirit and heart are linked and driven by this force that sustains all life. Our awareness enters a state of no-separation. We are alive in the center of our DNA, the link between life force and God force.

1. Bring your focus into your navel. Chant twice: *ah hay hu ay ya hey ah hey.* Then chant another two times: *Hey hey hu ay ah hey ya hay.*

   Pull energy up from the earth with your palms facing upwards. Move the energy through the center shaft of light in your body and through your crown chakra. Keeping your hands slightly cupped, circle the energy through your pubic bone and repeat the cycle. Continue to chant as you create a sphere of light in front of your lower belly. Move your palms down towards the earth and with palms facing up as you move the energy into your navel, keeping the circle moving.

2. Activating the Chakra Current: While standing, isolate the lower back by breathing into it. Reach your tailbone down and begin undulating your tailbone back and then forward while reaching the whole spine upwards. With palms facing upwards and elbows close to the body, begin to create a figure eight towards the body first, with both hands at the same time. Keep

the figure eight moving with your hands, lower arm and elbows moving in sync while within your pelvis is a current of light that undulates through all of your chakras, to then return back down to under the tailbone. Repeat 12 times.

Holy Grail Healing #11
Healing Birth Issues

It is common to feel suffocated in relationship, to reject intimacy and push away love because the energies in our mother's uterus before and during birth were energetically repressive. While growing up, we were not honored for who we are, nor were we given free rein to live based on our own energies. We attach ourselves to the dark and unconscious energies of another and remain stuck. By opening the navel energies and connecting them into the spiritual currents of our body, we are able to heal our pain.

1. Pull gold light up from the center of the earth into the navel and spin the gold light clockwise. Hook the gold light into the anger, darkness, despair and other dark emotions, and pull all of these emotions out. Send them deep into the earth. Focus light into your third eye and navel simultaneously. Place your left third finger on your third eye and your right third finger in your navel. Hold and breathe. Repeat 12 times.

2. Create a figure eight of gold light that moves up from the center of the earth, through the pubic bone, up through the center of the spine, through the back of the skull, through the third eye, through the tailbone and deep into the center of the earth. Repeat 12 times.

Chapter 24

When the Bodies Unite

"When you lose yourself, you find the Beloved.
There is no other secret.
I don't know any more than this."
~ Ansari of Heart

Just as the planets orbit around the sun, and the moon revolves around the earth, the energies in our body rotate around a central axis. The energies of the soul, emotions and physical life forces flow in currents of light to create vortexes of power in the body. The pivot point where all the bodies meet—physical, etheric, emotional, mind and soul—connects into the center of our consciousness, the Holy Grail.

Our consciousness interprets the forces of life through these elements. If the mind, psyche and spirit are out of balance, they become conflicted and cast the soul from its state of divine union. As the soul leaves its connection to Source, it enters survival mode and relinquishes the joy of living in union. In the soul's all-consuming quest for survival, it leaves behind aspects of self that have no place to live within the body. The more soul aspects that are forgotten, abandoned or betrayed, the more a person lives in the mind and experiences feelings of alienation and separation from life; or a person becomes attached to his/her viewpoints while ignoring or disparaging those of others. The physical body's internal space decreases, cutting off the flow of spirit within. Dogmas, religions, political extremism, misuse of sex and mind-emotional imbalances are created through such misalignment of the body, soul and spirit. This misalignment causes the mind to become fixated on possessions, knowledge, people or territory it does not possess. As spirit is opened in the body and the subtle bodies are cleared and aligned to the vibration of God energy, these potentially damaging illusions held in the soul are released.

The higher states of God connection can only be experienced when the emotional body is cleared, making it possible for all energy and spiritual levels to unite in the body. When our emotional body is cleared, we know the state of love—whether towards a partner, our self or every soul in which we come into contact. Love reconnects, clears and aligns all of the bodies. Love is the power that is revealed as we open to our spiritual force. We become impassioned to live this love and express it in every facet of our life.

There are masters of light on the higher planes who are always ready to meet us in love. As we extend our love to them and offer our love as a way to meet them, we are received. Love opens all higher spiritual doors.

The secrets of the universe are conveyed into our being through streams of love and light. Our hearts are conduits for the sensations and realizations of our connection into love. As spring breezes sing through the leaves and branches of trees, we are also connected to the softness and strength of life force.

Sexuality is a force of power capable of fully regenerating our body. When these currents fully express through our body, we can absorb cosmic energies and life prana, elemental essences, and unify heaven and earth within. When our sexual energy becomes transmuted healing energy and life force, we can soar into the gateways of God. By keeping our body open to these life-giving currents we are able to integrate the power and love of the divine feminine.

When we practice moving the cosmic currents in the body through the exercises of Babaji (chapter 21) or deep meditation, we open the portals into the deeper chakras. As the nuclei of the chakras are ignited, the body is illuminated in light.

Never is this more physically evident than during divine lovemaking. When we have a full body orgasm, we are experiencing the cosmic current flowing throughout our entire body. Men speak of full-body orgasms as profound release and union with the universe.

Some men experience the height and sensation throughout their bodies that, for them, surpasses a genital orgasm.

Women describe intense full-body orgasms as portals to dimensions of color, power, energy waves, music, light and oneness with the divine. Both men and women who open to God forces during lovemaking feel opened in their emotional and etheric bodies. The divine current of love that is interchanged awakens union between our higher and lower selves.

By absorbing this deep level of love into our body, heart and soul, we are touched by the inner essence of our existence. Its power and light bridges us into the love of God. Once we align to the highest ray of God in our body, we know the center of creation.

Living in this state of union inspires the creative process. When used to explore the hidden and unknown parts of our self, creativity becomes a gateway into living in the center of our self. Along the way, we move through the healing of our karma by reuniting the pure essence of our chakra centers with our highest rays of light consciousness. When we practice conscious connection in this manner, we live in a state of constant healing, regeneration and creative expansion. Writing, dancing, singing, sculpting, painting, filmmaking, photography, composing, cooking, healing, pottery, woodworking, and other creative pursuits contain the power and potential to become expressions of divine union. God power, when generated through creative action, unites our cosmic and soul forces and helps us enter into an eternal, indestructible state of consciousness.

Living each moment in the union of the creative and the divine joins our body and soul. Indigenous cultures are pure examples of this power. Their sense of play and vitality enables them to maintain a degree of alertness and sacred connection that is essential in the matters of life and death that define their daily lives—hunting, gathering, finding and building dwelling places, dealing with forces of nature. When our physical bodies resonate in these higher octaves, our inner sight, hearing and feeling nature becomes more pronounced and clear.

The following daily practices maintain the bodies in a state of divine union:

Divine Nourishment

Begin by breathing into your tailbone. Widen the core shaft of light with your breath. Bring your focus into this expansion. Move the breath from your tailbone into the back of your skull (medulla). Create two rays of light inside your skull and crisscross them through your chakras within the core shaft of light all the way down into the center of the earth. Pull the currents back up through your feet, feeling the currents as nourishment and as rays of life force while you crisscross them through all of the chakras into the third eye. Allow the rays to spill over into a waterfall over the top of the head into the area under your ribcage on both sides. Bring the currents up the center core shaft of light to the third eye and let it spill over again, pouring energy into the stomach (on the left side) and the liver (on the right side) under the ribs. Repeat the circuit 12 times. Bring the energy into a gold spiral within your solar plexus, and have it become larger and larger as it fills the core shaft of light in your body. Move it simultaneously into the earth, through your heart, and into your third eye. Become the center of the spiral.

Expansion of the Divine Feminine

Begin by breathing blue light into the navel. Bring in gold light and any other color(s) your navel area desires. Transmit light through your navel point into your spine. Move the light with your breath all the way into your throat center. Allow the color to change in your throat center and spin it, first counterclockwise and then clockwise. Send a ray of light through the core shaft of light into the pubic bone. Inhale a ray of blue light from the center of the earth into your pubic bone and up to your throat center with your breath. During your exhale, send the blue ray down into your pubic bone. With this blue ray, begin a circuit from the pubic bone through the core shaft of light into the third eye, into the crown chakra and then back down the core shaft of light to the pubic bone.

Place your focus inside the core shaft of light in the pubic bone and tailbone area. Fill the shaft all the way up through the center of your head with pure white light. The pubic bone area in the core shaft will be your grounding point. Allow the feeling of warmth and expansion to move into your entire belly. Allow your mind to move all the way down to the base of the core shaft of light.

From 10 to 20 feet above your head, send a beam of pure white light into the elevator shaft corridor in your spine and look for the part of your feminine self that has been trapped inside the base of the shaft. Dialogue with her. Hold her close. Hear her words and speak to her with love. When it feels right, invite her to walk with you into the core shaft of light. Share with her that she is safe, tell her you will protect her. Bring her into your heart and solar plexus. Honor what you feel and see. Honor the healing that occurs.

Cosmic Journey

Begin by breathing blue light into your lower belly. Inhale and bring blue light into your collarbone. Fill your whole upper shoulder area in light while exhaling. Repeat three times.

Create two strands of white light from your pubic bone area and loop them through the chakras. Inhale and arc the strands to either side. On your exhale, crisscross them through each chakra, slowly and deliberately. Go through each power center from the tailbone up through the second chakra, navel, solar plexus, heart, throat and third eye. Repeat the crisscrossing a few times in the third eye. Let the energy flow up through your crown chakra and flow down the sides of your body. Repeat 12 times. Then, create three strands of color on either side of your starting point deep in the first chakra, under the tailbone. Repeat the crisscrossing pattern with the three strands of color this time through the central core shaft of each power center, again bringing it through the third eye and crisscrossing a few times before moving it through the crown chakra and beneath the tailbone. Now, repeat the crisscrossing circuit through the chakras with 6 rays of gold light on each side, looping them through all of the chakras. When you arrive at the third eye, loop the golden energy nine times through the third eye, then bring the light upwards through the crown chakra, spilling it over and back down to the tailbone-pubic bone area. Once the rays of gold light have completed the circuit, unite the white, colored and gold strands together. Repeat the circuit until it is flowing like a swift river of light.

Speaking Truth

1. Bring blue light into the throat center and spiral it clockwise. Add silver, white and gold light into the spiral.
2. Send two rays of light deep into the center of the earth.
3. Spin a spiral of light within the center of the earth.
4. Loop the spiral around the earth, wrapping the earth with light.
5. Imagine the earth spinning on its perfect axis.
6. Move the rays of light up from the earth, into your navel.
7. Bring in a spiral of spinning light. Move it through the central core shaft to the back of the skull and to the third eye.
8. Send the light back down deep into the earth and spiral it inside the earth. Bring it back up through your feet, pelvis, solar plexus, center of the sternum and into your heart center.
9. Gently spiral the light clockwise in your heart center. Ask your heart center what color(s) it wants in order to unite all of your bodies.

10. Invite the ray(s) of color into the spiral, filling your heart center with its colors.
11. Feel your heart center.

Expanding into Stars

Bring your focus into the center of the earth. Create a spiral of gold light within the center of the earth and bring it up through your feet, legs and behind your tailbone. Slowly bring the spiral up through the core shaft in the center of your spine and touch a galaxy of stars within the shaft as you move up the shaft through your second chakra, navel, solar plexus, throat center, back of the skull, third eye and crown chakra. As the spiral touches your crown chakra, allow it to flow around your body (visualize it as gold glitter), then return it to the center of the earth. As the spiral comes up again, expand the space inside the core shaft to make more room for the stars to grow larger. Repeat this movement and push the sides of the wall to make more room for the stars to become larger. As the stars grow larger and take up more of the core shaft of light, merge the spiral and the stars. Become the expansion and space in your heart center.

Chapter 25

Holy Grail Emerging

Sent from the Power,
I have come
To those who reflect upon me,
And I have found
Among those who seek me.
Look upon me,
you who meditate,
and hearers, hear.
Whoever is waiting for me,
Take me into yourselves.
Do not drive me out of your eyes,
or out of your voice, or out of your ears.
Observe. Do not forget who I am.
~ "The Thunder: Perfect Mind," *Gnostic Gospel*

You are God's perfect creation; therefore, your only true safety zone lies in the strength of your alignment with God. No matter how hard you try to be someone other than your true self, you are always brought back to the recognition of this timeless truth. The way you think about yourself either disconnects you or honors your origin. Your true knowledge of self comes from acknowledging your alignment to Source; within this connection, you are divinely guided. Remaining steadfast to knowing your self each moment in union with Source grounds the unpredictable shortcomings of life into powerful mirrors of self-mastery.

I am the love living through me.
I am one in all-embracing light.
Remind one another of who you are.
Immerse yourself in the remembrance of this light
As God lives through you and as you.

Remember who you are every day. Make each day a practice of connecting into Source. Then you will know why you are here. Allow each day to activate the physical and emotional expressions of your soul. Make use of the night's internal protection of soul and dream traveling, and of being in spirit, to go beyond self-constructed beliefs and into your greater balance and truth. Become aware of the difference between your own dreamtime projections and light-inspired vision. What you think may be real in a dream may instead be the parts of your self expressing a viewpoint or feeling. The purpose of this latter type of dream is to make you question and find the part of yourself that you have given away or have not yet found. If you seek completion through others to fulfill your own disempowerment and soul separations, know that the ideas, beliefs, feelings and karma emerging in your dreams are areas being worked out. Follow your dreams' stories to help you take responsibility for the areas you need to "own." Before going to sleep, connect to Source by focusing on God's light and love. Ask your higher self to hold the connection for you to contact other progressing souls and spiritual teachers on the inner planes during dreamtime. Release burdens, resentments and fears to Source as you go to sleep. Ask to be placed in the light and healed of any corruptions or disharmonies in your energy bodies, soul and heart.

Before sleep, practice the following figure eight exercise: Pull a current of energy from under your tailbone to your solar plexus, through the back of your skull, crown chakra and into your heart chakra. Hold it in your heart chakra. Bring it down through your solar plexus, down into your tailbone and move the current back up through the core shaft of light through your genitals, through the center of your spine and straight up to your third eye. Hold the focus in your third eye. Beginning a circuit, move the current from your third eye into your heart chakra then back up to your third eye into your heart. Move your thinking patterns completely into the circuit of light. Circulate the love from your heart into your third eye and back into your heart. Absorb the love and drift off to sleep.

In the morning, greet God as soon as you open your eyes. Offer your humility and gratitude as a gift. Come into your self and give thanks for a new day. Connect your focus into your belly, heart and third eye.

By maintaining your connection to all of your chakras, it is easier to live in the world as one heart and one mind. Conflicts between parts of your self resolve as your power centers connect with light. Your etheric body becomes the protector of your heart center and energetically uplifts the burdens of the physical and mental body. A strong etheric body feeds the physical body with spiritual energy and light. Your etheric body will speak to you in a language of music, words, movement and color. It is through your heart center that your etheric, emotional and mental bodies integrate. Creativity flows with the universal design when we are integrated. We also restore a serious transgression that occurred to most of us when we were children—becoming separated from living in spirit due to peer, social, religious or family pressures, or other outer circumstances. To the soul, being taken out of our inner world of spirit and creative power feels like spiritual death. The grief and pain of this separation is healed when we return to the power of our spiritual connection. Only then can we live each day in the blessing of who we are. Once we enter into spirit and open the chalice within our bodies, we are able to fully find peace.

Expression of the Holy Grail

The Renaissance was a window of light through a time of repression and denial. Considered to be a time of creative, scientific and cultural exploration, the Renaissance was a bridge from the past to the future. Similar in many ways to our present culture, outer religious structures and political powers focused the attention on our ego selves, creating a split between our mind and body. A hearty few visionaries rose above this oppression and produced masterful, inspiring works—most notably Da Vinci, Michelangelo, Raphael and the Venetian painters.

Who is the master: the spirit or the mind? As the Renaissance visionaries, artists, artisans and principal financiers—Florence's de Medici family—clearly understood, souls require the nourishment found in the creative act. Throughout time, the energy of the Holy Grail has been expressed through the arts and sciences, much like the energy of a spiritual master has been transmitted through his or her eyes in photographs and drawings. A new renaissance will emerge as science and spirit meet once again, for our actual way of thinking will have changed as our higher centers of the brain become connected to the spiritual portals in our body. The renaissance of the mind will happen after we experience the dark becoming darker, and when the light of God opens our ability to see the cosmic forces and internal universes within. The ensuing creative power will extinguish dogma and belief systems that deny direct connection with God.

We all have within us creative power that becomes activated by the feelings and thoughts of our true self. We must go beyond the dead zone of numbing our creative drive and power. We have become a culture of idolizing the few who are not numb while our spirit and body further separate. The fear of wholeness is stronger than living in separation. When we recognize that music, art, the written word, the integration of our emotional, psychic, spiritual and physical selves and the soul journey of our lives must be honored, we have chosen the path of the Holy Grail. The Holy Grail emerges through the interaction of our creative, spiritual and sexual power.

This is the new Renaissance of the 21st century. We are all beginners on this journey. We all must find the courage and faith to face our own inner walls. As soon as currents of spiritual power flow through our body, the walls that separate our mind and body will collapse. It takes courage to face the pain within our stuck emotional bodies, but we must. Begin by recognizing how your self-love is limited, and remove or alleviate those limitations. For example, our corporate structures, energetically held childhood traumas and self-imposed limitations have warped our sense of self-love.

We need to learn how to backtrack a feeling to its original moment of conception. We may think we are out of love with someone, unable to heal, buried beneath our inner walls or afraid to rely upon someone else. The disappointments of our past create fear of real intimacy. When we fully surrender in our body, heart and soul to loving another person, we experience the beginning of living in God.

By living in the energetic flows of God as it pulsates through our hearts and souls, we learn to live in the Holy Grail. In this time of renaissance, we will each be given situations that will make us want to run, leave behind, escape or deny the challenges being given to us. They may feel impossible and life threatening. How we normally survive in our minds will be challenged. What we think needs to happen in a situation will not be the doorway to freedom. We will feel afraid and not know it. We will think we know what is right for us, but it will be the wrong solution. We may even be willing to break our own heart, as well as another's. Our fear, disguised as power, will misguide us.

However, our integrated selves will lead us to a new connection with life that feeds us. Everything else will feel like it is falling away.

We will want to grasp onto the moments in our life when we felt secure. They worked in the past, but not now. We will experience situations that will stimulate our deepest wounds, and it will be this stimulation that forces them to heal. We will go through physical challenges that confront us to face our weakest link—whether they be health matters, an emotional or mental box that must break open, or job stresses that force us to integrate our powers of love, acceptance and integration of all of our parts. Our souls will demand to attain this balanced state of being. No longer will an employer, employee, client, parent, child, lover or friend be able to feed our old self-constructed belief that we can only be spiritual or creative under certain circumstances. The days are over when their self-limiting images severely impact us. No longer will we feel the desperate need to repress, control or destroy our creative power in order to get through a day, month, year or lifetime. We are about to embark upon a new era of living in creative power.

The artist of life needs to be called a *creator with life.* As creators, we work with the forces of spirit that sustain and allow for the evolvement of our interactions and relationship with life. By coming to know these forces, we are able to create life expressions that touch and transform the people and circumstances around us, whether people are caring for another, healing another, finding new uplifting business solutions, writing screenplays or novels, rendering paintings or graphic designs, developing educational programs, finding political solutions, or composing songs, musicals or symphonies.

We must break down the walls from one part of our self to the next until we are whole. This is the work. As the walls crumble we find our deeper voice and truth. First, each room of our self must be cleared of the beliefs, residues and wounds of the past. After reconnecting your soul, heart and body with the highest light of self, you can successfully fill the room with the exact qualities, expressions and energies you and your soul most desire. Go through every room of your temple (house) and create what you want in each room. Create a communication system of love, acceptance and non-judgment between the parts of your self that seek recognition. Trust that as you come out of your illusions, you will have the opportunity to master everyday challenges, stresses and problems that currently bombard you, take you off center and exhaust you.

It is time to get out your paint brushes, crayons, pastels, mini tape-recorder, dancing skirts and pants, drums, flutes, empty notebooks and music composition paper and get to work/play. Take this joy and cherish it. Protect it and watch it grow.

Creators of the Holy Grail sing, write, compose, dance, envision, film, integrate, listen, evaluate, birth, feed and nurture the world through the power pouring through them from living in the center where Source meets the heart, body and soul. The rebirth during the Renaissance was the co-creative adventure of soul meeting spirit and its expression through the arts. The science of the universe, its law and forces in union with divine creation, guided the artist. "A man who has both science and art also has religion," Goethe wrote. Art was meant to be, and remains, the expression of God and soul in union. It is through reconnection with the divine feminine that art surpasses the limits of the human mind. "The eternal feminine draws us upwards," Goethe added.

The union of spirit in the body is the highest state one can reach while in a physical body. Becoming one with the vibrations, hues, feelings, movements and voice of spirit while meeting the Divine transforms artistic expression into a rite of spiritual opening and renewal. It takes dedication and focus to live in the center of the bull's eye. As innovative Russian ballet dancer Anna Pavlova said: "To follow, without halt, one aim: There is the secret of success."

When we love beyond our personal fears and projections, we enter the realm of the Divine. These fears and projections include having our love used or stolen, being abandoned, being lied to and not meeting the needs of the other person involved. We make use of anger as a mirror to heal our own lack of self-love. Suddenly, we find the part of our soul that needs to be filled, and we stop projecting our needs onto our lover. We no longer feel the need to leave our self because we want to be loved so much. When both partners in a relationship return to their centers and love themselves, then the act of loving one another becomes effortless. We begin to feel and honor the needs of the beloved and can express and communicate our feelings—not as ways to control and manipulate, but as actions of unconditional love. It is not until we embrace and love all parts of our self that that we can truly love another. Our powers of healing, vision and expression blossom as our soul becomes integrated.

To restore the original Holy Grail initiative of utilizing our social, educational, corporate and political systems to serve peace and light, rather than darkness and war, we must each first integrate the opposing forces of our spiritual and physical bodies. The positive forces within our spiritual bodies naturally want to resonate with beauty, truth, light, sound, nature and the higher centers of the brain. The negative forces within our physical body want us to abandon our self for God or another, maintain separation between good and evil and devalue the human spirit. The counterpoint of this duality is to align our physical and spiritual energies with the forces of creation: energy, color, sound, the five elements, imagination, inspiration, clairvoyance and intuition.

The container within our physical body becomes the balancing force that heals and integrates darkness and light.

The Holy Grail can emerge through trusting the power of sacred inner language. Language is created when the brain integrates the senses with spirit. When we listen, see and sense with our whole body, the unknown merges with the known. For our souls to touch God, we can no longer remain quiet; we must speak our truth, sing, write, speak, chant, dance and draw out our heart's power. Touching the etheric with our words, visual expressions and movements quicken and enlighten our soul's expression. The etheric realm activates the qualities of our divine feminine and masculine energies. Here, in the meeting space of these divine energies, dwells our creative sustenance, the generator of life force. By integrating the life force within our sexual, creative and divine spiritual energies, we arrive at the doorway to the temple of the Holy Grail.

When we enter, the Grail awaits to initiate the union of our body and soul in spirit.

Part VIII

Becoming the Holy Grail

Chapter 26

The Grail In Our Daily Life

"What do I have to do to get you to admit who is speaking?
Admit it and change everything!"
~ Rumi

I open my eyes to the fragrances of the day. I breathe in the colors all around me. Wild roses, lavender, oatstraw, buttercups, bleeding heart, morning glories and honeysuckle open their petals filled with dew. Wings fly by my blushing cheeks as I run my fingers through my hair.

When I close my eyes, I quiet my mind and feel a sense of peace infusing my body, for essence surrounds me. Two hawks, a bluebird, yellow finch and crow rest in communion. I sit with them. They are aware that I am the visitor. The breeze feathers my skin as I raise my face up to the sun. I wait and listen to the silence. My heart feels separate and I ask why. It aches. I wish it did not. I want the pain to go away. There is loneliness. Am I lonely for God? Am I so separate from who I am that I am lonely for my own self? I realize that each cell of this pain is created from an accumulation of abandoned wisdom and joy. I have been listening to someone else's view of my soul. How could I have believed them over myself?

I cry for those lost moments. They have become parts missing from my soul. The sun comes out and lines my face in its rays. I give to myself the compassion of fullness. I forgive myself for living in someone else's lie about who I am. There is no compromise now. I have learned to turn away from myself and I cannot continue. You only wanted to love me, to show me divine love, and I ran into my darkness —familiar and tempting, deceiving and captivating. I let so many take what is real about me and turn it into their interpretations.

Then I met you and all of my pain surfaced. I pushed away the light and pulled in the dark. I only knew how to survive by working for those split in the dark and light. I have served the wrong people, both men and women. I lost what and who is true.

Her green eyes come to me. They are soft, intense and vibrant. I had thought that she, too, wanted me to sacrifice myself for her. I stopped seeing the love she had for me. I fell into the numbing spell from all of those before her. Then, I lowered my knee onto the ground, realizing I had made a mistake. I took her for something she was not. But it was too late. I had become the person I was not and could no longer recognize myself in the mirror. I had covered over my own divine feminine for as long as I could. Raked over the coals of life by life itself, I gave her little room. She huddled into the only corner I allowed her. She could read, write and exclaim at the beauty of life through my eyes, not hers. I was blind, a fool stumbling in the dark, pretending to know where I was going and what I was doing.

Up until now, I had surrendered to the false personifications of divine feminine in all of her forms. How could I find her true form? Could I open my heart and surrender to her and to myself? I knew I had to go beyond myself so I could open the door jammed shut all of my life. I got stuck along the way, just like everyone else.

I close my eyes and perceive everything from the core shaft of light within the center of my body. My mind remembers that it is the doorway to the light and the gateway into my body. It is here that I can dwell in the pulsating rhythms of my internal flames of God/Goddess. The currents swell like the ocean and my body expands beyond what my mind has dictated. The Great Mother, the Furious, Loving, Intense Matriarchal Power of Divine Creation soars through my bodily elements of air, fire, earth, water and ether. I become the wave and rise up to enter the Holy Grail. I remember myself as the God and Goddess joining my divine feminine and masculine selves. Sophia, Inanna, Isis, Jesus, Babaji, Mary Magdalene, the Holy Mother, Mary, and so many others live in this divine union. One moment of receiving divine spark awakens the sleeping serpent in my body and soul. This caduceus carries the magnetic charge of the Holy Grail through my spine, nervous system and heart. As I ignite in its spark, I am brought into life force. As I awaken, receive, connect and become one with my spiritual nature, I become a chalice of light and power.

Awakening

Each morning, as the sun casts its warmth upon the earth and the sounds of life come alive, give your attention to the moment, the familiarities and differences of the day. Give your senses the opportunity to be in the moment, savoring and capturing the silence between the new rays of light and nature's awakening. Give yourself the moment of no-thought, changing your inner radio station to the frequency of God.

Keep your attention on your heart until you feel yourself settle into the center of the movements created by your thoughts and energies. Wait a moment before thinking about what you need to do today. Choose to make your time with the moment your priority, and fill yourself with its unknowns and life concerns. Feel what is in your heart and merge it with God.

Once you are fully in your heart, drop your attention into your belly, your second chakra, and dip into the well. If at first you do not feel or sense the well, stay with it, for in time you will. Connect your heart and wellspring together and begin your day dwelling in this calm depth. Ask yourself what comes next—a walk? Run? Yoga? Writing in your journal? Dancing? Or shifting into your day's responsibilities? Before you perform any function, awaken your inner self. Elongate the depth and length of each day, thus further receiving and awakening life around and inside of you. You will feel closer to everything within and without.

Nourishment

Take the time to fill yourself from your inner wellspring. You will know what to eat and will naturally seek out what feeds you most deeply. If you consume long-lasting fuel, your need to indulge in your list of "empty-hole" fillers will lessen. Your body, the temple for your spirit, wants to work effortlessly.

If you seek to open your body to spiritual food, your eating needs will change. The choice to numb or open your body is yours. Foods with preservatives, hormones, sugars and excess salt will numb your body, as will over processed cooked foods. To experience vitality in your diet, turn to foods that are organically farmed, grown on trees, or come from plants close to the earth. The more vegetables, fruits, whole grains, nuts and other body-friendly proteins you eat, the healthier you will be. If you have heart palpitations a half an hour after eating, you might be allergic to something you just ate. Instead of eating to drive away your hunger or emotions, plan ahead and consider how you want to feel after you eat and the kind of energy level you want to create. You are in charge.

When you eat properly, your sex life, work accomplishments and efficiency as a student or parent will increase. Your entire attitude will improve by eating foods that do not deplete your endrocrine (glandular) system or over-stimulate your digestive system. Caffeine, processed foods, alcohol and sugars will keep you swinging and hitting the wall of your fears and life challenges. The struggle over weight gain and loss, cancers, diabetes, arthritis and other chronic diseases is a battle over what controls your body. It often comes down to dietary choices. Your fears, denials and various forms of pain often lead you to the foods that split your mind from your body so you do not have to feel. Instead, keep a journal of the foods you crave and what you are feeling when you desire them.

Your feminine and masculine energies want to be fed. If you find yourself craving dairy products such as cheese, ice cream, milk or baked goods with wheat such as pastries, cookies or muffins check in with your feminine self. Does she need more time to express, be alone, say what she feels? Does she feel supported? Ask her. Make sure you also ask what she needs from you or the people in her life. Instead of over-indulging in foods that are feminine in nature, fill your feminine self.

Food of the Divine Feminine

Herbs are the most powerful food God has put upon the earth. For every disease and imbalance in both mind and body that we might experience, an herb exists on this magnificent planet that will assist healing. Herbs are a feminine food, a great gift from the Divine Mother. However, they can also carry masculine energies.

Medicinal plants supply herbs that fulfill and help to balance our feminine and masculine energies. American ginseng, grown predominately in Wisconsin or New York, is more feminine. It helps to strengthen the immune and endrocrine systems for both men and women. Siberian and Korean ginseng build the forces of the body and energize masculine protective systems that may be sleeping due to dietary or psychological imbalances.

Most illnesses are connected to imbalances of the four major systems: endrocrine, digestive, nervous or immune. Instead of first reaching for the pharmaceutical drug prescribed to you (unless it is an emergency), research herbs and receive professional assistance from a qualified herbal or botanical medicine practitioner. If you strengthen your four major systems with herbal medicines, you will avoid many of the pitfalls connected to those systems' imbalances. Avoid doctors who operate from a mind set that herbs and natural medicines can be harmful or a waste of time and energy. This usually indicates a significant lack of herbal and medicinal plant knowledge on the part of the doctor. There are now qualified herbalists, naturopathic doctors and a few medical doctors located all over the country thoroughly trained in botanical medicine who can assist you to dig deeper and return to the roots of your body's core cellular structure, which will innately respond to herbs.

The following is a list of herbs that have been used for centuries to help maintain strong minds, bodies and spirits. Many of these herbs have been Holy Grail medicines used for centuries to assist the level of connectedness between the inner bodies, soul and physical body. Remember: Herbs nourish your body on a very deep level. When you combine spiritual nourishment with these plants, you create powerful medicine.

Red Clover	Dandelion Root	Shatavari
Burdock Root	Marshmallow Root	Lavender Flowers
Yellow Dock Root	Eleuthero	Passionflower
Schizandra	Astragalus	Chamomile
Lycium	Ashwaganda	Kelp
Ginseng	Triphala	Oatstraw
Nettles	Peppermint	Horsetail
Hawthorne	Watercress	Fo-ti-Tieng
Cayenne	Wild Yam Root	Boswellia
Guggula	Ginger	

Reishi, Maitake, Shitake Mushrooms

Receiving Yourself

Receiving the Holy Grail begins with a subtle and life-affirming gesture of connecting into our pure and holy self. It is possible to connect to our self from an essential, spiritual level and fill our self with this energy, but to live fully empowered lives, we must be able to funnel our power into our energetic body alignment.

All of the exercises laid out in this book assist in learning to receive our self. By clearing the chakras of control, pain, disconnection, betrayal, abandonment and rejection energies, an open vessel can be created to the whole self. Receive your divine inner male and inner female and unite them by seeing, feeling and hearing them as one. They stand ready and waiting to receive the spiritual ignition of the Holy Grail. Their union in soul is the catalyst to receiving remembrance and recognition of their life path. Their way is the open portal to divine happiness. This is the True Tantra, the true way of transcending into God (see Chapter 29).

Receiving the essence of our inner divine feminine and masculine and embodying their power happens after we release and let go of what we assimilated into our emotional, etheric, causal and mental bodies in past lives and earlier in this lifetime. Rather than receiving more pain, we receive the love that resides in the core of our being. When connected to our self, we are able to run self-love and vital energy through our own circuitry.

As we practice receiving each day, the walls that separate us from universal love energy begin to collapse. Breathe, bathe, create and play in the love within yourself and the universe. Take time to receive the natural beauty of life around you and the voice of the life energy moving through you. Instead of pushing your inner programs onto someone else, listen and feel the rhythms of your thoughts, perceptions and life within you. Between the heartbeats lives a spiritual wholeness that is the gateway to your divine, powerful and determined Holy Grail nature.

Creating Our Self-Image From Divine Union

Defining our beauty by comparing ourselves with another person is a common occurrence. It can happen from personal observation, watching TV and movie stars, or through examining fashion magazines or Internet ads. For a moment (or more), we are suspended in time as we notice our subject's total absorption with themselves, their rapture with the moment or complete detachment from it. All the while, they emanate beauty, grace or complete vanity.

It has become increasingly difficult for people to identify whether a beautiful person on the outside is a loving, soul-centered and self-empowered person on the inside. It is rare to know someone who sees the divine beauty within another and is not fooled by the exterior masks of the ego. Being centered in such a flow of life expands our hearts and radiates light through the pores of our skin and soul. Our inner divine masculine and feminine join to weave our physical and spiritual bodies together. How we dress, speak, move and what colors we wear become expressions of our integration with spirit and the heart. When we are touched with this divine beauty, we are inspired to write poetry, stories, wear clothing true to our most authentic selves, paint, sing and create our home to reflect ourselves. We are moved to transcend the everyday perception of just getting by and living in a one-dimensional mirror.

By discovering the eternal beauty of our inner nature and fully accepting it, we are freed of the mind games of deception, lying, pretence, influence and conquest. The essence of the rose, the majesty of the sea and the hues of color in the mountains at sunset are not mere experiences for the mind. They reflect the soul's most powerful and liberating energies. Their divine energies spin, hum, sing and dance in thousands of colors, some of which we have never even seen before. Our divine self-image is mirrored in the beauty of creation, the portals into nature. Here, our spirit is recognized and nurtured.

The damage we inflict upon our soul and body when we leave our authentic self can be healed. When we live in the realm of what is possible, we enter the Divine. If we focus on living in perfect beauty, we create harmony. When we align our body, soul and spirit in harmony to universal forces, we are free to experience divine beauty and bliss. When we leave it, we create madness, pain and strife. We forget that we are spinning atoms in the universe of light, and we spin downward into survival thinking.

When we allow God to touch our hearts, overflowing streams of life energy and love spark us. We can stare into a leaf and see its veins feeding its form. We can watch clouds overhead cast their shadows upon the land before receding. We can witness our own hearts opening in the center of a flower. Our vision, both visible and invisible, connects us to the realms of beauty.

Look into the mirror and see beyond your visual image. Look for the light and the innocence under your skin. Now look for the false projections, negative self-indulgences and emptiness. Have compassion and empathy; establish a rapport of heartfelt acceptance. Allow self-judgment and condemnation to melt, and with love see your most vulnerable self. In the solitude of being present with your self, remove your illusions. Through love, reveal to yourself the beauty and light with which you were born.

Enjoy re-imaging of your self. Take a moment to imagine how you want to express your inner beauty. Hold the vision in your heart and begin to take the steps to transfer this image of beauty into how you present yourself. Just by holding the vision each day and doing what you need to do—changing your diet to more fruits and vegetables, exercising, meditating, smiling more, emptying your feelings into a journal or to God each day, will help to manifest your divine presence.

Remembering Who You Are: Six Steps

1. See yourself as a child relating to nature or a scene of magic, innocence and wonder.
2. Visualize an image of something to which you connect and relate.
3. Allow the colors, scents, movement, textures and feelings to fill you.
4. Fill yourself until you are one with the image and your mind is at rest.
5. Experience the sensations as a link to your divine nature.
6. Take them into your heart.

Reconnect Your Spirit and Body

We need an inner container in our emotional body to hold our feelings. Without an energetic container, we are unable to nestle the feelings that arise from our childhood, teen years and adult experiences. Those of us who grew up in families that did not allow us to express our feelings—the majority of people in the U.S. and abroad—never created energetic containers.

If you anger easily, talk too much, don't know how to deal with intense feelings, avoid communication in relationship, need outside distractions to function, stay in your head and close your heart, or hold secrets or lies and cannot handle the unknown, you lack a container in your emotional body. Whether you were bombarded by family dysfunctions such as alcoholism or drug problems, control issues, rigidity, obsessive-compulsive behaviors, poverty or conditional love, you were never allowed to be your own person. The act of creating a container in the emotional body never happens unless you are fortunate enough to have a parent or teacher who encourages you to be with your feelings and not abandon your self.

Within your emotional body is an oval of light. It extends from your pubic bone, surrounds your lower belly and moves into your solar plexus. The energies of the navel are safely protected in this cocoon. Without the container, you probably will have lower back pain, stomach problems, arthritis, kidney stones, a heart condition or diabetes at some point in your life. By creating a container, you are allowing your spiritual energies to fuse with your emotional energies.

The clearer and stronger you become inside the inner core column in your body, the more your Holy Grail chalice can be filled. When building this inner chalice, trust that it will be a container for your life force. The more light you can contain, the greater your spiritual, creative and soul power will become.

Building Your Inner Container

Connect With The Earth

1. Receive the light of the deep earth through your feet.
2. Bring light up into your body, raising it through your legs, pelvis, solar plexus and heart center.

Connect Your Solar Plexus

1. Connection with the solar plexus is the first step to anchoring your energy and mind in your body and to building a container for spirit to exist within.
2. Breathe into your solar plexus and fill it with gold light—sunshine.
3. Send this gold light to every part of your body, down to your feet and into your palms.

Connect Your Bones

1. Inhale breath into your bones through your mouth. Exhale through your mouth, expelling any stale energy inside your bones. Inhale light into your bones.
2. Inhale energy and light through your skin, then exhale.
3. As you exhale, allow the energy to remain inside your body, under your skin and around your bones. Breathe deeper into your bones until you feel a pressure surrounding them.
4. Direct this energy deeper and deeper into your bones as you hold your breath for 10 counts.
5. Exhale slowly, keeping the energy in the bones. Repeat eight times.

Connect Your Life Force

When we clear our navel center of the cords implanted by parents, family members, friends and past relationships, we free up vital soul, emotional and physical energy. Once bonded with our self, we are able to fulfill our soul's creative and spiritual challenges.

1. From ten feet above your head send a ray of light down into the open elevator shaft in your body. Look to see whose energies are in your navel area.
2. Ask why they are there and dialogue with them.
3. View the cords and decide if they add or take away your light.
4. Ask your body what color is needed to unhook the cord(s).
5. Send the cords into universal light.
6. Fill the hole where the cord was with a color your body chooses.
7. Send white light into your navel area.
8. Receive the light as love and allow it to fill you.

Living Inside the Chalice: An Exercise

Close your eyes and visualize a translucent oval in the space between your solar plexus, second chakra and pubic bone. Invite in a color to fill it up and bring your focus inside the oval. Fill the oval with your love.

Invite a part of your wounded past self to step into the oval. This could include an angry pre-teen or teen self, an ignored or unseen five year-old, a seven year-old puppet or "doll" for needy relatives, or a ten year-old shut down by parents who violated and ignored your personal space and your needs (a home life without stable boundaries). Allow these feelings to come into the oval. Breathe, be with this part of your self, and permit the oval to energetically hold the emotion.

In your heart, be present with the emotions of the younger part of your self. Feel, hear or see who he or she *really* is beneath the emotion. Be with that person. Do not abandon him/her. Stay truly present. You may experience living in your solar plexus, second chakra or inner space above the pubic bone for the first time in your life. Allow your heart center to expand by taking in this person's true presence, power and light. The container bridges your spiritual and soul nature with your body.

Send the color of your inner oval into your outer oval. Increase your outer oval until you can breathe fully into it. Breathe into both ovals at the same time until they become one circle of light and color.

Chapter 27

Living in the Holy Grail

"In the center of your soul lives truth.
Gift your heart with its wisdom and know thy self."
—Iana Lahi

I live in the center where flesh, spirit and life force meet. I am the union of your masculine and feminine soul. I come to you as the flame of oneness. I will love you as I love myself, for I am here to free and comfort you so that you and I may live in joy.

I live in the union of my heart. Here in the center of spirit, I am the current of life. I am the worshiped and the worshipper, the song and the singer, the beloved and the lover.

In love with the One, I caress and awaken your longing to touch God. I come to you from deepest honor and respect. I come to your temple and enter paradise. Together our forces are joined. Two currents of light become one. I honor you.

As we unite, we become ecstatic bliss and happiness. The currents of dark and light have joined within our selves. Our hearts transform our darkness into awakening light. Here I stand, open in all ways to you. Rays of gold and white light dance in my soul.

My legs are my roots absorbing the power of your earth. My hands are leaves emitting the light of the moon and sun. My throat is the voice of life moving through me. My belly generates the fire; my solar plexus spins the light of the sun to give these wings flight. We soar into the heavens, leaving the earth beneath us, yet still within us. The rapture of surrender fills and completes us. We know each other as God—the creator living within.

Becoming the Bridge for Union with the Divine

The Holy Grail's vibration is a stream of consciousness that creates, preserves, nurtures and sustains the light of life. It is the ultimate food flowing from the center of creation. When we live in the center, we become one with its flow and liberated from the need to direct it. We co-create the direction of our lives by shifting our flow of power, much like changing course while skiing down a mountain.

For many, this creates fear of the unknown. Will we have enough worldly security and personal "creature comforts" to continue to help us feel in control?

When we co-create from the power of love in our soul, we are able to trust, acknowledge, allow and stay focused within our energetic power. This power works as a conduit for creative forces to build into spiritual power, during which every creative expression is fuel for our ever-expanding souls. As our spiritual power is growing, it is important to be conscious of the circular flow of creative energy. If we express our creative energy into the world, but disengage from receiving the return of our own creative energies we become empty and eventually encounter the dangerous crossroads of physical and mental health breakdowns. Conversely, when we're connected in Spirit, or God, the creative process will re-emerge and express again through us, no matter how busy we've been in the everyday world.

The physical source of creative expression lies in the cross at mid-chest, between our nipples. Press the middle finger of either hand into the hollow in the middle of your sternum, at the midpoint between your nipples. This is the cross of the beloved. God flows into and out of this point horizontally and vertically. The symbol of the cross represents this energy point, an ancient code for living in union with divine universal forces. It is also the portal into inner dimensions of creative energies. By living in the cross, we are able to sustain spiritual and physical union. Living in the center of the cross prevents work burnout, co-dependency, the impulse to look outside of our self to fulfill emotional needs, eating for instant gratification and living in a matrix of routines that lack meaning and purpose.

Many touch into higher spiritual power through meditation, but neglect the equally important work to clear lower energies of survival, existence, abandonment and pain. An endless cycle of disappointments and heartaches transpire time and time again. Potential is felt but never fully realized, because we get to the point of overcoming those lower energies, then succumb to them. This is often seen with authors who can't finish books, musicians who can't write songs, or creative geniuses who work blue-collar jobs to avoid tapping deeply into themselves—where their mastery lies.

Universal Laws

If we each take responsibility for our thoughts, and alchemize them with our feelings and soul, we can help to shift our consciousness—and the world's. Our thoughts will form into matter that prevails in our lives. Ask and you shall receive.

When breathed into action, these universal laws can bring sacred solutions to volatile situations:

- **The Law of Oneness** teaches that everything we think, feel and say connects us to the divine source.
- **The Law of Cause and Effect** teaches that how and what we set into motion in our lives must be acts for which we are responsible. We create our outcomes.
- **The Law of Action** teaches us to choose actions aligned to what we want to create.
- **The Law of Vibration** teaches that when our words, feelings and actions are aligned to our highest vibration of love, light and truth, we connect into original creation.
- **The Law of Attraction** teaches that we create the situations and people that enter our lives through our thoughts, words, feelings and actions.
- **The Law of Polarity** teaches there is a positive and negative pole in the body and universe. By connecting, aligning and balancing the poles, we are able to create integration between our mind, body and spirit.
- **The Law of Non-Interference** teaches that as we lovingly allow others to act according to their free will, we also offer them the opportunity to grow and learn by their choices.

• **The Law of Unconditional Love** teaches that loving without controls, manipulations, and judgments provides the opportunity for another to receive true love and to merge with universal love and acceptance.

A circle is made up of two arches, or bridges. When we place one arch on top of the other arch, a defined center is created. This center is the bridge between our spiritual and physical self.

When we live inside the meeting place of union, we become a bridge between spirit and matter. Our hearts become the rendezvous location for our spirit and body, the completion of a sacred circle.

To become a full bridge, the complete circle, we must receive our own heart energies as well as the hearts of those in our life. When we cross half of the bridge of our inner circle, we merge matter with spirit. We become adept at manifesting ideas, making a living and caring for others. The other half of the inner circle requires bringing spirit into matter. When we accomplish this, we bring inspiration, sacred values and higher dreams into our lives. When we cross one bridge but not the other, we tend to over identify with an outcome (matter to spirit) or to live only for creative nourishment (spirit into matter). When the two arcs unite, there is full union of body, soul and spirit.

When we fail to identify and merge with the bridge within our self, our relationships and work fall apart. By serving solely the bridge for everyone around us, rather than living as a bridge of divine creation, we generate self-betrayal. It is a one-way street to a painful journey of picking up the pieces. Likewise, if we hold onto identifying our self with thinking about how we are creating, manifesting or working, without receiving the creative juices of the universe, our lives become void of joy. The result? The world lures us to seek and find the next fix that promises temporary fulfillment but which also leads to an eventual lack of meaning, purpose and joy. Until we let go and stop fighting the need to be in control of our creative power and understand that it does not define who we are, but rather only characterizes one side of our power, we will continue to hurt our self and the ones who love us.

Creative nourishment transforms the need or attachment to an outcome. We are able to release the need to receive recognition or fulfillment from worldly affairs. We are filled through the *act* of creating and manifesting without judgment or fear. Then, by living in the center of creative power, our mental will shifts from being power-centric to becoming a *vessel* for spiritual and material wealth.

When we cross the bridge into our self, we merge spirit and matter without losing the self. We enter the space where pure power exists, rather than force. We stop the counterproductive practice of forcing or making things work, and instead live in a space of oneness with the power that creates all life.

The higher the spiritual force we bring into form, the bigger the fall when we identify with its power. This is both the meaning of the allegorical battle between God and his counterpart, Lucifer, and the pitfall of the Holy Grail path. Many fall off the bridge because they identify with their power or lack thereof.

The fight between the mind and higher self prevents the great crossing. The only way to cross this bridge is to stop battling the forces created by our own struggles, cover-ups and negligence to Source. Through our heart center, we can stay connected to the parts of our self that call out to be heard, seen and felt, and then surrender to the state of divine union. When we reach this point, the drama of fighting for our own interpretation of life ceases to entertain us. We learn to release our incomplete stories, and reach into living and manifesting a universal mission.

As we settle into our sacred circle, the passion of love grows out of the fountain of compassion. Joy flows as our hearts open to the connection of love. Living in the original vibration of our light, our eternal connection opens our heart to receive divine power. Everything else dissolves into the beauty and majesty of uniting our hearts in the one. It becomes easier to accept that what enters our lives in the moment is the perfect vehicle to transcend our own self-made limitations. When we keep passion alive by living in the center of duality and being empowered by its forces, we begin to open to living in universal union.

Your Limitations

The voice of your soul is the presence of your truth. If your mind interprets truth through its ego rather than through your heart, the communication of your "truth" will cause harm to another. Until the part of you that has heretofore been shown little compassion is embraced in love, giving compassion to your self is an enigma. When you are willing to melt into the compassion that already thrives in your heart, you will be able to heal what limits you.

Each sorrow, tragedy, desire or physical pain is a potential gateway into greater love. It exists as a voice in your head that tells you how impossible it is to have what you want. It can take you right out of yourself. Such a separation can hold you in its addictive power of not having, not being and not receiving. Each time you choose the belief that something else is preventing you from living your truth, you are living in limitation. In this case, one often feels as though there is not enough love in life or enough money in the bank. If you refuse to communicate with your pain and funnel it instead through the portal of love, it will engulf your body, mind and soul. It will consume you even while you pretend it is not there. When you think that your thoughts alone are the extent of your reality, you are living in an illusion. It is only when your thoughts are free of pain that you can fully trust them. To become free, they must surrender to the true self who lives inside the soggy cloak of pain. Until then, every action in your life will run the risk of creating limitation rather than expansion.

Your Sanctuary, Your Chalice

Until our divine and human selves are reconnected and merged within our physical and etheric bodies, we will often feel lost at sea. As the reconnections are made, space is created within our inner sanctuary to experience our divine self. Our human self will feel safer to expand into its own home—a womb of light and power shared by men and women alike. This is the cradle of intuition. To achieve this state and subsequent strength, all cords to past relationship that originate in the lower emotional body need to be cleared or transmuted to a higher connection.

To unite the divine and human selves, we need to create a sanctuary—a chalice—large enough to contain the universe within ourselves. Deep within the solar plexus, we will find a portal inside the navel area and lower belly that opens into this safe sanctuary. After you create the inner space of your chalice, reach into the universe within your heart, plant a seed and grow a tree with deep roots. Nurture your light. Extend it from your heart to beneath your pubic bone. Receive the life-giving parts of your divine feminine and masculine and observe the love that pours into you. Energetically align your inner original self —all the ages of your inner child and adolescence to the light emanating through your eternal love. Fill the empty spaces within yourself.

Expand into the space within your interior self. Become intuitive by moving "into it." Trust, surrender and release how you think you need to function. Fill the moment with a sense of union between your frightened part and universal love. Union with the essence of light and power in your inner sanctuary is what *makes* you intuitive.

Connect your third eye into your sanctuary; swing open the gateway into the infinite. Feel, see and hear the inner currents, rhythms and voices of this planet, other dimensions, your heart and the hearts of others. Bring this gift into your life and apply it to your relationships with everyone. Utilize as much space as you can within your inner sanctuary, and offer this space to your work and life.

Bring the sanctuary—the chalice—to others. When we teach and help children to hold open this space, they feel valued, honored and creatively limitless. Help them remain open to their power; guide them to self-nourish. Teach them to water their inner gardens and forests. Help them keep the light radiating in their sanctuary.

Igniting the Feminine Flame in Your Sanctuary

The flame of divine light is ignited in the inner sanctuary of the first and second chakras. As the feminine fire within the center of the earth ignites the spiritual and creative flames within the chakras, all burdens and negativities burn away. The true voice of the body is uncovered by sitting in the flame of God, located within the core of our spine.

You must grow toward the heavenly rays to find your voice. The feminine fires burn away all falsehoods of our true power. She exposes them in the light. All of our projections burn in this fire of passion. She is the initiator from death to rebirth. There she sits within her clouds of wisdom and fires of transformation. The feminine transmutes the collective consciousness of all lifetimes through your body and expands your heart to meet the vibrant world. She meets with you in your inner temple through the rays of the Divine. Through the spine, she transforms matter into spirit and ignites the channels of the *ida* and *pingala*—the solar and lunar pathways. This caduceus of the serpent energy awakens the Godhead in the body.

Whether from higher sex or deep meditation, the lower self is ignited in the second and third chakras and uplifts the reincarnating soul into its true identity of eternal soul—awakened and transformed into everlasting love. This happens through the heart and higher centers in the head. The five-pointed star, or pentacle, opens the gateways into the Divine when ignited at the top of the head. When these energies are brought into the body and circulated, the Divine and human merge. We experience the direct voice of God within. Our life feels integrated as the transformative flames burn away everything obstructing the heart center. The inner and outer universes merge to become the spiritual voice that connects all of our bodies. Spirit begins to sing with us and from us.

This is the ancient practice that was kept secret from the masses for two millennia.

Live in Fearless Joy

Many leave their soul's design and take on another's. It takes fearlessness to live in the true beauty of one's divine self. The prevailing mindset of the world tries to mold you into something you are not. Your inner world has been formed by dogmas, ideologies and myths based upon duality, and the everyday outside world will constantly encourage you to add to that duality. No one can permanently sustain such a false identity. Know what you are *essentially* made of—whether a rose, dewdrop, plant root, perhaps the flame that burns the wood to ashes or the stream pushing everything out of its way.

Such oneness offers us the experience of creating a new story. The old duality model is based upon "nots" and "shoulds." Your story is created by what is *not* regarding your self, what *cannot* be true about you and who you are *not.* Take the word *not* out of your vocabulary and see what happens. Review your old story about how you see the world and others treating you and change the story. Hear the story of your masculine and feminine selves, then bring them together to create a new story based upon empowerment and love. Become the full expression of who you are in divinity. Stay with your heart.

By leaving the self, we leave God.
When we stay with our self, we are making love with God.
Live this joy.

Move into Your Cosmic Design

To move into our true God design and leave behind the body-mind structure we created for self-protection, we need to acknowledge our body as a chalice for the divine. Our misuse, abuse or acceptance of our chalice defines how we relate to our divine nature. When we choose joy, we're able to walk through and overcome thoughts created from past pain, sorrows and disappointments. Joy is a choice that manifests through finding the connections between our self-imposed pain and radiant creative-spiritual action.

The universe mirrors itself through our bodies. We are perfect configurations of nature's designs. The leaves, trees, rocks, plants and stars are patterned like snowflakes; no two are exactly alike. So it is with us. We carry unique patterns. No one else owns or creates them. If we close our spiritual eye to the design of our eternal self, we become inwardly blind and unaware of how we are connected. By visualizing the pattern of our light body and mirroring its image onto our physical and etheric bodies, we are able to stay aligned with creation.

Our spiritual eye is the conduit between our higher and lower selves. It serves as a conductor of the currents of energy between the bodies. When the spiritual eye is closed, the body's energetics slow down; sometimes, they decrease in motion so dramatically that illness in mind, body and soul results. Once we learn to keep our spiritual eye and heart center open and connected, we can heal ourselves. When the spiritual eye is united with the points directly above the pubic bone, sacrum, tailbone and the back of the skull, we begin to know our self as a vessel for consciousness. Then, as we clear and open our solar plexus and heart centers, we can circulate and maintain our own God flow.

Let us see ourselves as our own teachers. Let us own our wisdom and replace the fears that are lodged in the solar plexus with the movement of spirit power, and move our sense of spiritual knowingness into our solar plexus. Infuse this center with the light that connects all of life. Connect mind and soul to this point, then journey into the origins of *where* and *how* we are connected. By rediscovering our original connection, we plug all of our selves into that divine power and sometimes to our amazement realize that we're already divinely empowered!

When we bless the world around us with our offering, we make a difference. If our offering is to live in the fire of creative power, the spirit of peace, the vigilance of truth, heart and soul vitality, spiritual integrity, soulful acceptance or illusion-breaking power, we shift the minds and hearts of those around us. By living in the center of our light, we enlighten the world around us. The gateway to the kingdom of heaven on earth opens in our heart. It is the mirror of the life within. Keep it intact and do not allow it to break. "With utmost concern, take care of your heart" (Proverbs 4:23).

The pattern of creation is your holiness. It becomes known as a blueprint of God's existence within your body.

World Thought Forms

Our collective mind is made up of a grid pattern of thoughts that can disempower or empower our selves, others and the world at any given moment. Our thoughts are controlled and influenced by the messages we have received about how we are supposed to see the world and our self. By learning to see through the eyes of authenticity, we are given the freedom to navigate into the highest purpose of our lives.

As long as thoughts and feelings are kept separate, we can be controlled. Thinking without the co-action of feeling creates separation. Knowledge held separate from self-empowerment creates numbness. Blend together fear and visual imagery, and you will find a way to control how people think. Give people a reason to fear and they will relinquish their own thought process. Kill, enslave, imprison, censor and judge those who think authentically and are sourced to the power of masculine-feminine balance, and you will control a culture.

Our world history to this point has been written by the blood of these truths. Universal thought forms that laid the foundation for our thinking for over two thousand years include:

Hell

Hell is depicted in bright red flames. It usually includes a devil and burning people. They do not know why they are stuck there; looks of eternal damnation cross their tormented faces. Western religions created hell as the punch line of a three-part tumble from grace into sin, guilt and hell. We are told it is a place that God created to punish those who have sinned. Some believe they go to hell if they do not put the Son of God on a pedestal to which even *he* would have objected. Others believe if they do not sacrifice themselves for a political mission of God, they will suffer in fire and brimstone. Some believe that pre-marital sex or—God forbid—pregnancy while unmarried results in a trip to hell.

What is hell, really, but a creation of our consciousness that denies our intuition, passion for life and secret dreams? When activated in the body, the element of fire lives in the genitals, lower belly, solar plexus and heart. It is the power of regeneration, procreation, creativity, desire and sexuality. The fire of God is in the center of spirit. It dissolves thought forms, burns away false desires and illusions, and transforms darkness into light. When disconnected from spirit, we are pulled by our thoughts. When grounded into our creative power, heart and spirit, we avoid the self-centered pull of the mind. The ego fears the flames of transformation. It wants to detach from the lessons that the fire of spirit teaches.

Religions preach consequences of sin and transgression for one's actions, rather than teaching seekers to face themselves and walk through the fire of the soul. Even though we are taught not to sin, our mistakes are the "sins" of our unconscious trying to express itself. Rather than learning how to use our powers of sexuality, creativity and spirit, we are taught how to judge and separate them from the fire.

To fear hell is to fear these powers. If we acknowledge our desires and thoughts and take them into the fire of spirit, we can find the awaiting truth and follow its divine inspiration.

Sin

When repeatedly denied and repressed, our soul will eventually express itself with misguided actions that could be called sins. However, these "sins" of our mind are *doorways to greater awareness and responsibility.* Sin is the soul or the heart trying to be heard and carried into higher understanding. When the mind is separate from the soul's callings, we live the betrayal of our true nature—sin. We want to express our sexual, soul and creative nature, but we are taught not to commit these acts. For instance, if we confuse being a good person with always putting another first, we do not even know how to begin feeling what we need. When we do, we become confused—especially when our churches or peers label us as "sinners" when we think and respond to our soul's need for authenticity. By living in the duality of what is good and bad, it is impossible to avoid lying to our self and making a mistake. When we do make that mistake, we are trained to yield to actions that avoid conflict rather than to break open the fear of what others may think. We ignore the voice within that always speaks a higher truth. Consequently, we live within the boxes that we created in order to avoid our sins, or passions of our soul. We develop cancers, co-dependencies, power struggles, we lose relationships and we develop weight problems. When this happens, we've clearly listened too much to the voice of the world, which is constantly telling us to forget who we really are, who we are at the soul level. That is the real sin.

When we stop judging our self and ask our soul what it needs or seeks, and listen, we open the possibility for expansion. Once we realign our life to the voice of truth, we step out of fear. We leave the box; we reunite with the passions of our soul. We walk beyond the fires and gates of our own self-created hells.

Guilt

The voice of guilt speaks the soul, heart, body and verbal language of shame. When we feel we do not exist, we experience that feeling as shame. The shame of not being who we are creates guilt. The shame of continuously avoiding our most authentic selves, or acting in a way that denies our soul's purpose, creates guilt. We perpetuate disempowerment by teaching our selves and others how to think/act/perceive, rather than how to live authentically. World religions and dysfunctional families teach that unless we feel guilty for being who we really are, we are social and personal disgraces. When we hurt another or stunt our own soul evolution in any way, we spiritually must take responsibility for our actions—not through caving into guilt, but through recognition of how we abandon or betray the voice of our hidden pain. The key is to locate the original circumstances that caused us to feel we did not exist and communicate total recognition and acknowledgement to this part that lives in the energetic shame and guilt for not being allowed or supported to exist. Through complete self-acceptance of the pain that evolved through needing to remain separate to survive, we can move through the darkness of guilt.

Suffering

We accept suffering as a collective consciousness. In many western cultures, it's even considered a badge of honor! Generations of family suffering are perpetuated by holding family members captive in judgment, condemnation and fear if they leave the long bloodline of pain and choose spirit and light instead.

Suffering is created when we disconnect from spirit and live in isolation. We begin to identify with how others hurt us, what we do not possess and how alone we are, rather than with the oneness of all life. We fill the holes in our soul with illusions that involve judging our self, blaming others, and power struggles that perpetuate greater suffering. If this continues, we shave away dignity and self-respect from others and cause personal and more wide spread suffering. We see the "other" not for who they are, but for how we need and want them to be.

When our ego surrenders the need to have others acknowledge our importance and significance, we end the cycle of suffering. Acceptance of our own light enables us to walk through our points of resistance with calm detachment and humility. Suffering is alleviated.

Chapter 28

Living in Full Activation

Transform your inner and outer worlds to become one

According to the Mayan calendar, August 1987 marked the beginning of a 25-year cycle—the Harmonic Convergence. The period of time, to conclude in August 2012, is to serve as a great cleansing for the people of the earth and the earth itself. The prophecies of the first-millennium Mayan prophet Quetzalcoatl, the "Bird God," averred that in the future, there would need to be a return to a 13-month moon calendar. This calendar would ultimately assist in shifting the planet into a fourth-dimensional reality that would then elevate all aspects of human consciousness.

These dimensional shifts are occurring now and are causing us to face, run, change or hide from the higher tests of spiritual progression. We are being gifted and challenged daily with activations of profound light, clarity, integration, love and vision that are gateways to unifying time, mind, soul and spirit into oneness.

Each of us is preparing to move beyond our belief systems to receive the incoming higher frequencies of light that are returning to our planet, as promised, after the great fall of consciousness many millennia ago. The shifts we are presently making in our body and spirit are for the sole purpose of assisting us to align with these higher vibrations. The biochemistry of our bodies, including our cells, must shift to accommodate these higher frequencies. Our hormonal, endocrine and nervous systems are realigning to the light of our christed self as we experience this shift. This alignment will make it possible for us to walk through the upcoming spiritual and physical changes on this planet. As our proficiency at receiving transmissions of the Divine increases, and our ability to live at those high frequencies and express those vibrations through our hearts and souls grows, our bodies will become greater messengers of divine intelligence.

When we clear distortions in our thoughts, emotions and memories, we can change the flow of energy in our bodies and better prepare the body for this more refined alignment. Beware of sabotaging belief systems; they will prevent your body cells and systems from shifting. The more you can hear your body and live in the awakened state of your divine feminine and masculine energies in deep harmony and communication, the easier it will be to recreate your self in the image of your God self. That is what this time period is all about.

Observe Your Body's Messages

Give your self a few hours to be alone and fully present with your mind and body. During this holy time, observe how your mind responds to the messages of your body. It might surprise you to see how many times your mind stops the truth in your body. Watch how your noisy lower mind finds or invents excuses to do things its way while shutting down the quieter voice in your body. You have a higher mind and a lower mind: Your higher mind seeks to free your emotional body, while your lower mind—the negative, insecure pole of the ego—wants to compress and lock down your emotional body. Once your physical and emotional bodies open to spirit, the lower mind will mirror the lower emotional body and act out energies still lodged in the emotional body. These include anger, verbal and emotional abuse, shame, guilt and repression. Due to thousands of years of social and family training, our lower minds have become very adept at suppressing the vibrational levels in the physical and spiritual bodies. However, an activated higher mind will work with the emotional body's transformation into living from the heart.

The voice of spirit, feelings and the physical body all in union, *the voice of the feminine,* will push up against the domineering force of the lower mind until the lower mind's resistance is broken through. A few examples of ways to support the voice of the feminine:

- We are working and our body wants to get up and stretch, but we have been forcing our body to sit still. A solution: We can plan three stretching exercises to do ahead of time when our body calls out.
- A man creates a partner in his life who likes to tell him what and how to do something, which mirrors his need to dominate his own body voice. A solution: He chooses to take responsibility for completing the chores and work he agrees upon doing in advance and asks his partner to trust his motivations and to focus upon what she wants to accomplish.
- A woman who values her own material success suppresses the message to write, paint, sing or dance that her body transmits to her. A solution: She shifts her picture of success into one that includes giving herself the time to express her soul.

Bring Spirit into the Moment

As soon as we bring spirit into the moment, the boxes we have placed upon our mind and body can dissolve. Our relationship to our work, life, love and significant other can emerge out of a deep freeze. When you unite your mind, body and spirit with the forces of creation, miracles happen. Instead of thinking if your mind can bend a spoon or not, realize that *you* are the power bending or straightening the spoon.

Vibrations of light in the body are stabilized through unifying the lower forces of our self with the higher forces of light. As your consciousness enters a higher frequency of movement (light), listen to the voice of your body and it will guide you to the light. In the heart exists the light and consciousness of your true self. The incomplete stories that surround our heart cause us hurt. The center of the heart is always aligned to peace and love. When we become attached to the stories of our past, whether on the memory, emotional or mental body level, we replay the feelings that cause us to become separate. Go into the feelings and let them open you all the way to their roots. Embrace them with your heart, and release their cords of discontentment into Source.

We nurture our self as we love and live in our divine essence. This abiding commitment to oneness deepens our ability to love our self and shifts how we love our significant other. We move from pain and disappointment to joy and honoring. The work of a relationship becomes the practice of receiving, giving and being willing to let go. The work of intimate loving takes the place of fulfilling the false expectations that we alone create in our minds.

The parts of your self that avoid their true identity hide in the dark; when recognized, they will run so as not to be seen or transformed.

Know they are veiled aspects of your power that seek to return to the light. As you release their aberrations, their true identity will flood new energy through your inner bodies. This activation takes the patience of a surgeon as blocked life forces are released and returned into your body. There will be places in your self that want to remain in the dark. Until they trust that you are there to love them and able to heal by returning to their original self, your persistence to hold unconditional love will be tested. Persevere and give them your light to guide them out of their darkness.

If you ever find yourself rigidly holding onto a belief or stance with a person or situation, to the point of stubbornness and frustration, let it go and give it over to God. By letting go, you are choosing to free your self from external limitations and controls. As soon as you surrender in this way, your power can return to you. You can welcome the shift into being one with your self, rather than becoming caught up in outside circumstances. Then, you will be released to love your partner and your self while discovering the patience that arises when you unfold into your true self. Love yourself completely so that it becomes an honor to do your own work as you bring about greater shifts in consciousness.

Activating Full Consciousness

To activate full consciousness, root your self in your body and recognize who you are in your body. Acknowledge the eternal presence underneath every aspect of your heart and soul. Focus into the eternal part and expand that as you accelerate your vibration through recognition of your whole self. Expand beyond the walls of your physical body into your true self. Your power and light will feel like rays, waves and currents of energy that can meet and encompass the world. Allow your light to expand and fill the void within you and in all life.

Activating God Forces

To activate the God forces in your body:

1. Transform the aspects of your soul in the dark into light.
2. Learn to move universal life force currents through your chakras.
3. Connect your purified etheric and emotional body energies into your higher chakras.

4. Align your heart chakra, second chakra and eternal self.
5. Awaken and transmute the forces of light in your spine.
6. Release the emotional and mental body blocks that keep you entrenched in your past.
7. Integrate the energetic forces in your emotional, mental, etheric, spiritual and physical bodies.
8. Speak and walk the truth of integration, integrity and oneness.

Activate your highest self each day and invite him/her to engage fully with your activities. Bring the insights of your highest self's eternal sight and wisdom into your life. Concentrate and focus your desire for truth, beauty, integrity and expression into a daily prayer of action. Make this your highest thought in prayer, meditation and silent contemplation and introspection. Create the high integrity of always living in the moment, rather than dwelling on the past or projecting into the future.

You Are Never Alone

Know that you are never alone, but in the universal presence of great love and support for all that you are. Feel this power of love activating your heart, and practice receiving divine love and gratitude deep within you. Your divine purpose will be revealed and activated as a sacred act of honoring your self. God activation occurs by letting go of illusions, self-doubts, transgressions to others, fears and self-disempowerments. When this happens, we can become greater channels of clear power and love. New pictures of life-connecting images need to be given to your mind and body. Create a circle of light around your self and fill it with your images of what generates the life forces in your body. Stay within this safety circle and circulate the life-giving forces from your belly into your heart and hold your light power in your third eye. As your spiritual recognition of higher forces develops, you will experience feeling one with beings on the other side who are assisting your progress. Ask them to help you during your clearing process and make your self available to serve at higher levels.

Every day, re-affirm to the universe your intention to be totally responsible for all of your past, present and future actions. Take on a vow of total responsibility to live in full light, truth and integrity. Free up the relationship between your higher self and your soul by making the commitment to cancel all contracts, vows and agreements that you have made against your higher self. Activate your divine free will and end all your cycles of self-betrayal, sabotage and abandonment.

Yearn for the higher path of union with the divine—then embark on it.

Part IX

Fulfillment and Completion In the Holy Grail

Chapter 29

Sexuality as a Chalice

Know your sexuality as you know your soul.

She has cleared the emotions of the day and waits in peace, the desire of her fire growing. The light in her temple begins to fill her body. He has quieted his mind into the peace and serenity of the ebbs and flows of his life. The light in his heart fills his body. They know themselves as holy vessels for divine current. She creates the container within her body to receive the seed and light of his rod, and he creates the container within his body to receive her fire and light. Their nectars are each other's elixirs. The woman's juices are the arousal of her fire. The man's juices are the expression of his desire for union.

She prepares her body for him. He comes to the temple. Her body is adorned in shimmering love, cleared by scented waters and powerful practices of meditation. Aligned in herself, she welcomes him. He has inwardly journeyed far to reach this point. His thoughts are calm, focused only on their union. His hands are charged with the light of heart, the temple of his soul. He feels whether his mind is one with his heart. He takes his time. This is his walk down the aisle to his sacred home. She knows that her womb and her heart are one in spirit.

She welcomes him to her temple. Through her united hands and heart, she begins to transmute his worldly energies into the divine openings of her body and soul. Her senses feel him completely as she begins to move his energies into higher frequencies of love. She recognizes him as a man connected in God and offers her heart as a passageway to the Divine. Her love melts away his resistances and fears as she sings the light of the invisible—visible through his heart.

Their chamber of love is made ready by the meeting of their cosmic forces. Their hands and body vibrate with the joys of entering the unknown and surrendering to the love waiting in their hearts. The fires of the divine ignited by each kiss, their tongues quaking, awaken the serpent power. Each caress carries them into the ecstasy of opening to light meeting dark, God meeting body. As each current is awakened, breath sustains the movement.

They find the gateway into God as they merge into their unified energy. Their minds surrender to the light moving in their bodies, transforming all darkness. They move deeper into their souls, touching one another through love alone. God takes over completely as their bodies disappear into the waves of the Divine.

The Holy Grail chalice of divine love is the reward of conscious preparation. As a chalice of life through divine union, sacred partners can consciously create a womb of love and dwell within it. The feeling and beauty of the outer environment reflects the light of the inner sanctuary. Both partners take to heart their own union in God and individually practice daily alignment of their cosmic and life forces. The light created when two individuals meet through the body and spirit multiples the love of God in the physical and inner worlds. Their united spiritual and physical forces rejuvenate their bodies and the body of life. Together, their absorption into God opens the gateway into eternal bliss.

Divine sexuality bridges God connection into the body. Sexual pleasure between two partners who learn to responsibly open spiritual, emotional, etheric and physical currents together can realize bliss. The beauty of sustaining pleasure and sharing in the expansion of light in our body opens the heart to receive and give ecstatic love.

Making love with divine consciousness offers the opportunity to love God with or without a partner. As a pathway to spiritual evolution, divine union with a partner is a doorway to surrender and spiritual completion. By offering our higher energies to one another we create a daily practice of living in union with God.

Sex and the Holy Grail

The light of our true self fills the chalice of our body. Through the union of our body and soul, our authentic nature becomes the vessel for our God self. The sacred home for our heart's love is created through balancing our divine feminine and masculine powers. By acting upon the feelings of our heart and soul in union we learn to paint with love the eternal landscape of our whole self. When we open to the colors of universal love and apply them to the canvas of separation and pain, we assist the unraveling of old cords that have attached our emotions and willpower to feelings of lack and control. The presence of our true self always exists; by the grace of spirit, we are destined to live in this magnificence.

The spirit and heart of sex is an expression that flows like a river bursting with life energies from the desire to be one in self. It takes courage to hold that space with another human being. It takes the willingness to be seen, heard and received. It means that we must deal with lifetimes of our human patterns to control and separate just to stay safe, and emerge from our cocoon to determine how we want to live in God—or outside of God. We must be willing to go beyond our own definition of how things are supposed to be, and heal our shame caused by past actions, projections and loss of self. By doing so, we feel connected to our true self and enter the presence and sustainability of living in our own wholeness.

When we truly surrender to *living* in God, we enter the meeting point where body, spirit and heart meet. Our mind becomes the benefactor of blessings and radiates love and acceptance, making it possible for our heart and soul to surrender into union. These blessings open the temple of our body to contain the initiating flames of the Holy Grail by becoming living prayers, walking ceremonies of joy and oneness. As we prepare for receiving holy love in our body by absorbing the gold and white light of God, we can remember the peace and union of our eternal self.

To make love to life, our self and to a beloved heart-mate, our mind, body and soul becomes a living shrine and altar to the heart of devotion. This decision lifts us to Source and calls forth our desire to dissolve, awaken, recycle, translate and unify everything that separates us from oneness. By serving the God/Goddess in one another we can awaken to the divine bliss of love without separation.

The alchemy between a man and a woman begins with creating a loving and magnetic field of safety and love. All foreplay, lovemaking and time spent together after lovemaking creates the divine harmonics that bring about entering into a higher consciousness together. When the woman feels adored and safe with her partner, she can move into an alchemical bonding with her partner—a chalice of love—that carries them both into the higher initiations of sex.

Whether practicing these activations of light alone or with a partner, always give your self plenty of inner space and unlimited time to feel every nuance of sacred union with your own heart, body and soul.

Creating Sexual Union

Sexual union with your own forces:

Men: Move your heart energy into your penis. Learn to contract the anal sphincter muscle. From above your crown chakra, send light into your heart and create downward loops through your solar plexus, second chakra, genitals and perineum. Bring the light above your crown chakra and repeat while drawing the sexual energies up as the loop reaches its highest point in the circle.

Women: Create your womb to be the temple of bliss and chamber of cosmic desire. Learn to open like a flower to receive the God Forces of your lover. Learn to contract and master your vaginal muscles. Pull cosmic current into your vagina, creating multiple upward loops through your second chakra, navel, solar plexus and heart center. Send the current back into your vagina and repeat until high arousal.

Together: Breathe in moving your tailbone towards the sky and contract your anal sphincter muscle. Extend your tailbone towards the earth as you exhale and release the muscle. Inhale. On the next exhalation, press your middle back into the ground and reach your tailbone up to the sky. Pull up energetic flames of fire into your vagina/scrotum and into the second chakra. Push these flames into your genitals and pull them back up. Breathe into your chakras one by one and learn to open them. Hold eye contact as you remain open.

Sexual union with each other's forces:

For Men: Take your lover's nipple into your mouth and suck upon it, receiving and absorbing her divine mother energy until she is highly aroused. Practice receiving your lover's essence of love into your heart to help melt away your emotional armor.

For Women: Take your lover's penis into your mouth with passion and worship it with adoration. Send the love of your heart into his testicles as you lick them with devotion and gratitude.

Together: Connect your chakras together with light and send love to each other's heart. The man receives her love and sends her his love, the woman receives his love, and they circulate this flow. Take turns placing your right hand on your lover's sacrum and your left hand beneath your lover's medulla oblongata (base of the neck). Place your right hand on your lover's lower belly and your left hand on your lover's forehead. Allow the energies to flow between your palms.

True Tantra

Tantra is the practice of realizing union with the Divine through energetic principles that raise the vibrations in the body and soul to attain universal oneness. Does that definition sound a little different from the way tantra is often marketed today, as a physical reflection of the words and diagrams of the *Kama Sutra?* While the *Kama Sutra* does illustrate many positions and attitudes for the practice of tantric sex, it does not adequately address the deep divinity of tantra, nor tantra's place as a central Holy Grail experience—what I know as True Tantra.

Whether practiced alone or in partnership, True Tantra reconnects the God forces in the body to experience divine bliss. To practice True Tantra is to embrace expansion. It returns us to a state of wonder, innocence and oneness with the universe and with our self. True Tantra teaches us to identify and sustain the state of divine essence with our partner. It unifies female and male energies into divine union and aligns them into the expansive creative forces existing in the universe. By entering into this full heart space, the essence of light and love can merge. The joy of surrendering to the Divine in our partner opens our heart center and serves to hold the relationship in the highest light. The gift of receiving another completely with an open heart dissolves the fears and mistrusts of past relationships. It also breaks open the ego self by teaching us to give and receive levels of God energies that release karmic, family and past relationship issues in the body.

Before taking this vital step into a True Tantric relationship, both partners need to face and deal with past childhood developmental issues, wounds and abuses in order to experience total sexual-spiritual fulfillment. It is difficult for a man to remain and surrender into an intimate relationship when, as an infant or young boy, he experienced power struggles with his mother. The male child must be able to push his mother away without a battle of wills and enter autonomy with himself. If his childhood experience was traumatic and left an imprint, it may be difficult to fully surrender and deeply engage with a partner without feeling the need to fly or run away. The fight-or-flight response needs to be healed before the deepest love can be realized so the man can learn to take flight in divine ecstasy.

A woman who was constantly belittled, unsupported and judged as a young girl for her spontaneous creativity, sexual joy or outspokenness needs to heal these wounds before she can receive the adoration and attention of a divine lover. Her reconnection with her divine feminine must occur to trust the transformative journey of love.

In preparation to practice True Tantra, we also learn to transform primal and earth energies in the psyche and body, increase breath and body awareness, reunite the soul, heart and belly and begin to recognize one's true self as light. When the frequency in our light body can match the frequency of our emotional, etheric and physical bodies, the finer and more enlightening aspects of True Tantra can be achieved. By making your intention the full activation of God Realization while in a physical body, your growing chalice of divine masculine and feminine union can hold the spark to full realization.

True Tantra unites energy and consciousness. A spark of bliss is ignited between the male and female generative fluids during lovemaking. A woman releases her nectar, amrita, after multiple orgasms; the act serves to cosmically bless the universe. The union of the male and female fluids can heal, sustain and build life force energies. Their combined light and power transform and uplift mind and body into pure ecstasy. We unite with our other half of our God self, whether male or female, when we purposefully practice tantra. When both partners are integrated in their own divine masculine and feminine energies, the power of oneness can be deeply celebrated. This is known as the hierosgamos, the sacred inner marriage. By first reuniting our unique and authentic divine masculine and feminine energies, we are able to live in this inner marriage whether in partnership with another or at one with one's self.

The secret to experiencing deeper and more meaningful sex is to remain integrated in the core of the chakra centers. By bringing your focus into the core column of light in the spine and learning to master the currents in your body, you are able to approach sex as an initiation into the Divine. As with any higher meditation practice, it is not possible to plan the outcome. The power experienced creates high-level joy and is honored, revered and recycled as spiritual energy. As both partners learn to let go into the transcended energies of love, and sustain them in their daily living, the walls to God can dissolve.

The divine feminine will want to express all aspects of her self with her partner. This erotic experience is a gift to both partners. The divine aspects of her goddess self will want to give and receive pleasure, accessing all her powers in the process, as symbolized by a number of immortal reflections of the divine feminine: Kali, the Hindu goddess of transformative death and rebirth energies; Lakshmi, the abundant Hindu messenger of life wealth in all of its forms; Isis, Ancient Egypt's regal guide through the esoteric mysteries of the universe; Aphrodite, the radiant Ancient Greek beauty of love and seduction; Inanna, the creation goddess of sexual love and fertility who reigned over Sumeria; and other life-giving manifestations. The embodied energies of the Goddess in a woman awaken the Shakti and Shiva (life force and kundalini energies) present in both women and men.

When practicing True Tantra, time becomes a window into love without restrictions, fears or limitations emotionally, spiritually and physically. Extending the element of time gives a couple the opportunities to explore love's deepest intimacy and connections. Giving and receiving one another within eternal time allows the body, spirit and heart to merge, creating profound and beautiful orgasms.

During True Tantra practice, a man's penis channels the energy of full consciousness, ready to become one with the universal body of God within a woman. The energy in a woman's vagina opens to receive unified light and power during True Tantra as she unites with love to experience union with her partner. This Holy Grail rite is a direct experience with the Divine. By visualizing the vagina opening into a full lotus or rose, a woman can begin to open to universal energies of love. A man can maintain his sexual excitement through deep connection with his body and natural forces. As he receives her divine feminine power and all of her manifestations, he can move the energetic charge through his whole body and simultaneously feel himself becoming erect in his light body, core self and genitals.

When engaging in higher sexuality, transforming the forces in your body to become one with God forces takes the willingness to overcome all obstacles. Any couple desiring to improve or relight their sexual relationship or reach God together can do so by learning to see, feel and move the currents of power within their own bodies. Your expression of transformation into True Tantra can begin by breathing light into your core column. Move the light through the spine and into your third eye, and clear and integrate your chakra centers with higher intention and integrity. The resulting removal of your unconscious cords and imprints will change your life. The darkness you will uncover reflects parts of your self that have separated from your core life force energies.

In Kabbalah, it is taught that, at the onset of Sabbath, a couple engages in divine sex to honor God. Hopefully, as we evolve through this time period of planetary awakening to divine order, all religions will embrace and honor the spiritual function of conscious sexuality.

There are also important spiritual practices that rejuvenate the life forces and assist in greater self-realization and God realization; they require sexual abstinence. These times are sacred and meant to be honored. Celibacy can rebuild and generate powers in the body that can be used for personal transformation, rejuvenation and spiritual evolution. Time alone with the forces of the Divine can initiate the deepest personal connection. When used consciously, celibacy can be a portal to God and creative empowerment.

Bring to a close your days of considering your relationship with sex separate from your relationship with God. The only way to experience christed or divine consciousness is to open the body vessel all the way up to God. Divine sex is a way to extend longevity by creating union with God in the body. Even the highest Buddhist monk who takes a vow of celibacy experiences union with the infinite through the sexual act after leaving the body at death.

The days of viewing higher chakras as being good and lower chakras as being bad are over. The integration of the higher and lower chakras is a gateway to whole thinking, being and creating. As long as you are committed to clearing old wounds, hurts and traumas from your inner energy circuitry, you have the potential to experience incredible sex that touches the face of divinity. Flowing, integrated beings do not need pornography to ignite their sexual energies. Hearts alight with streaming rays of gold currents pulsate and magnetize on their own. The senses opened by the inner melodies of enlightenment and bliss help us become balanced and integrated sexual-spiritual beings.

Sexual Circuitry

Visualize a solid gold, silver or white beam through your core inner shaft of light. Create a globe of light inside of each chakra center.

1. Begin in the solar plexus center and turn on its globe of light.
2. Pull in its light into the core shaft of light.
3. Feel its glow in the shaft.
4. Turn on the globe in your navel and heart centers.
5. Connect the light in your heart, solar plexus and navel globes. Feel their connection.
6. NOW turn the globes on in your pubic bone, throat chakra and third eye. Feel their connection.
7. Focus upon all of the globes lit at the same time.
8. Open the light first in the back of your eyes. Heighten the globe's light in your second chakra and then heighten the light in your third eye. Connect their light and hold the focus of all three at the same time.

The Female Gateways

Knowing how to build the energy in our female palace creates physical wellbeing, a healthy mind and spirit. Rather than thinking of stimulating these points in the vagina, think of bringing light into these gateways.

The three female gateways are the clitoris, the G-spot and the area around the entrance to the cervix. Focus light into one gateway at a time. When both the receiver and her partner focus light into these areas very slowly, allowing them to open, a woman's flower blossoms with great potency. This is particularly true of the G-spot; opening is achieved through touch and sending light energy through the fingers, palms, third eye and heart. Many times, an activated G-spot will also open the other two gateways. Meditate into the light present within each gateway and invite your partner's touch, or touch your self on your G-spot (Goddess spot) with a conscious, gentle and steady light pressure. Gently touch your clitoris with your right hand and your third eye with your left hand, then send light into both places at the same time. Feel the circuitry of light flow between these two points of power. Hold the contact as the energy begins to increase, and then:

a) Pull the light up towards the navel, then send it back down into your vagina.
b) Spiral the light through all three gateways.
c) Move light up through the core column in the spine to the third eye as the contact is held and the energy increases.
d) Activate the light further by moving your finger(s) on the contact spot.
e) Expand the light throughout the whole body and back into the vagina.

Your partner can receive and circulate the chi through his or her body and send it to you through the energy body, heart center, third eye, hands and genitals. As a woman approaches or has begun to climax, her partner can ignite her energies further by entering divine space with her while deep within her palace. By connecting their light together and circulating their energies through their core shafts of light, they initiate an exquisite journey together into God.

Sexual liberation is the opening of the combined chalice to the light of God. Profound climaxes are miraculous expansions of light, in which partners experience oneness in God. As enlightened energy currents open a woman's womb, lovemaking becomes an inner meditation of focusing powerful light. By channeling light into the G-spot, the gateways in the vagina and womb open. From here multiple colors, light and energy can travel through the inner circuits of the spine, third eye and heart. If a male partner is attuned to bringing light through his genitals and through his spine, the couple can move the currents of light with intense love and surrender to one another's circuitry.

This is far beyond isolated lower chakra sex, in which a woman must work up against a man's penis to begin to open her womb. A man may feel inclined to help her find herself, but he is setting himself up to not be fully received. When a man focuses only upon sensations in his penis, he is forfeiting the full transformational experience of sex. Enlightened sex begins with an energetically clear, receptive and divine feminine womb and a heart-connected divine masculine phallus seeking oneness into the female nectars of divine love. From there, the couple moves into ecstatic bliss.

Creating a Sexual Chalice

- Every day, practice moving pure energy through your core column of light from under your tailbone to your third eye and back down.
- Create a space(s) of beauty and peace to meditate alone, together and for making love.
- Your space needs to be a container to build a positive sexual charge rather than a place to merely release negative stress.
- Relax and unwind together before making love. This will create the proper energetic conditions for later exploration and sustenance of your sexual vitality and connection.
- Clear any issues, emotions or negative energies that may be obstructing full intimacy before you engage sexually, so you can open to higher feelings and energies together.
- Bring light into your etheric (Ka) body and draw it into your physical body and chakras.
- Practice energy current exercises each day to build your body and mind as a chalice of light.
- Offer devotion and love through your touch and your eyes as you practice presence with your partner.
- Settle into the container of light and energy within your pelvis.

- Holding sacred space as partners, inhale light up through your genitals and into your hearts, then exhale as you both send light back down to your genitals and tailbone. The female breathes light into her genitals, moves it up into her heart and exhales it through her heart as her partner inhales her light into his heart, pulling her love into his genitals. She receives his love through his genitals into her vagina, while moving his love into her heart. The longer this circuit is engaged, the higher the levels of arousal and love. As the energies build, both partners will be ready to enter into coitus.

- Follow the same exercise as you move into deeper union. After you bring light into your heart, draw this light into your third eye, hold it there and absorb it, then send or receive your light or your partner's light through your heart center.

- Move the light through your own chakra centers and into the other's heart while circulating the light through your chakras together at the same time. Enter into your light bodies to hold the energies of love.

- From inside the perineum (the area between the anus and genitals) pull light inside the tailbone. Create two rays of light, one that is the Sun Current and one that is the Moon current. Move them as a caduceus of ascending power, crisscrossing them through each chakra. As you feel the movement of the caduceus, feel the development of the accompanying magnetic charge. As you approach the heart center and pineal gland (third eye) within the center of your head, create two chalices of light: one in the heart and one in the third eye. Simultaneously with your partner, move your light up through the central core column of light and feel the caduceus moving into the crown chakra. Allow your consciousness to meet your partner's consciousness at the crown chakra and concurrently move into the light above your heads, creating an *Antakarana*, a bridge into the power and love of God. Join with your partner in God light and receive the nectars of energy flowing into the chalice inside your head, illuminating all of your chakras and transporting you into bliss. Open the chalice in your hearts to receive the overflow.

- During your orgasms together, experience the full charge of the semen as the carrier of light.
- After climax, rest together and receive the light generated. The male partner should refrain from going to sleep, instead dwelling upon and taking in the energies created. This creates a circuitry of spiritual fuel for both partners. The act of remaining sensitized dramatically assists the man to recharge and strengthen his energy bodies while resting in the peace and love of his Beloved.

Chapter 30

The Offering

Just forgive everything that is going to happen.
~ Vajra

Every step we take in this time period of global and personal change potentially empowers us to establish our soul's freedom—and on a larger scale, contribute to the greater cause of planetary unity and harmony.

Bringing the pieces of our soul together after lifetimes of creative, financial, survival and love commitments is necessary to repair the power and strength of our soul. We become recharged by the fuel of our own spirit returning to the framework of our soul. Our feminine body stores the memories of our separation from Source and works to create union and connection, while our masculine side steadily moves us forward to make changes, create stability and develop new contracts of empowered survival. It is important at this time to release our existing contracts with our personal power and welcome new agreements that align us to serve the forces of Oneness and Light. It is here that freedom and responsibility take on a whole new meaning.

By releasing all blame, judgment and condemnation, we release our old contracts. When we feel the pain caused by keeping our attention off of our connection with the light, we need to recommit and hold the connection. We must deeply commit to living in the center of our selves, in the *nous*, the treasure, and refuse to emotionally and spiritually leave our selves. We must practice gratitude and faith while living in our heart and soul at the same time, leaving no stone left unturned. Look closely at the elements and energies that motivate your will to succeed. We must turn away from habitual ways that ultimately harm us and face the light within. We must also change our inner and outer direction. Rather than looking straight ahead, we must remain open to finding the passageway in a new direction. Try this quick exercise: Close your eyes, and while in a contemplative state, inwardly turn to the right and look for light. If you see darkness, turn to the right again, and again until you see light. Align your daily choices to this light and trust it.

To make room for the full power of your true self, learn to release the abuse in your physical and subtle bodies from this lifetime and all lifetimes. Our feminine sides need this respect and tender attention in order to move into living without the fear of success, pain, light, recognition, empowerment or intimacy. Our masculine sides need to clear the cellular memories of being destroyed after expressing ourselves to the world, and begin to implement truth that is unified in light. By releasing all abuse from our cellular structures and removing the numbness from the traumas we have undergone, we can live in our body with attunement and heightened awareness.

What does it require today to remain open and connected to what we know as the truth, beauty and light of our soul? How do we handle watching and experiencing war, famine and dehumanization as it spreads across our planet right before our eyes, while many of our world leaders act with deep insensitivity and impunity? We must learn to step out of the way of our projections and respond in the moment from our connection in Source. We must remain connected to Source, no matter what, and we must say "no" to the voice that wants to react with its self-important response. Whether we are facing global warming, family dispute, financial loss or death, the only solutions are *aligned* solutions, those that are realized through conscious or chosen union with Source. If there is one thing we can teach our future generations all over the world, it is this: we are the carriers of truth. You are, and so am I. When we know ourselves as co-creators with divine forces, we can live with purpose. When we awaken to the reality that divine energies are the matrix of our lives and the connecting link of our existence, and we live in relationship to these energies and forces, our views of our selves and the world will shift. We realize and recognize that who we are is enough, and that our presence truly matters when we are connected into our wholeness. When we are whole—one in body, soul, emotion, mind and spirit—we feel our spiritual power in concert with everyone else's power around the world. It may or may not instantly change the power imbalance currently rearing its head and trying to consume this planet, but it can eventually make possible the tilt needed to restore balance.

Your personal alignment in spirit, body and soul creates your wellbeing, relationship to the universe, and integration of love and power. The alignment of your chakras and your emotional, spiritual, etheric and mental bodies fuel the push or pull toward your center of power.

During this time of global change, pay close attention to how you use your energies. Your past ways will serve you less and less. For those of you who reach out into the world to make things happen, take one step back and view all of the times you have climbed to the top of the mountain. Notice how you got there and what you put aside along the way. For you, the mountain is no longer the goal. You need to spend your time in the valleys below, resting and taking in the more feminine giving aspects of your self. Then integrate your abilities to climb your mountains with a steadfast focus that can literally move mountains and cause change on a global level.

For those of you who have felt content with silence, your cup of tea in hand, contemplative and listening to your deepest self, this is your time to reach into your communities and make a difference. Give what you know and help make others aware of their place in the universal order of life.

For those of you who have something to say through the creative planes, do it now, in a more assertive and divinely connected way than you've ever created before. Trust your self and follow the voice and power of integration.

Become aware of your denials and fears surrounding being exposed in the light. Find how you separate your feelings and thoughts about love, intimacy, connection and power. Place your attention on the part of your self that dwells under your mask of protection. Ask it why it has been on this planet and listen for its response. It will share its deepest connection with you and touch your soul. There is a saying, "Stay with your self." Pay attention to the energies inside you that are hiding behind and beneath your light. These energies will run your life without you even knowing it. They await your return to guide them into wholeness.

The way to live integrated within the light of the inner self alongside the desire to be seen, recognized and accepted in the world, is to live in the center point that connects both. All attachment to outcome must be released. Deeply feel, with sincere devotion, every emotion while discovering the profound and beautiful being that lives inside each of those emotions. Until you know your emotions as gateways into your true self, they will run you, inspire great creative expressions, create romantic encounters and entice you all at the same time to run from your emotions until you can no longer put them into separate compartments in your mind and soul. Your emotions are the powers that, when honored and followed to their core, will take you into and through your darkness. This journey can only succeed when the ego surrenders to the light of the empowered self. Become the singular force of enlightenment that runs through you, rather than a force split into separate shafts of light and dark. An alignment to God force will gift you with greater stability and clarity.

Imagine for a moment a highway running through your spine within the center of your body. At each chakra center is a light bulb wired to high voltage. Bring your attention to the first light bulb inside the space above your tailbone and directly above your pubic bone to keep the bulb dimly lit. Move along the highway, a current of energy that may also be called your *sushumna*, turning on each bulb, one at a time, to match the glow of the previous bulb while looking for the next portal of light. Travel through this wide channel of light, a super highway, seeing each sphere of light emanating a warm glow. When you arrive at your crown chakra, begin the descent down to your base chakra. Each time you ascend up the highway, brighten the intensity of light blazing from the bulbs, while on the descent, keep the illumination of the light bulbs constant.

Align your consciousness with the center of the highway igniting the light bulbs. Balance your self in this moving energy, from your crown chakra to your base chakra. Feel what happens to you when you move either to the right or to the left side of your body. Each time you enter the light along the center of your highway, open to fill your body with light. Place your focus within this center. From this point of view, love your self and enter your heart, filling it with the life-giving forces of God. Acknowledge the feelings in your heart when you are in the *sushumna* or are on the outside. Gently, call attention to the part of you that needs things to be a certain way. Notice how it projects fictional pictures of a secure reality onto the moment. You no longer need its distractions; communicate this. Return to your super highway of light and true power. Sit and stay awhile. Welcome home.

Home in the Body

Use the third finger of your right hand to make contact with the point below your pubic bone. Move your finger directly above your pubic bone while breathing into each point, then gently press it into the center of your pubic bone. Pull gold light from the center of the earth and spiral it into this point. Contract and expand this gold spiral into your pubic bone, feeling it grow wider, then contract it 12 times. Suck in your lower belly and navel area so it presses into your middle back. Pull the gold spiral into the point where your back and belly meet. Breathe into the point and expand and contract the gold spiral 12 times. Pull the energy up into your solar plexus, maintaining the contraction in your middle back. Elongate and straighten your upper back. Pull the energy into your solar plexus and repeat contracting and expanding the golden spiral. Send a clockwise circuit of light from your solar plexus into your pubic bone and back into your solar plexus.

Hold the connection in your middle back. From the earth, draw gold, violet, blue, red and yellow flames of fire of into your second chakra. Contract the anal sphincter muscles 12 times as you pull up the flames of fire into your navel area. Pull your belly in with strength as you exhale out of your mouth. Repeat 12 times. Draw the energy into your heart center, through the back of your head, into your third eye and down through the core shaft of light in your body until you reach your tailbone. Next, pull the light up through your spine, igniting each power center along the way, until you reach your crown chakra. Send it back down to the tailbone. Repeat 12 times.

The Choice

Every one of us *must* eventually choose to serve either the light or the dark. It is the most empowering decision we can ever make in a lifetime.

Most of us put off this decision until our life is in crisis. Perhaps we can learn how to make this choice before we develop a serious health condition, create relationship difficulties or endure work-related problems. Choosing to serve the light not only connects us to Source, but it also clears the bonds we created when we served the dark. These bonds may have been formed during a time we were struggling to simply survive. We can only be in the light with someone else, however, when we shed the patterns and behaviors formed during our time serving the dark. Most of you reading this book came into this lifetime with the intention of bringing light and reconnected consciousness to this planet. You may not yet know how it works, but this purpose becomes evident when you step out of your own separations into the power of oneness. Your light-filled consciousness can change the thoughts on this planet. Once you learn to hold your vibration of light and stay in the frequency of your spiritual self, you can create change. Your desire to love will grow and you will be faced with learning opportunities that test your endurance to stay with your self.

Others around you may have drug, self-esteem, ego, health, sexual and self-destructive problems that you have to face. It is not your place to lecture, preach the light, make wrong or try to get them to see another way. Your place is to stay connected with your light and highest truth first. Then ask them if they want to live in a different way. Let them come to your wholeness. Know that your wholeness is a safety net, a warm fuzzy blanket in the midst of a spiderweb of conflicting messages. Stay connected to all of your chakras and do not give your self away. Trust in your love and be strong in that love. Ask them questions so they begin to see their own choices from their own light. Where they are is perfect for them. It is our responsibility to stay connected to our self, no matter what, even if the other person is in the deepest depression.

Our light empowers others. Beware of those who use their darkness in the name of the light to create change. They will always take away something and replace it with their personalized solution to a problem. If someone does not address the real power struggle existing within her self, know the dark is using her light for its own gain. If someone is trying to get you to do it his way, know he is in denial of his own dark and is utilizing the dark as his comfort zone. All of his actions will be taken to protect that comfort zone. You must protect yourself by holding your light within all of your chakras at the same time and maintaining a pearl of light around your self that is as strong as steel and translucent as rain.

When we begin to heal and integrate our feminine and masculine energies we become the elements of air, water, ether, earth and fire. We are living in communication with our essence as it integrates and blends with the forces of soul alchemy. When we have spent enough time learning to move these energies in our body we can become a healer of life. As our inner masculine and feminine selves become active and involved in our lives, the light of love is then able to instigate awaiting transformations. We become skilled at holding the space for others to reclaim their parts, love themselves and find the fearlessness to expose their deepest self in our presence as we learn to hold space for the precious and powerful beings within our self. The space we hold is the power received by living in the Holy Grail, our divine union with oneness.

The Holy Grail Empowerments

1. Listen to the inner flow of light and energy through your core shaft of light and through your body. Quiet everything within to feed your self with spirit.
2. Allow your light and energy to flow through and relax all your joints—shoulders, elbows, wrists, fingers, hips, knees, ankles, toes.
3. Breathe light and energy into the back of your skull, reaching your occipital ridge, then up to your crown chakra towards the sky as you stretch the vertebrae in your neck.
4. Circulate the energy to your crown chakra, pineal gland (third eye), down the inner spine, tailbone, genitals, solar plexus, back of the heart chakra and back to the occipital ridge.
5. Expand light into your heart center and radiate it.
6. Simultaneously open currents of light in the soles of your feet and in your throat chakra.
7. Envision a gold chalice with its base in your solar plexus and its top rim in the center of your head, on line with your lower eye socket bone in your face. Fill it with liquid light.
8. Listen to the pulse and rhythm of the gold light pouring into the chalice.
9. Align your root and crown chakras to a star of light three to ten feet above your head.
10. Remain connected in all of your chakras at the same time.
11. Create a Shield of David, with its center in your heart chakra. The lower triangle point is on your pubic bone and the upper triangle point is in your third eye.
12. Live in the center of your mind, body and spirit by placing your focus in the "valley point" above your solar plexus, in the center of your breastbone—perpendicular to your nipples.
13. Focus your attention in your solar plexus. Gently look up with your inner vision and watch the light as it pours from above your head as it flows into you.

14. Awaken the serpent of light through your perineum to your crown chakra by purifying your mind and emotions and by opening your core shaft of light through the center of your body. Raise your divine feminine power from the earth to meet your divine masculine power as it flows in from above your head. Meet the light in your body.

15. Absorb the healing power of the serpent into your thymus gland (approximately two inches below the center of your collarbone).

16. Focus inside your third eye and look up through your crown chakra. Bring into focus a geometric design of pastel hues and white light. Allow it to ignite your chakras with its light and align you with your higher soul energies.

17. Mentally, physically and spiritually align with spirit every moment.

18. Maintain your endrocrine system with green foods, amino acids, compatible proteins, Omega-3, Omega-6 and high-enzyme foods.

Chapter 31

Drinking of the Rose

"The rose, wherein the world divine makes itself flesh."
~ Dante

In many pictures of Mary Magdalene and Mary the Mother, a lavish and deep red rose extends from each of their hands. The symbolism is direct, divine and intentional. The all-pervading presence and intoxicating aroma of the rose in bloom fills our every sense. We become one with the rose's scent only by lifting our complete attention into the rose. For that moment, we enter and become the rose. From this delicate, precious place, we wonder how it is possible to ever forget this heightened state.

The rose never ceases being a rose. It lives and dies remaining a rose. Its petals are connected to form the scent of its essence. As its petals fall to the ground, its essence remains. For its entire existence, the rose knew itself as a rose and nothing else.

Throughout time the rose has represented eternal love, union with the Divine and the purity of devotion. Mystics and spiritual avatars have been known to manifest through the ethers often carrying with their presence the scent of the rose in full bloom and magnificence.

In the first century, when the two Marys walked the planet and were energetically planted in the earth, each moved the heavenly energies of oneness through her united body and soul. Through their example, the Marys taught how to live in the state of being one with the rose. Through the centers of their hearts, they could enter into other realms of light that could remove obstacles and blocks to the most serious conditions and situations. Jesus knew in his deepest heart that Mary Magdalene would carry the torch of this integrated spiritual power into time and space. He also knew that until men and women embraced the divine male christed energy and divine feminine enlivened rose, the legacy of the Holy Grail would lay dormant. His vision was in not in vain, because we are still struggling to unite our masculine and feminine energies, and as such we have not yet attained unity. Just as opposite sides of magnets are attracted to each other, however, the masculine and feminine will become integrated; this is the direction occurring on this planet, no matter what external forces wish us to believe or follow.

Why were there so many Marys during the time of Christ? We had Mary of James, Mary of Salome, Mary Magdalene and Mary the Mother, among others. The answer to this question lies in the name itself: Mary originates from *Mri*, an Ancient Egyptian word meaning "beloved." These women were higher initiates who were given the respected title *Mri*, which later became known in Hebrew as "Miriam." They lived in their essence of love, the essence of life: God.

The opportunity to live within our christed light while receiving the spark of love and power from our divine feminine opens the door to true love. Together, as one weaving of ecstatic union, the body-soul drinks from the chalice and is restored in God. Imagine for a moment what it would feel and look like to be living within the holy chalice. It is filled with the colors, scents and currents of a light-filled divine inner marriage. As you enter into the hues of tangerine, aqua, purple, pink, blue, yellow, violet and gold currents of bliss, a sanctuary of peace connecting heaven and earth nurtures your heart. There is a sense of motion around the serenity that continually embraces and connects you into larger stratospheres of energy and light. The cup of receiving that lives within your solar plexus, navel and lower belly becomes filled with gentleness and soothing strength and trust. Each moment spent in the beloved union of your inner feminine and masculine creative forces opens your heart further to the unlimited resources existing in this divine union with universal forces.

When union with your divine self is maintained, a natural protective shield is formed around your core self. It serves as a powerful replacement for fear. Any emotional or mental armor can be put to rest as your light unites with your power.

Most of us spend our lives leaving our essence. One moment, our ego demands that we deserve more acknowledgement, appreciation and attention. In the next, we are consumed with how much money we have in the bank. Later, we may seek acceptance and throw ourselves into someone else's life drama. We fight with our demons that block us from feeling accepted, seen or wanted by life, our loved ones and the world.

Then one day after we have spent years on a rollercoaster ride through life, we decide that we will no longer leave our temple of worship. After thousands of moments of going to our inner temple, we choose to dwell and drink of the love we have found within our self. There is no other place to go. We must live in the temple. Its walls reflect the color of our soul. Its scent comforts us and intoxicates our mind. We choose to live in the center of love.

We find that whenever we leave the love, we create pain. Eventually, we tire of feeling our heart center close. It takes so much time and work to reopen it. We grow weary in spirit because what we have accomplished means so little compared to the joy of living in the love. Affirm in the core of your being: *I love and acknowledge myself. I live in the love that I am. I am love. I truly am of the Divine.*

When you are immersed in love, it becomes possible to understand the path of duality and separation, create great works of art, love a partner passionately and completely and perform acts of kindness. Your mind will always try to construct a "valid" reason to leave the love and cause you pain; that is the action of a desperate ego that has been wounded in battle with spirit. It will continually want, and when it cannot have, it will attempt to sacrifice something very precious to you —love.

Refuse to leave yourself even if others taught you as a child that you had to relinquish your true being. Leaving yourself means abandoning the very love that is the core of your soul. As you reclaim the love and essence of your true self you can empower your self. Your power and love is reintegrated and made use of to grow and transform into *who* you are—your whole self. When you end the cycle of abandoning your true self, you stay planted in living your truth and vision. You are able to remain within the center of your self while the world works out its issues and the people around you face their lack and poverty of their own heart and soul. *Stay in your love*. You can be busy from daybreak until sunset and yet still remain united in your love. All health, relationship, career and family issues will resolve themselves. Honor the love in your self. Work hard, love hard, play hard and laugh hard.

What do you have to give up? How about the dramas of your control struggles, which include the need to feel and look better in comparison to others, your rescue attempts of friends or family from their dealings with their dark sides, your angry struggles with God for not being able to do what you want how you want, your attempts to impose on another your beliefs that certain things should be done your way, the distractions you create to avoid the pain within you, and the attempts you make to keep the parts of your soul and heart separated so the addictions to loss, loneliness and extremes live on.

Once you are back in the venerable love that has always been alive within the essence of your heart, you are free. Allow this love to fill every cell in your body, and you will feel joy. Feel the power of love fill your mind, body, soul and spirit. Then live in the center of this love. Enter it. Practice it over and over again. Keep filling yourself in love. Close your eyes many times a day and observe the love turning into light until you are living in the light as it fills your entire body. As you drink from this chalice of light, the Holy Grail will ignite your passion to accomplish your life dreams, heal relationships, overcome health challenges, realize career goals and offer higher service to this planet.

We are all carriers of the Holy Grail. By following the desire to live in union with the power of our hearts and light combined, the legacy of the Grail touches all life through our authentic unconditional love.

Chapter 32

Replenishing the Planet's Cup

Treat the earth well.
It was not given to you by your parents,
it was loaned to you by your children.
We do not inherit the Earth from our Ancestors,
we borrow it from our Children.
~ Ancient Native American Proverb

Throughout our lifetimes, we have given life various degrees of our love, faith, promises, hopes and dreams. It has been easy to separate our mind and soul to believe that we can come and go from our relationship with spirit instead of living in the true reality of who we are as the embodiment of life itself.

Many of us carry the wound created by giving to life what is most precious in our soul and experiencing having it taken away, used, ignored or judged. Many of us have wanted life to give us more of a return; consequently we carry resentment, arrogance, pride, greed and the need for recognition. We often have out-of-balance expectations on relationships and work. We hold a grudge, whether with life, someone else or God.

While we are figuring out our day-to-day life, we walk upon Mother Earth interacting with her as we go about our daily routines. Ever at our side she is taking on our problems and woes. She pours her nourishment through the air, water, animals, plants, food and beauty on our planet. We use her and we do not give back. Many who can feel her know she is crying or is angry because of what we are doing to this planet and to one another. But, underneath the anger is a heart of serene and gentle love welcoming us to become one with her heart. She wants us to feel her love. As we enter into the deepest love of our heart and integrate this vital knowingness into our lives and invite the Divine Mother into our life picture, we are often given the roadmap to full awakening.

Gaze upon the earth with loving attention, feeling yourself embracing the planet, and send out a vibrant call to bring back all of the soul pieces of your self that were previously expressed into life, people and situations, given conditionally or unconditionally. Then, state your commitment to return back to all beings and life the energies and soul pieces that you took from them. Offer back to the earth and all of her beings all that you have taken and received. Allow this to be a gift of forgiveness to the Divine Mother. Giving back to her honors the life forces she sustains and creates, allowing us to experience our highest nature; we come away living in oneness with the Divine. As you take back all of your soul pieces, you can begin to release the memories of your past. This ceremony is a transformation into the heart of your true inner home and honors your relationship with the planet that you have called home. Instead of constantly giving energy to past memories that resonate with your struggles, pain and victimhood, release these memories from your body-mind-soul and choose to empower the memories that serve your highest good. Send them through your heart and release them for all time. Ask the universe to bring up to you every memory that needs to be returned to the Creator. Release all connection to those memories. You will remember your true self as you become uncluttered from all that you are attached to. As you give back to the planet everything you have received or taken, open your self to live in a state of for-giveness and be here for giving.

The Mother wants to receive the armor of your heart. Each time you bring light through your heart and use your breath to open your heart, the cement walls surrounding your heart can begin to break open. You have to really want to open your heart. The experience can be frightening in the initial moment; you may feel exposed and you may question what is going to happen when your light and love will be seen and felt by everyone around you. Give over your armor, peel it off of yourself and ask Mother-Father God to penetrate your heart with enough love to heal you.

Trust that as you heal your heart, you will feel one with God—the full presence and union of Mother-Father God. A specific exercise brings this to bear:

Bring light through your crown chakra into your third eye. Hold the light in your third eye as you bring white light up from the earth, through the center of your feet, legs, lower belly, solar plexus and heart chakra. Send light out through your heart and circle it down into your first chakra (inside the tailbone), absorbing and raising the light back up through your spine. After you get this circuit moving, visualize a star of blazing light above your crown chakra and send the light down through your third eye, into your heart center, out through your heart chakra, up and back into the star of light above your head, down through your crown chakra and into your heart. Practice circulating and sending both circuits of light through your heart at the same time, as they will cleanse and purify your heart center with divine love.

When you send love to the planet and envision her healing, call upon the beings of Mary Magdalene, Mary the Mother, Yeshua and Babaji. Feel their essence and send them your love. Harmonize your heart to their vibration and ask them to align you to their frequencies. Feel your heart unite with their hearts and ask to be guided as a bringer of truth, wholeness, integrity, honor and love. They will guide the restoration, transformation and remembrance of union with your divine masculine and feminine aspects into oneness and reveal to you who you are and have always been.

At the time of this writing, I am being asked to invite you to call upon Archangel Michael for healing all issues regarding justice, personal power and in clearing attachments, St Francis for healing and the power of prayer, Melchizedek for serving the new planetary design, Archangel Gabriel for healing, Archangel Raphael for creativity and inspiration, St. Germaine for claiming your spiritual identity, Paramhansa Yogananda for karmic awakening and spiritual empowerment, White Buffalo Woman for restoring balance on our planet and to Merlin for learning to live in the center where all life forces meet.

They all send you their blessings of peace, light and love and want you to know that you are never alone. Live with self-respect and honor for others. Speak only truth and walk with humbleness and gratitude. Practice love in every moment and integrate your power with your heart. Call in your higher self and integrate her or him into your body. May you drink with joy from the Holy Grail cup and have returned to you the spiritual freedoms known through direct connection with Mother-Father God.

Bibliography

Drinking of the Holy Grail celebrates the teachings and traditions that, in past millennia, occupied a few select centers on Earth, but were scattered and hidden during the onslaught of the patriarchal religions and societies. Besides the deep spiritual origins of this work, I have pulled small pieces from numerous text sources to again reconvene the sacred teachings. Rather than diminish the flow of the narrative with source notes and other academic citings, I list below the books and other major texts from which I received some of the historical information. I recommend these books as your continue your own exploration into this remarkable path to divine communion.

Ashe, Geoffrey, *The Virgin,* Arkana, London, 1976

Cerve, Wishar, *Lemuria: The Lost Continent of the Pacific*, Supreme Grand Lodge of Amorc, 1931

Davies, Steven, *The Gospel of Thomas*, Skylight Paths Publishing, Woodstock, Vermont, 2002

Ferrini, Paul, *Dancing with the Beloved: Opening our Hearts to the Lessons of Love*, www.heartwayspress.com, 2001

Gardiner, Philip and Gary Osborn, *The Serpent Grail,* Watkins Publishing, London, 2005

Gardner, Laurence, *Bloodline of the Holy Grail*, Barnes and Noble Books, NY, 2003

Ghose, Ashutosh, Swami Abhedananda, Ramamkrishna Vedanta Math, Calcutta 1967

Hassnain, Fida, *A Search for the Historical Jesus*, Gateway Books, Bath, England, 1994

Jordan, Michael, *The Historical Mary*, Seastone, an imprint of Ulyssses Press, Berkeley, CA., 2003

Kenyon,Tom, and Sion, Judy, *Magdalene Manuscript:The Alchemy of Horus and The Sex Magic of Isis*, Sounds True, Inc., Boulder, Colorado, 2006

Leloup, Jean-Yves, *The Gospel of Mary Magdalene*, Inner Traditions, Rochester, New York, 2002

Leloup, Jean-Yves, *The Gospel of Phillip*, Inner Traditions, Rochester, New York, 2004

Lucius Apuleius: *Metamophoses* or *The Golden Ass*. Book 11, Chap 47. Adapted by Paul Halsall from the translation by Adlington 1566 in comparison with Robert Graves translation of 1951

Maharshi, Ramana, *The Essential Teachings of Ramana Maharshi: A Visual Journey*, 2002, www.ramana-maharshi.org/books.htm

Matthews, John, *At the Table of the Grail,* Watkins Publishing, London, England, 2002

Massey,Gerald. *The Historical Jesus and the Mythical Christ.* Escondido, California: The Book Tree, 2000

Missett, Bill, *Awakening the Soul, Book 2: Our Suppressed Spiritual Nature*, AuthorHouse, Bloomington, Indiana, 2005

Morgan, James Coyle, *Jesus and Mastership*, Oakbridge University Press, WA, 1989

Notovitch, Nicolas, The Unknown Life of Jesus Christ 1890, Kessinger Publishing, Kila, Montana, 2004

Pinkham, Mark Amaru, *Guardians of the Holy Grail*, Adventures Unlimited Press, 2004

Price, John Randolph, *The Jesus Code*, Hay House, 2000

Prophet, Elizabeth Clare, *The Lost Years of Jesus*, Summit University Press, Montana, 1984

Prophet, Elizabeth Clare, *Mary Magdalene and the Divine Feminine*, Summit Publications, Gardiner, Montana, 2005

Starbird, Margaret, *The Goddess in the Gospels*, Bear & Company, Sante Fe, New Mexico, 1998

Szekeley, Edmond Bordeaux, *The Essene Gospel of Peace*, International Biogenic Society, 1981

Yehling, Robert, *Shades of Green,* Koboca Publishing, Tampa, Florida, 2006

Yogananda, Paramhansa, *Autobiography of a Yogi*, Crystal Clarity Publishers, Nevada City, California, 1995 reprint of the 1946 First Edition

Yogananda, Paramhansa, *The Divine Romance*, Self-Realization Fellowship, 1986

Iana Lahi
About the Author

Iana Lahi is the creator and director of the Spirit Gateways™ Trainings and the author of *Drinking of the Holy Grail* (Koboca Publishing: 2007) and the forthcoming *Spirit Gateways: The Union of Love and Power*. Iana has worked with thousands of people from all over the world assisting their healing, soul and creative integration, personal and business relationships, physical and emotional healings, heart and soul journey and spiritual growth for 30 years. A Divine Feminine Initiator, Spiritual Teacher, Healer, and Movement Innovator, Iana assists individuals to source their own soul and spirit to embody their highest light.

Trained in NYC in modern dance and ballet with The Alvin Ailey American Dance Theater, Martha Graham, Jose Limon and Merce Cunningham, Iana majored in dance at The Boston Conservatory of Music and California Institute of the Arts under the tutelage of modern dance master Bella Lewitzky and the Ballet Russe's Mia Slavenska.

Iana is trained in eighteen different healing modalities including: bio-cellular breathing, rebirthing, polarity therapy, bioenergetics, energy healing, kinesiology, lomi lomi, huna kane, shamanic medicine, soul recovery, past life work, chakra clearing, cranial sacral therapy, botanical medicine, expressive and dance therapy, jungian psychology, and holistic medicine.

Iana Lahi initiates individuals into the union and integration of their Divine Feminine and Masculine Self by opening, clearing and reconnecting their spiritual, physical, soul, etheric, emotional and essential God and life force energies. Her work helps to clear and align karmic, ancestral, energetic and soul level patterns and restore the original blueprint of spiritual power and light in the body.

For more information on the Teachings of the Holy Grail Trainings contact Iana Lahi at www.spiritgateways.com

Printed in the United States
72290LV00001B/4-51